ARMOURED FIREPOWER

ARMOURED FIREPOWER

THE DEVELOPMENT OF TANK ARMAMENT 1939–45

PETER GUDGIN

SUTTON PUBLISHING

First published in the United Kingdom in 1997 by
Sutton Publishing Limited · Phoenix Mill
Thrupp · Stroud · Gloucestershire · GL5 2BU

British Library Cataloguing in Publication Data
A catalogue record for this book is available from the British Library

ISBN 0 7509 1387 8

™ ALAN SUTTON™ and SUTTON™ are the
trade marks of Sutton Publishing Limited

Typeset in 10/13 pt Sabon.
Typesetting and origination by
Sutton Publishing Limited.
Printed in Great Britain by
Butler & Tanner, Frome, Somerset.

CONTENTS

ACKNOWLEDGEMENTS

To write a book such as this without outside help would require a knowledge very much greater than mine, and I therefore acknowledge with grateful thanks the assistance given me by David Fletcher, the librarian at the Tank Museum at Bovington, with regard both to the supply of photographs and to the extraction of data from his extensive archives. I am grateful too to the Curator of the Tank Museum, Colonel John Woodward, for granting permission for the reproduction of Tank Museum photographs in the book.

My thanks are also due to Avimo Ltd., Scicon Ltd. and Messrs Barr & Stroud for permission to reproduce certain photographs from their collections, and to the Public Record Office at Kew for their help in locating certain wartime intelligence documents. Certain private photographs are reproduced by kind permission of Hptm (a.D. (retired)) Wilhelm Hartmann and David Dring.

Peter Gudgin
Leamington Spa, February 1997

GLOSSARY OF TERMS

Term	Meaning
AA	Anti-Aircraft
AFV	Armoured Fighting Vehicle
AP	Armour-Piercing
APC	Armour-Piercing Capped
APCBC	Armour-Piercing Capped/Ballistic Cap
AP/CNR	Armour-Piercing/Composite Non-Rigid
AP/CR	Armour-Piercing/Composite Rigid
APDS	Armour-Piercing, Discarding Sabot
APHE	Armour-Piercing High Explosive
ARV	Armoured Recovery Vehicle
AVRE	Armoured Vehicle, Royal Engineers
BEF	British Expeditionary Force
BL	Bag Loading
BT	Bystrokhnodnii Tahk (fast tank)
CinC	Commander-in-Chief
CS	Close Support
DT	Degtyarev (type of machine-gun)
DTD	Department of Tank Design
ETO	European Theatre of Operations
FlaK	Flugabwehrkanone (AA gun)
GHQ	General Headquarters
GQG	Grand Quartier Générale (GHQ)
HE	High Explosive
HEAT	High Explosive, Anti-Tank
HVAP	Hyper Velocity Armour-Piercing
HVSS	Horizontal Volute Spring Suspension
HWA	Heereswaffenamt (Army Ordnance Dept)
KwK	Kampfwagenkanone (tank gun)
L/C	Ratio of Length to Width (of a tank)
le.F.H.	Leichte Feldhaubitze (light field howitzer)
MAN	Maschinenfabrik Augsburg-Nuernberg
MG	Machine-gun
MNH	Maschinenfabrik Niedersachsen-Hannover
NGP	Nominal Ground Pressure
Pz.Jäg	Panzerjäger (tank destroyer)

PzKpfw	Panzerkampfwagen (tank)
QF	Quick-Firing
RAC	Royal Armoured Corps
RNAS	Royal Naval Air Service
RNVR	Royal Naval Volunteer Reserve
ROF	Royal Ordnance Factory
RTC	Royal Tank Corps
RTR	Royal Tank Regiment
SdKfz	Sonderkraftfahrzeug (special vehicle)
Sf	Selbstfahrende (self-propelled)
s.I.G,	Schwere Infanteriegeschuetz (heavy infantry gun)
SP	Self-propelled
Stu.G	Sturmgeschuetz (assault gun)
Stu.H	Sturmhaubitze (assault howitzer)
Stu.K	Sturmkanone (assault gun)
Stu.Mrs	Sturmmoerser (assault mortar)
SU	Samokhodnaya Ustanovka (SP)
TZF	Turmzielfernrohr (turret sighting telescope)
Wa Prüf	Waffenprüfungsamt (Weapon Testing Office)

ILLUSTRATIONS

INTRODUCTION

The history of warfare throughout the ages reflects the continual see-saw battle between the attack and the defence. As the advantage has passed initially to the side introducing a new tactic or weapon, so inexorably has it been lost as the other side introduces a successful counter to it.

Nowhere was this better exemplified than on the Western Front in the First World War from 1914 to 1918, where the machine-gun, coupled with the barbed wire entanglement and the artillery barrage, produced a stalemate in which the defence triumphed over any attempt at manoeuvre by the attacking side. This stalemate resulted in two opposing trench systems stretching in a continuous line from the Belgian coast in the north to the Swiss frontier in the south, any attempt to break out of which was immediately defeated by the enfiladed fire of innumerable machine-guns covering the defenders' wire entanglements. Attempts to destroy the wire by means of artillery bombardment were not only largely ineffectual but were also counter-productive in that they reduced the ground to a quagmire in wet weather and a Martian landscape of shell holes and powdery soil in dry. Although the American Civil War and, to some extent, the Crimean War, had alerted military thinkers to the problems posed by trench warfare, the conventional peacetime military mind had thought of no counter to it beyond bigger and better traditional weapons, especially artillery, in ever larger concentrations.

War, however, is a great stimulant to the inventive mind, many of which volunteered their services in the outburst of patriotic feeling on both sides, generated by the declaration of war. As a result, many ideas for breaking the stalemate on, and reintroducing mobility and manoeuvre to the Western Front were mooted by the more unconventional thinkers in both the German and the Allied armies. One of these ideas, poison gas, was tried with some initial success by the Germans, but was soon countered by the Allied introduction of the respirator. Britain and France, on the other hand, were more preoccupied with mechanical methods of crossing wire entanglements and trenches and getting their firepower through the enemy lines to his rear areas. Independently of each other, from 1915 onwards, they examined many ideas for doing this.

There was, of course, nothing new in the idea of using an armed and armoured vehicle to penetrate enemy defences. Armoured chariots have been reported as early as 2,000 BC, while the wooden horse of Troy and the armoured elephants of Kubla Khan are the stuff of legend. Armoured war carts were used in the fourteenth and fifteenth centuries, and Leonardo da Vinci's drawing, dated 1482, of his proposal for a manually-driven vehicle is famous. He wrote:

'I am building secure and covered chariots which are invulnerable, and when they advance with their guns into the midst of the foe even the largest enemy masses must retire, and behind these chariots the infantry can follow in safety and without opposition.'

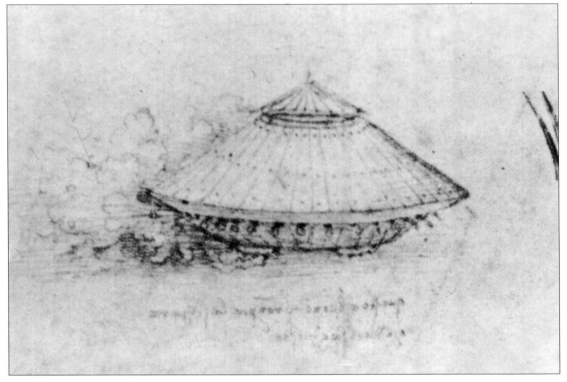

Leonardo da Vinci's design for an AFV.

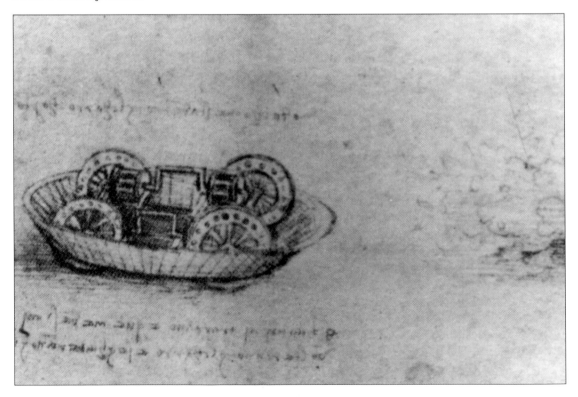

Model of Leonardo's vehicle. (SD-Scicon)

This was an uncannily accurate forecast of the performance required for such a vehicle on the Western Front in 1915. It was, alas, unobtainable in Leonardo's day, or for several centuries afterwards, as the weight of the armour protection required was too great for the crew to be able to propel the vehicle, even on flat ground. The invention of, first, the steam engine and, second, the internal combustion engine in the nineteenth century at last gave designers the power source necessary to drive vehicles of a greater weight than could be propelled by men or pulled by horses. For such vehicles to be of use in land warfare, however, they must be able to cross rough terrain, such as the no man's land between the opposing trench systems on the Western Front, a task for which the wheel was manifestly unsuitable. It was the search for a replacement for the wheel, which would give the required cross-country performance, that proved to be the stumbling block in 1915. Although Britain, France and Germany were all simultaneously searching for a solution to this problem, it was the British who found the best answer and who first produced and used the resulting vehicle, later known as the tank, in battle.

CHAPTER ONE

TANK DEVELOPMENT UP TO 1939

THE FIRST WORLD WAR

For the purposes of this background narrative it is proposed to follow only the British route to ultimate success in some detail. They found the best answer to the problem of crossing trench and wire systems in 1916 and were the first to produce it and use it in battle. French and German (and later the American) requirements and solutions will be covered only briefly.

Although the first British armoured car had made its appearance in 1900, the War Office had shown little interest in it or in several others which appeared in the period before the outbreak of the First World War. The soldier, with some notable exceptions, is a conservative creature, in whom forward, far-ranging thought is not one of the chief characteristics; this has never been more evident than in the history of the AFV in the British army. It was therefore left to the Royal Navy to appreciate the potential of such vehicles, and the Eastchurch Squadron of the Royal Naval Air Service (RNAS) made good use of them in Belgium in 1914, operating, in conjunction with the aircraft of the Squadron, against the enemy cavalry patrols and the exposed flank of the advancing German army. The emphasis in all these vehicles was on protection at the expense of firepower and mobility; converted as they were from civilian designs and carrying much more than their designed weight, they could operate only on roads, and were armed only with machine-guns. When,

therefore, the Western Front degenerated into trench warfare, there was little opportunity for mobile action and the armoured cars were transferred to other theatres of war, where they were later handed over to the army.

The potential for armoured vehicles in the land battle had, however, not been lost on those personnel of the RNAS who had been involved in the fighting in France and Belgium, and some of the more inventive minds among them sought to adapt the idea to the then-prevailing stalemate on the Western Front. An experimental RNAS squadron, No. 20, was formed at Wormwood Scrubs, against some Admiralty opposition and massive War Office disinterest, to test some of the less outlandish proposals. This move was backed by the dynamic First Lord of the Admiralty, Winston Churchill, who was instrumental in forming the Landships Committee in 1915 to oversee its work. This Committee later became an inter-service one, with the Navy input gradually becoming less as time went on and War Office interest in the project increased. Initially, the Committee's task was to select, from the mass of well-meant advice and ideas proffered, those which seemed most practical and offered the prospect of providing a solution to the problem of crossing and passing through enemy defence lines while minimizing casualties to the attacking troops. In the end, the choice was narrowed down to vehicles mounted on either big wheels, of radius sufficiently large to span enemy trenches without falling in, or caterpillar-type tracks, which were designed in the USA. It soon became apparent that the 'big wheel' idea in the form originally proposed (a vehicle with a body 100 feet long, 80 feet wide and 46 feet high, running on three 40-feet diameter wheels) was beyond the capacity of British industry of the time to engineer; a smaller version, an articulated machine running on four 15-feet diameter tractor-type wheels, was therefore put forward. A mock-up was built and demonstrated to the Landships Committee, but it was soon realized that it too was impractical, as the pressure exerted by the four wheels would be too great for use on soft ground. The 'big wheel' idea was thus abandoned in June 1915 in favour of a tracked solution, after abortive or partially-successful trials of various other wheeled and combined wheeled/tracked vehicles had been carried out.

The American Holt tracked agricultural tractor had made its first appearance in Europe in 1911, at the behest of an Hungarian farmer, and interest had been shown in its military possibilities by both the Austrian and the German military authorities. The latter had carried out comparative trials against a Mercedes FWD vehicle, of which they thought very highly, in which the tractor's performance proved vastly superior. Due to vested interests in the car and a divergence of opinion on policy in the High Command, no further action was taken regarding the Holt tractor until after the British introduction of the first tank on the Western Front in 1916. The Holt was among a number of tracked tractors of American design imported by the Landships Committee and tested by No. 20 Squadron RNAS, but it was soon apparent that, however suited they might be to agricultural use, none was strong enough to be used as the basis for an

armoured vehicle; the tracks in particular could not accept the weight of an armoured body. The Landships Committee, under the firm guidance of its dynamic secretary, Lieutenant Albert Stern, RNAS, therefore placed the task of developing a suitable track-laying vehicle in the hands of two engineers of genius and breadth of vision, Lieutenant Walter Wilson, RNVR, and William Tritton, the managing director of the Lincoln firm of agricultural engineers, William Foster & Co., Ltd. With full justification could these two men be called the fathers of the tank, and their capacity for invention and innovation as well as for action bore fruit in a remarkably short space of time. From many claimants, the Royal Commission on Awards to Inventors in 1919 judged their contribution to have merited the highest accolade.

Tritton soon got down to developing a track of his own design, and it is clear with the benefit of hindsight that it was this development that gave the breakthrough necessary for the successful development of the British tank. No longer were the designers to be limited by the capacity of a track developed commercially for a completely different purpose, as were those of other countries who opted to use the Holt tractor as the basis for their armoured, tracked vehicle designs. The first tank prototype, known initially as the No. 1 Lincoln Machine, ran on a specially extended set of tracks made by Bullock of Chicago. It had run at Lincoln on 10 September 1915 after a month of concentrated work, but trials had soon proved that the Bullock track was not suitable. The vehicle was accordingly modified to run on the Tritton-designed track, on which, now known as 'Little Willie', it commenced trials on 30 November 1915. It passed its trials successfully, but had unfortunately been rendered obsolete before it completed them. The War Office had finally issued an Operational Requirement in late August, having belatedly recognized that it would have to take over responsibility for the Admiralty's brainchild and decided that, if so, this brainchild might as well conform to War Office needs. Based on the latest information from the Western Front on German trench system design, the new machine would have to be able to cross a trench 8 feet wide and to lift itself over a vertical step 4½ feet high, figures almost twice as large as those to which the Landships Committee had previously been working. This performance could only be obtained from a completely redesigned machine, and this redesign was started on 24 August 1915. The trench-crossing requirement was met by increasing the length of track in contact with the ground and the vertical step capacity was increased by raising the height of the front idler wheels. The resulting rhomboid shape

gave the early tanks their distinctive outline, incorporated in the badges of the armoured corps of many armies, the British, German and American among others. Between the two rhomboid tracks, the crew was housed in a box-shaped hull with a raised cab at the front. Due to the overall height of the tracks and because of possible stability problems, it was decided to dispense with the turret with all-round traverse originally proposed both for 'Little Willie' and 'Big Willie' – as the prototype of the new design was called. Instead of being turret-mounted therefore, the armament (two naval 6-pdr guns of 57-mm calibre, mounted one on each side, and three Hotchkiss machine-guns) was mounted in projecting 'panniers', or sponsons in naval parlance, on each side of the hull between the top and bottom 'runs' of the tracks.

On 13 January 1916, less than five months

'Little Willie.' (Author's Collection)

'Mother', the prototype of the first British tank. (Author's Collection)

after design had started, the prototype of the new vehicle ran in Foster's yard, and preliminary driving and firing trials started on the 20th of the month. The vehicle, initially known as 'Big Willie', was now known as 'Mother', possibly because 'Mother' had been the invention of necessity! It was later also known as 'HM Landship (HMLS) Centipede'. On the 29th it was taken to Hatfield Park, Lord Salisbury's estate north of London, where it was demonstrated on 2 February, across a replica of a German trench and wire system, complete with shell-holes, to Lloyd George, Lord Kitchener and others. It performed faultlessly, crossing a 9-foot trench and impressing all who saw it with the exception of Lord Kitchener, who dismissed it as 'a pretty mechanical toy' with no effective part to play in the winning of the war. Despite Kitchener's disparagement, an order for 100, later increased to 150, was

placed after the demonstration. Some people, however, felt that in action a tank armed with 6-pdr guns would lack the means to deal with a determined attack by massed infantry, or even to clear infantry from trenches, so it was decided to complete only one half of the order with tanks armed with 6-pdrs, the other half being armed with Vickers machine-guns only, mounted in sponsons of reduced size. Tanks armed with 6-pdrs were known as 'male' and those armed only with machine-guns as 'female'. The original tactical idea was for the male tank to bolt enemy troops from their pill-box or trench with the 6-pdr firing high explosive shell, while the female tank stood by to kill them with its machine-guns as they tried to escape. All tanks produced in fulfilment of this first order were known as Mark I, and they differed little from 'Mother', the most important difference being that 'Mother' was built from mild steel while the Mark I tanks were of bulletproof armour plate. To maintain secrecy, a large area of land was required for driver, crew and tactical training, and a suitable site was ultimately found on Lord Iveagh's estate at Elveden, near Thetford in Norfolk. Training of 6-pdr gunners was to be carried out at HMS *Excellent*, the Royal Navy's gunnery school at Whale Island near Portsmouth, while machine-gunners were to be trained at Bisley, near Aldershot. To maintain secrecy in industry and when tanks were being transported by rail, the name 'tank' was used, as the riveted construction was similar to that used in the construction of large water tanks. Prior to this, the machines had been called 'Trench-Crossing Machines' or 'Landships'.

In March 1916, a new unit to operate the tanks was formed by the British army under the command of a Colonel (later General Sir Ernest) Swinton. To maintain secrecy as to the unit's function and equipment, it was concealed under the title of 'Heavy Branch, Machine-Gun Corps'. By June, the first Mark I tanks were delivered to the troops for training at Thetford and in August the first tank companies moved with their tanks to France, where they arrived as the Battle of the Somme was in full swing. They were first used in the attack on Flers-Courcelette on the 15 September 1916, but as has so often been the case with a new weapon whose function and capabilities are only partially understood by the higher echelons of command, they were used prematurely, in much too small a quantity and over unsuitable ground, with the result that their success was limited and the advantage of surprise soon lost. Nevertheless, the surprise they achieved in their local sector of the front was complete, although, out of the sixty tanks available, only forty-nine were in running order and of these only thirty-six reached the start-line. The panic in the German lines soon spread well beyond the limited area in which the tanks had operated,

provoking the German High Command into issuing deprecatory reports decrying the tanks' effectiveness and usefulness, while simultaneously beginning both to design their own tank and to plan a force to use it. There were detractors in the British army also, who made much of the failures of the tanks and dismissed them as a technical nine-days' wonder – many who had expected much of them were disappointed by the tanks' performance. Haig, the British C-in-C, was luckily not one of them. Only four days after the Flers attack he was asking the War Office to order a further 1,000 tanks.

Heavy tanks built in fulfilment of this and later orders all had the same outline shape as 'Mother'; basically similar in design to the Mark I, they differed from it in only minor details. Fifty each of the Marks II and III were built, divided equally between 'male' and 'female'; the most noticeable external difference between them and the Mark I was the abandonment of the Mark I's wheeled steering 'tail' and the wire mesh, anti-grenade screen over the hull roof. Mark II and III tanks began to be delivered to the new tank training centre at Bovington Camp, near Wareham in Dorset, towards the end of 1916, as the new Mark IV, the subject of Haig's order for 1,000 tanks, began to enter production in the proportion of one 'male' to two 'females'. While the placing of this order showed the Commander-in-Chief's confidence in the new weapon at a time when considerable doubts as to its value were being expressed elsewhere, it was premature in the sense that insufficient battle experience had been gained with the Mark I for an objective assessment to have been made of any design deficiencies and areas for improvement. The Mark IV tank, therefore, entered production with only marginal design improvements over its predecessors. Among the most obvious was the substitution of a shorter-barrelled (23 calibres in length as against the 40 calibre

British Mark IV heavy tank. (Author's Collection)

length of the original weapon) 6-pdr gun in the 'male' tanks, as the original gun had proved too long and fragile for land use; it tended to bend if struck by a tree or building and to bury its muzzle in mud on steep descents. The shorter-barrelled weapon was, of course, less accurate and had a shorter maximum range, although these disadvantages were not noticeable at the ranges at which it was used. What could have mattered, had the enemy possessed armoured vehicles at the time, was the greatly reduced armour penetration performance of the shorter gun. In the 'female' version of the Mark IV, the heavy Vickers machine-guns of the earlier Marks were replaced by the lighter and more portable Lewis light machine-gun, a reliable enough weapon in ground use but

one which, in the enclosed confines of a tank, produced too many fumes. The Hotchkiss machine-gun used in the 'male' tank, on the other hand, had proved perfectly adequate for tank use, and it might be thought more logical for the tank arm to have standardized on one type of MG throughout its tank fleet.

The Mark IV heavy tank was the mainstay of the British tank fleet in the First World War; a total of 1,220 was ordered and produced, of which 1,015 were delivered as fighting tanks and 205 as supply tanks without sponsons, between April and December 1917. It was followed by the Mark V, of which 400 were delivered between December 1917 and June 1918, the Mark V* (327 delivered from June 1918) and the Mark V**, of which 300 were ordered but only 25 delivered in anticipation of the Marks VIII and X to come. A mock-up of a Mark VI was produced, but further work on it was abandoned in February 1917 owing to the urgent demands from France for tanks. It was interesting in that it abandoned side sponson mounting of the main armament in favour of a single 6-pdr mounted in the front between the tracks, a solution later adopted by the Germans in their A7V Sturmpanzerwagen (Assault Armoured Vehicle) and the French in their Saint-Chamond 'Char d'Assaut'. The Mark VII, produced in October/November 1918 had been only partially completed by the time of the signing of the Armistice. This tank reverted to the Mark V configuration, but with a lengthened tail. The Mark VIII was a completely new design throughout; it was the largest, heaviest and most powerful of all the heavy tanks and was more heavily armoured and carried more machine-guns than any of its predecessors. It had been intended to produce 1,500 jointly at a new factory to be set up in France, with a further 1,500 produced in the USA and 1,450 in Britain. In the end, only one each of the joint Anglo-US and US versions was produced and three of the British version, of which one was in mild steel and the other two in armour plate. The Mark X was the tank that never was. It was to have been an improved Mark V design, intended for the great tank army which was envisaged for 1919; 2,000 were scheduled for production, but again the Armistice had been signed before production lines had been established.

To cope with the increased production and employment of tanks, the British army had rapidly expanded its tank training facilities in the UK and France, as well as recruitment into its tank user arm, the Heavy Branch, Machine-Gun Corps. The latter changed its title to Tank Corps in June 1917, by which time several battalions had arrived in France, together with their Mark IV tanks. There

were now nine battalions in all, including two still in the UK, and four more were formed in August of that year. By now tanks were in demand for any offensive, however small, but the Battle of Cambrai on the 20 November 1917 was where the Tank Corps achieved its greatest success. All nine battalions of the Corps took part, involving a force of some 300 tanks supported by five infantry divisions and five cavalry divisions, in an attack in which the preliminary artillery bombardment, normally thought to be an essential in any offensive, was dispensed with. Thus the ground over which the tanks were to attack was not broken up by shell holes and the element of surprise was increased. The attack was a complete success but, if the German High Command had been surprised so had that of the British, by a breakthrough that had succeeded beyond all anticipation. Unfortunately, they had no reserves with which to exploit their success so that, two weeks later, most of the ground so easily won had been taken back by the Germans. Nevertheless, although the victory at Cambrai was shortlived it had shown beyond question the value of tanks used properly in quantity rather than in penny packets. This victory is celebrated annually on the 20 November by the Tank Corps' successor, the Royal Tank Regiment.

The inability to exploit fully the breakthrough at Cambrai had confirmed the need, long foreseen by the thinkers in the Tank Corps, for a lighter and faster tank to operate in support of the cavalry. The maximum designed speed of the heavy tanks was only 4 m.p.h., and this was much reduced on shell-torn ground and the heavy mud in which they had to operate. To meet this requirement for a lighter and faster tank, four Marks of medium tank were designed and built by the British during the First World War, of which only one was used in action.

German A7V heavy tank. (Tank Museum 358/F1)

French Saint-Chamond heavy tank. (Tank Museum 573/B4)

British/US Mark VIII heavy tank. (Author's Collection)

Sir William Tritton had designed a high speed, lightly armoured tank known as the 'Tritton Chaser' in 1915, and the first medium tank, the Mark A (letters were used to distinguish the Marks of the medium tanks from those of the heavy), evolved from this in December 1916. Known as the 'Whippet', the Mark A entered production in 1917 and was first in action in France in March 1918. The Whippet was designed to a configuration completely different from that of the heavy tanks; the tracks were no longer overall in a rhomboid shape, but the top run of the track, the idler wheel and the sprocket were much lower, with the superstructure projecting above it. Weighing only 18 tons, it was armed with four Hotchkiss machine-guns mounted in a box-like superstructure towards the rear of the tank, and was manned by a crew of three men; unsprung, like the heavy tanks, it had a maximum speed of 8–9 m.p.h., although one prototype, fitted with sprung

tracks and a Rolls-Royce Eagle engine, managed to reach almost 30 m.p.h. Exactly 200 Medium Mark A were ordered, of which 195 were delivered to the army and went to equip the III Tank Brigade in France.

The Medium Mark A was to have been superseded by the Mark B, which incorporated the Whippet's superstructure and armament on a track configuration similar to the rhomboid shape of the heavy tanks. Of these, 450 were ordered and production started in September 1918, but only 48 were produced and it never saw action. The Medium Tank Mark C, sometimes known as the 'Hornet', was probably the best British design of the First World War. Designed by Tritton, but in full consultation with battle-experienced Tank Corps officers, it again was of rhomboid shape, with a top run of track slightly lowered from that of the Mark V. Again, 200 were ordered and production was started in

British medium tank Mark A (Whippet). (Tank Museum 1128/B5)

December 1918; only 45, all 'female', were delivered to the army, however, before production was cancelled. A 'male' version had been planned which would have mounted the 23-calibre long, 6-pdr gun in the front of the vehicle, but none was produced. The Medium C tank remained in British army service until 1925.

Various derivatives of the heavy tank were produced during the war for various purposes, such as carrying personnel or stores, or as artillery gun carriers or recovery vehicles. These, however, were not strictly tanks and were armed with one machine-gun at the most. Of these, the most numerous was the Gun Carrier, produced to overcome the problem of moving wheeled guns and limbers over the waste of mud and shell-torn ground of the Western Front no man's land. It was designed to carry either the 6-pdr gun or the 6-in howitzer of the Royal Artillery, although only the howitzer could be fired from the vehicle. Known as the Gun Carrying Tank Mark I, the vehicle used the power plant, transmission and running gear of the Mark I heavy tank, but there all resemblance between the two ceased. Of the fifty vehicles ordered, forty-eight were delivered to the army between November 1916 and February 1917, the first appearing in France in November 1916. The remaining two carriers from the order for fifty were diverted in December 1916 to become Salvage Tanks (their successors were known during and after the Second World War as armoured recovery vehicles) and sent to France on trial. There they proved very satisfactory, and more would have been made had it been possible to spare the carriers from their work as supply vehicles. The salvage tanks carried a crane on the platform which could lift, luff and slew a load of 3 tons, as well as sheerlegs which increased the lifting capacity of the crane to 10 tons.

As the Mark IV tanks reached France, the Mark Is which they replaced were converted to carry stores by substituting mild steel, box-shaped sponsons some 3 feet wide for the tank's normal armoured, weapon-mounting sponsons. These vehicles, known as Tank Tenders, were first used in the battle of Messines in June 1917 but, in the third battle of Ypres later that year, the ground conditions were so bad that many of them stuck because the square edge of the sponson dug into the ground, thus preventing any further movement. Later some 205 Mark IV tanks, not needed for battle, were similarly converted to tank tenders in the same way. Later still, in the latter part of 1918, the Mark IX supply tank was ordered. Out of the initial contract for 200 vehicles, however, only three had been delivered by the time of the Armistice. This vehicle, which resembled the Mark V* in outline but without either sponsons or the turret of the heavy tank, had two large loading doors on either side for loading of stores or personnel. It could carry 30 fully-equipped men or 10 tons of stores, and weighed 37 tons loaded.

By the end of the war, British industry had designed and produced more than 2,000 heavy tanks, 200 mediums and 85 special-purpose tracked vehicles, for a Tank Corps which had expanded to 25 battalions. As David Fletcher says in his book *Landships – British Tanks in the First World War*:

'Perhaps, in the end, it is fitting to ask just what contribution the tanks made to victory in 1918. No mechanical aid could be a substitute for the enduring courage of the Allied infantry. However, it remains a fact that, from Cambrai onwards, a series of massive and successful assaults were made, upon increasingly well-defended enemy lines, which showed hitherto unequalled gains for substantially smaller losses, and it was precisely these actions in which the tanks were used, and used properly. . . . Had it not been for the tank, it is almost certain that the war would have dragged on, at least into 1919.'

Similar views were expressed by the British Commander-in-Chief, Field-Marshal Sir Douglas Haig in his final despatch:

'Since the opening of our offensive on August 8, tanks have been employed on every battlefield, and the importance of the part played by them in breaking up the resistance of the German infantry can scarcely be exaggerated. The whole scheme of the attack of August 8 was dependent upon tanks and ever since that date on numberless occasions the success of our infantry has been powerfully assisted or confirmed by their timely arrival. So great has been the effect produced upon the German infantry by the appearance of British tanks that in more than one instance, when for various reasons real tanks were not available in sufficient numbers, valuable results have been obtained by the use of dummy tanks painted on frames of wood and canvas.'

An officially-inspired paragraph which appeared in the German press in October 1918 confirmed the important part played by tanks in the Allied offensive:

'The successes which the Allies have gained since the first battle of Cambrai do not rest on any superior strategy on the part of Foch or on superiority in numbers, although the latter has undoubtedly contributed to it. The real reason has been the massed use of tanks. Whereas the artillery can only cut wire and blot out trenches with an enormous expenditure of ammunition, the tank takes all these obstacles with the greatest of ease. . . . They are the most dangerous foe to hostile machine-guns. They can approach machine-gun nests and destroy them at close range.

The great danger of the tank is obvious when one considers that the defence of the front battle zone chiefly relies on the defensive value of the machine-guns, and that the armour of the tank renders it invulnerable to rifle fire, and that only seldom, and in exceptional cases, is machine-gun fire effective.'

The tanks had thus fulfilled the purpose for which they had been designed – to regain mobility and the capacity for manoeuvre on the battlefield, to break the stranglehold imposed for so long on the Western Front by the machine-gun and the barbed-wire entanglement – and they had been the first troops of the warring nations to do so. Their success in battle had assured them of a future in the army, despite persistent but finally unsuccessful attempts by vested military interests of the old school after the war to abolish the Corps.

Having followed in some detail the development of the tank in Britain, it is interesting to compare the progress of the other combatants along the same path. While the British had been developing their ideas for breaking the Western Front stalemate, the French had, independently and unknown to their allies, been pursuing similar ideas of their own under the driving force of Colonel (later General) Jean-Baptiste Eugène Estienne, a far-sighted artillery officer who played a similar role in the French development of armoured vehicles to that played by General Swinton in British tank development. There was a fundamental difference in thought between the two countries regarding the purpose of the armoured vehicle; in Britain, it was seen as a means of supporting the infantry in the assault, while in France, the prime mover being an artilleryman, it was regarded as a source of mobile firepower, 'Artillerie d'Assaut'.

Estienne's interest in the tracked armoured

vehicle as a possible solution to the problem of defeating the machine-gun's stranglehold on the Western Front was aroused in 1915 when he saw the cross-country performance of the Holt tractors being used in the forward area by the British artillery. As a result he put a succession of proposals for tracked armoured vehicles mounting a light gun and two machine-guns, towing an armoured trailer carrying infantry, to the GQG, the French general headquarters in France. At his third attempt he was granted an interview with the Deputy Chief of Staff at GQG at the beginning of December 1915, by which time his arguments were supported not only by the costly failure of the French autumn offensives that year but also by the practical success of a tracked machine capable of breaking through wire entanglements, produced by the Inventions Committee. He was granted leave to visit Paris, where he consulted M. Brille of the Schneider Creusot works and with him worked out a design for a tank based on the Holt tractor, for which Schneider were the French agents. After further discussions and trials with a Holt tractor, GQG was persuaded to place an order for 400 of these machines without waiting for the construction and trial of a prototype. Shortly afterwards, on the initiative of M. Breton, the Under-Secretary of the Inventions Committee, an order for a further 400, of a different design, was placed with the Saint-Chamond company. However, starting from scratch and hampered by much official obstruction, the French tanks were not ready for use until six months after those of the British and it will be remembered that the British trials of the Holt tractor had proved it unsuitable both to carry the weight of a tank and to cross a typical German trench-and-wire system.

The Schneider vehicle weighed some 14 tons, had a maximum speed on level ground of only 2½ m.p.h. and was armed with a 75-mm gun mounted on the right

front and two Hotchkiss machine-guns. The Saint-Chamond tank was also armed with a 75-mm gun, mounted centrally in the front, but carried four Hotchkiss machine-guns instead of two, weighed approximately 23 tons and had a maximum speed on roads of more than 5 m.p.h. Both tanks had a box-like body with an excessive overhang at the front, carried on short tracks with a low profile; their trench-crossing and cross-country capacity were therefore very limited compared to the British rhomboid configuration. On the other hand, there was much to be said for a front-mounted gun, rather than side sponson mountings. The British sponson mounting meant that, when engaging a target, the tank tended to present its broadside to the target, but the French front mounting exposed only the smaller front elevation. The French mounting had the additional advantage that the driver could help the gunner by traversing the whole vehicle if a target presented itself outside the limited traverse range of the gun mounting. These French tanks were known as 'Chars d'Assaut' (Assault Vehicles) Modèle 1916, and they were first used in action on 16 April 1917 in the Champagne offensive. Instead of the expected 800 tanks, however, only 8 groups of 16 Schneider tanks apiece were available due to prolonged delays in delivery, while only one group of Saint-Chamond tanks could be mustered on 5 May and failed miserably. Deliveries of the Schneider had begun in December 1916 and, by May the following year, 300 had been delivered; the remaining 100 were delayed until 1918, work on them having been slowed down in favour of artillery tractors. The Saint-Chamond order was similarly delayed, the last tanks of the original order not being delivered until March 1918, when they were used as supply vehicles. No great success was gained with either of these tanks, due really to the design faults which had been earlier spotted, and eliminated, by the British in their assessment of the possibilities of the Holt tractor. As a result of the failure of the French-designed vehicles, the French army in October 1918 ordered 150 British Mark V* tanks, but the war's end the following month prevented their use in action. They were replaced after the war by the French Char 2C.

Estienne meanwhile had been gazetted on 30 September 1916 as 'Commandant de l'Artillerie d'Assaut aux Armées', a long-winded way of saying that he was commander of army tank troops, and was actively pursuing his idea for a light tank both to support the infantry in taking advantage of the fire effect of the heavy tanks and to exploit success by armoured action. He had been influenced by a demonstration of the capabilities of the British heavy tanks which he had attended in June 1916. These could obviously out-perform the French equivalent, and he felt that it would be logical for the British to concentrate on the design and production of heavy tanks while the French developed smaller and faster machines. After the failure of the French heavy tanks in the Champagne offensive, it was therefore decided to suspend the building programmes for these vehicles and to concentrate instead on the production of the new Renault light tank, a two-man tank weighing some 6 tons and carrying either a short 37-mm gun or a machine-gun in a rotating turret with 360° of traverse. An order for the production of 1,000 of these vehicles, known as the Renault FT, Modèle 1917 light tank, was placed and it was first in action on 31 May 1918. It performed well, although its low maximum speed of 5 m.p.h. limited its value in the exploitation role. The Renault light tank was the most successful French tank of the war, many also being supplied to the US army in France; the most innovative feature was the mounting of the gun in a traversing turret, originally proposed for

Little Willie and the Medium B by the British but abandoned.

The rotating turret was also a feature of the heavy tank, Char de Rupture C, for which the French issued a specification in 1916. This was to be a heavy tank weighing about 40 tons, of which two prototypes were produced in 1917–18. One, the Char 1A, was to mount a 75-mm gun while the other, Char 1B, was to carry a 105-mm weapon. Neither prototype was ever armed, their real value being as test-beds for Char 2C, an even heavier machine weighing some 70 tons, armed with a 75-mm gun and 4 machine-guns and with a crew of 13 men. The French seem to have been mesmerized by size and weight in the design of tanks, rather as the Germans were, as will be seen later, with their proposals for the K-Wagen. Ten of the Char 2C were produced after the war, the last being delivered in 1922. They remained on the strength of the French army until 1940, when they were destroyed in a German air attack on their way to the front by train.

The American Army was a late entrant to the First World War and, prior to its entry, had no experience of the design, production and tactical use of armoured fighting vehicles. Its knowledge of these vehicles was obtained second-hand, via its military intelligence network and latterly from information supplied by its allies. The Americans were thus able to stand back and take an unprejudiced view of the efforts of its allies and, with their characteristic ability to sort the wood from the trees, were quick to appreciate the British advantage in heavy tank design and the French superiority in light tanks. For the equipment of their own tank force, therefore, they opted to work with the British on the joint design and co-production of a heavy tank, the Mark VIII already mentioned, and with the French on the production of their Renault FT under licence.

French Renault FT light tank. (Tank Museum 3243/E4)

This, however, was only after the US Military Mission in Paris had reported unfavourably on tanks at about the time the United States entered the war in 1917. After General John J. Pershing arrived in France, special committees were set up to study possible American use of tanks, and interest increased after the battle of Cambrai in November 1917. The Anglo-American Tank Treaty was signed on 19 January 1918, under which the new Mark VIII heavy tank (the 'International' or 'Liberty' tank) was to be built jointly in large numbers. Despite almost complete industrial confusion in the United States, Pershing's HQ was constantly quoted firm production dates for the US version of the Renault FT light tank, even though at the time the drawings had not been converted from the metric system. It was not until August 1918 that order began to emerge from chaos and several factories began the building of this tank. At the end of the war, of the 23,405 tanks on order only a few hundred were completed, 10 of which reached France and none saw action. The contribution of the Americans to tank design in the First World War can thus be seen to have been negligible.

The part played by the Germans in the development of the tank before and during the First World War can now be examined. Their High Command had given no serious consideration to the possibilities of mechanized warfare prior to their encounter with British tanks at Flers-Courcelette in 1916; why should they have done, when it was their overwhelming quantitative superiority in machine-guns, and superiority in their tactical employment, that had been very largely responsible for defeating all attempts by the Allies to initiate a war of movement on the Western Front? Their only unconventional attempt to break the impasse there had involved the use of poison gas, but after the initial surprise which it created the

Allied introduction of respirators and other anti-gas precautions had soon nullified its effect and stalemate again prevailed.

As in Britain and France, various ideas for military armoured vehicles had been produced in Germany before the war and had met the same apathy in the Kriegsministerium as had been manifested in the British War Office and the French War Ministry. The Imperial German army did, however, experiment with a few armoured cars from 1905 onwards. These were seen primarily as reconnaissance vehicles, gun carriers or observation balloon destroyers, and their value in a fighting role was not appreciated by the German General Staff. No attempt, therefore, was made in official quarters to investigate them further.

It was not until after the first British tank attack at Flers-Courcelette in September 1916 that the German War Ministry began to make active efforts to develop similar vehicles for the German army. Although the surprise appearance of the British tanks had a very demoralizing effect on the troops facing them, the German General Staff had been aware from Intelligence reports and prisoner-of-war interrogation that the British were developing some sort of armoured cross-country vehicle since the first appearance of 'Mother' early in 1916. British security had been so good, however, that little information as to its appearance and characteristics had reached them. A committee was set up, formed from members of the German automotive industry and the old Commercial Testing Commission, under the aegis of A7V (Kriegsdepartment 7, Abteilung Verkehrswesen: General War Department 7, Traffic Section), the express function of which was to assume responsibility for the design of German armoured fighting vehicles.

Several proposals from engineering firms for armoured vehicles were submitted to the A7V Committee during 1917, of which one or two reached the demonstration prototype stage; none impressed sufficiently to be carried forward to production. Meanwhile, the A7V Committee, as the British and French before them had done, showed great interest in the US Holt tractor, a sample of which had been acquired in 1916 from Austria. An engineer member of the A7V design team, Obering. Josef Vollmer, drew up plans for a chassis, based on a much-lengthened Holt design with three bogies instead of the one of the Holt tractor. By modifying an existing, proved system, much design time was thus saved, and a prototype of the chassis, fitted with a steel superstructure, was demonstrated to the German High Command in May 1917 at Mainz. As a result of this demonstration, ten pre-production trials vehicles were ordered, to be delivered by the following summer. The vehicle was now called the 'A7V Sturmpanzerwagen' (A7V Armoured Assault Vehicle).

The German army requirements were for the vehicle to be capable of crossing a trench 5 feet wide, of climbing a 1 in 10 slope cross-country and a 1 in 4 slope on roads, of carrying a load of 4 tons, having a maximum road speed of 8 m.p.h. and mounting a big gun front and rear with machine-guns mounted in the hull sides. To meet these requirements necessitated considerable redesign, but the Holt running gear was retained unmodified, the standard Holt tractor units being obtained from the Holt subsidiary in Austria. Firepower was a problem. It was originally intended to mount a 20-mm Becker TuF gun (Tank und Flieger: anti-tank and anti-aircraft) at each end, but trials proved this gun to have inadequate armour penetration. It was therefore decided to use the captured Belgian 57-mm (6-pdr) Maxim-Nordenfeldt gun in its place. However, there were too few of these guns available for one to be mounted front and

rear, so it was decided to mount only one, at the front, and to substitute two additional machine-guns for the rear-mounted 6-pdr. Production of the A7V was considerably delayed by shortage of materials, other war material being considered in 1917 to be of more importance, and by mechanical failures which surfaced during prototype trials.

In the event, before the end of the war, only some twenty A7Vs were completed and issued to the three tank companies formed to use them. The A7V was the only tank designed and built by the Germans in the First World War to see combat, but the overall design showed a fundamental failure by the design team and the German General Staff to appreciate the need for a high leading track wheel, an overall track and a long length of track in contact with the ground if the vehicle was successfully to cross wire and trench systems. These were the very reasons why the British had rejected the Holt design in favour of the rhomboid track layout for their heavy tanks. It is interesting to see how two great industrial powers, Germany and France, made the same mistake and produced heavy tanks of very similar design and poor performance.

The main strength of the German tank force lay in their supply of captured British Mark IV heavy tanks, most of which had been captured after the battle of Cambrai in November 1917. The German High Command in December 1917 made plans to expand their tank force to twenty-two companies in the following twelve months based on this windfall, as a start forming four additional companies that month to man captured British Mark IVs. These vehicles, known by the Germans as 'Beute Panzerwagen IV' (Captured Tank IV), were refurbished and modified at a depot set up for the purpose at Charleroi, the British 6-pdr guns being replaced by the Belgian 57-mm guns in the 'male' tanks and the machine-guns in the 'females' by standard German Model '08 Maxims. Use was also made of captured British Medium Mark A 'Whippet' tanks, with which one company was equipped. The captured British tanks were usually used in support of A7Vs but, due to shortages of materials and consequent delays to the A7V production programme, the German tank force never consisted of more than eight companies, five of which were equipped with British tanks. Despite their superiority, these were never too successful in German hands, due partly to inadequate training, partly to the fact that the German tank units were ad hoc units composed of men drafted in from other arms and units, and thus lacked the *esprit de corps* of the British Tank Corps, and partly because the Germans had played down the significance and capability of British tanks for propaganda and morale purposes.

Despite this propaganda, the German army was sufficiently convinced of the superiority of British heavy tank design to commission the design of a modified A7V based on the British overall track layout and rhomboid outline, with main armament mounted in side sponsons. The resulting prototype, which was tested at Mainz in June 1918, was known as the A7V/U, the 'U' indicating that it had 'Umlaufende Ketten' (overall tracks). It had a much-improved performance over the A7V, crossing a 9 foot trench, climbing a 30° slope and attaining a maximum speed of 7½ m.p.h., but at 40 tons was heavy and the Holt tracks tended to jam in muddy conditions. Only a 'male' version, mounting Belgian 6-pdrs in the sponsons and four Model '08 Maxim machine-guns, was built, although a 'female' version (the A7V/U3) was designed. In September 1918 twenty prototypes of the 'male' A7V/U were ordered, but the Armistice, with its halt in German arms production, supervened before any had been built.

Like the French, the German army was fascinated by size where tanks were concerned and tasked the A7V Committee in December 1917 with designing a 'breakthrough tank' of vast proportions and heavy armament; the resulting 'K Wagen' corresponded to the French 70-ton Char 2C, although twice as heavy. The vehicle, again designed by Vollmer, was of vast proportions, weighing some 140 tons, carrying a crew of 22 men and armed with four 77-mm guns mounted in sponsons and six Model '08 Maxim machine-guns. Two prototypes were under construction but incomplete when the war ended. They were destroyed by the Allied Control Commission.

Vollmer pointed out to the High Command that such super-heavy tanks were a waste of valuable resources and of only limited tactical value, and recommended instead the building of simple light tanks. He thus echoed the ideas of both the British and French, with their Medium Mark A Whippet and Renault FT, respectively. Asked to design something on these lines, he produced a design very similar in outline to the British Whippet, known as the 'Leichte Kampfwagen 1' (Light Tank I, or LK I). It had the advantage over the Whippet of having its machine-gun mounted in a revolving turret, but this advantage was discarded in its successor, the 10-ton LK 2, a three-man tank mounting a 57-mm gun in a fixed turret. Two prototypes were completed for trials and an order placed in June 1918 with the Daimler company for the building of 580 vehicles in 1919. None was completed, however, before the war ended.

That then is the story of the German contribution to tank design and production in the First World War. It was not great: the Germans were late starters in this field, having failed to realize soon enough the possibilities which armoured vehicles possessed for breaching trench systems protected by machine-guns and barbed wire and reintroducing mobility to the battlefield. Although the French as well as the British were ahead of them in tank design, it is interesting to note some similarities between the German and French approaches to the subject, namely:

1. The adoption of the Holt tractor running gear, despite its poor weight-carrying capacity and unsuitability for trench- and wire-crossing.
2. The mounting of heavy tanks' main armament in the front of the tank.
3. The adoption of a hull-shape whose overhang front and rear precluded a good cross-country performance.
4. The fascination with super-heavy tanks, shown again by both countries prior to, and during the Second World War.
5. The far-sighted introduction of revolving turrets for the mounting of armament, if only on light tanks.

The tank's characteristics of firepower, mobility and protection had been clarified during the war, although Britain, France and Germany had differed in the priority given to each. The French, for example, had given firepower the highest priority, only to be expected when the man behind their tank programme was an artilleryman by profession, while the British had given the greater priority to mobility and protection. The Germans appear to have given none of these a clear priority but rather to have followed in the wake of the British and the French.

Mobility of First World War tanks was of a rather specialized nature, slanted towards the crossing of trenches and barbed-wire entanglements at a slow infantry walking pace. It was not until the success of the British heavy tanks in accomplishing this had been recognized that attention was turned to the design of lighter, faster tanks with a more generalized cross-country ability, able to exploit the breakthrough achieved by the heavy tanks, and the war did not last long enough for such designs to be available in the field. The speed and manoeuvrability of the British Medium Mark A and the French Renault FT light tanks were not sufficiently great for mobility to have played a large part in vehicle protection.

Protection of the tank crew was achieved by armouring the tanks with riveted bulletproof plate. This was adequate against machine-guns and rifles firing ball ammunition, but little use against the same weapons, or other larger calibre weapons, firing armour-piercing rounds. It did not take long for the Germans to realize this and to introduce AP ammunition for small arms, and the specially-designed anti-tank rifle of larger calibre. The joints between plates and the spaces around gun and machine-gun mountings and sights also attracted aimed small arms fire, and the lead 'splash' from bullets hitting these was another source of injury to tank crews. The need for thicker armour was further emphasized during the first tank versus tank battle, at Villers-Brettoneux on 24 April 1918, where the tanks' main armament was employed against other tanks and easily penetrated them. It was this action that first pointed to the fact that the tank was a tank's worst enemy and therefore its prime target, a fact that was to colour tank armament, design, protection and tactics up to the present day.

Firepower of the tanks deployed by both sides in the First World War was made up of a combination of one or more guns, ranging in calibre from the 57-mm of the British and German to the 75-mm of the French heavy tanks, and several machine-guns. The purpose of the main armament was to destroy enemy trenches and machine-gun posts, as well as personnel. The British 6-pdrs were therefore provided with high explosive (HE) and case-shot projectiles in the first instance, although, as a naval weapon, an armour-piercing round was also available. As befitted a tank with an artilleryman as its design prime mover and which in consequence had first priority allotted to its firepower, the French heavy tanks were armed with a 75-mm gun, the famous French 'Soixante-quinze'. This too was provided with HE and case-shot rounds. The ammunition provided for the German tanks' 57-mm guns is not known, but is likely to have been similar in nature. The machine-gun secondary armament was air-cooled in most instances, although the British Mark I female tank was provided with water-cooled Vickers MGs. In later British tanks Hotchkiss or Lewis guns of 0.303-in calibre were standard. The French also used the Hotchkiss, but in 7.92-mm calibre. This calibre was also used for the Maxim Model '08 MGs in the German tanks.

1919 TO 1939

At the end of the First World War, it can be seen that the head start gained by the British in tank design and operation during the war ensured that they were the world leaders in these fields. This lead did not last for long after the Armistice due partly to the rapid demobilization of a majority of officers and men with experience of designing and operating tanks in war, partly due to a parsimonious Treasury and partly to jealousy of the new arm by other arms of the service, frightened of losing their pre-war roles and influence. The War Office had no clear idea of what tanks would be required to do in the army of the future or whether indeed there would be any need for them and, even had they known what they wanted, they would have been faced by an engineering industry tooling up for civilian products and with little interest in the small quantities likely to be involved in tank-building contracts to be forthcoming from a cash-strapped War Office. Apart from Vickers and the Government-owned Royal Ordnance Factory at Woolwich, there was no repository of tank design knowledge left in the country by the mid-1920s, so it is not surprising that the lead which had existed in 1919 rapidly disappeared.

In the absence of a direct statement of requirements from the War Office and with the failure of the Department of Tank Design (under threat of imminent closure) to design anything suitable for issue to the Tank Corps, it fell to Vickers, with some help from the Royal Ordnance Factory at Woolwich, to produce the most significant British tank of the interwar years. This was the Vickers Medium Mark I, a tank mounting a 3-pdr (47-mm) high velocity gun in a turret with all-round traverse, carrying a crew of five men and weighing approximately 12 tons. Originally called the 'Tank, Light, Mark I' until lighter tanks were introduced in the 1930s, this machine was ordered off the drawing board and production started in 1923. It remained as virtually the only tank in service with the Tank Corps until the mid-1930s and was still in service in the UK as a training tank in 1942, nearly twenty years later. Its origin is something of a mystery; the Tank Design Department was closed in 1923 and no trace of any correspondence, trials reports or memos has been found in either War Office or Vickers archives to indicate where, when or by whom the design was originated. There is no doubt that it was ordered and produced in a hurry, mainly in order to commit the funds allocated for a new tank by the Treasury before the financial year ended. There is no doubt either that it continued the wartime British lead over any tanks produced elsewhere. It was the first British production tank to carry its main

Vickers medium tank of C Squadron, 48th Battalion RTR. (Author's Collection)

armament in a turret with 360° traverse and to be carried on sprung running gear. Both of these innovations were rendered possible by dispensing with the overall track layout of the wartime heavy tanks and lowering the top run of the track, now that the necessity for crossing complex trench systems and wire entanglements had lessened.

The War Office must thus have specified at least the requirement for the tank to carry a high velocity gun as main armament, and for this to be mounted in a fully-rotating turret. Similarly they had laid down earlier the likely tactical role for the medium tank as one of exploitation, requiring a higher maximum speed than the infantry-supporting heavy tanks of wartime. This had led to the provision of sprung suspension and the abandonment of overall tracks in the Medium Mark I. The choice of a high velocity gun capable of firing only armour-piercing (AP) shot showed that the lesson learned after the first tank v. tank action of the war, that the prime target of tanks was the enemy tank, had sunk home in the War Office. It was the task of the auxiliary armament of machine-guns, or the few special purpose, close support (CS) tanks armed with a 3.7-inch howitzer, to take on the anti-personnel role. The need for speed in production meant that existing components were used wherever possible, and the same frame construction with armour plates rivetted to it was employed as had been used in the heavy tanks during the war. The art of electric welding and casting of armour plate, which enabled the frame construction to be abandoned, had not yet been learned.

Vickers 16-tonner (on left) and Independent. (Author's Collection)

But if the War Office was having a hard time defining its AFV requirements and acquiring the necessary funds with which to order its tanks, Vickers was enjoying an export-led boom in tanks on the back of Britain's wartime lead in their design, production and use. This was of considerable significance, not only for the country's balance of payments but also for the effect which it had on the design of tanks all over the world, as British design trends tended to be copied by other countries even if not customers of Vickers. Certainly this was true of Germany, whose own designs, produced and tested clandestinely in contravention of the Treaty of Versailles, were almost direct copies of Vickers' vehicles. The Soviet Union on the other hand, while permitting the testing of Germany's illegally designed tanks at their test facility at Kazan, bought Vickers tanks and set up their own tank factory with Vickers' help. Of the other wartime allies, France began the interwar period with a large stock of Renault FT tanks but little else, without either the desire or the money to replace them. Some development work took place from 1931 onwards, but most of the money made available for the defence budget

was poured into the construction of the Maginot Line defences. As in Britain, it was not until the effectiveness of the German tanks used in the Spanish Civil War was realized that any worthwhile funds were made available for the replacement of the Renault light tanks. In the USA too, shortage of funds in the postwar period limited tank production, but considerable experimental work took place on designs which could, if the need arose, be put into mass production. As in Britain, armoured thought was far from clear.

Almost throughout the industrial world, however, armoured thought in the 1920s and 1930s gradually settled on the need for three main categories of tank:

1. Light, for reconnaissance.
2. Medium, for exploitation.
3. Heavy, for infantry support.

It became universal practice that all tanks should mount the main armament in a turret with 360° of traverse, that the running gear should be sprung and that the top run of the track should be low. Generally, too, it was almost universal practice that all tanks should comprise three main compartments:

4. The driver's compartment, at the front, often also accommodating a hull machine-gunner.
5. The fighting compartment, containing the turret and turret crew.
6. The engine compartment, containing the power plant.

Thus the general design of tanks became almost standardized, differing only in the details of armament, size and weight, armour thickness and distribution, engine power and performance.

It was in the details of design, and particularly with regard to firepower, that Britain came to lag behind Germany by the outbreak of the Second World War, and behind the USSR and the USA as well during the war. Germany had never recovered from the shock of encountering British tanks in the First World War and in consequence paid more attention to the lessons to be learnt from the encounter than had any other country except the USSR. Britain's postwar tank designs were closely followed by the Germans, as were the tactics being developed by the Mechanised Force in the late 1920s and by the 1st Brigade Royal Tank Corps in the 1930s, on manoeuvres in the south of England, as well as the writings of such British tank protagonists as Basil Liddell Hart and General J.F.C. Fuller. Apart from developing armoured tactics and the organization of armoured formations, the Germans correctly placed greatest emphasis on firepower as being the most important tank characteristic; mobility and armour protection, the other characteristics, came poor second. The German superiority in firepower stemmed firstly from their having designed a range of guns suitable for tank mounting and secondly, from having tank chassis suitable, by virtue of their design of superstructure overhanging the tracks, for up-gunning when necessary. The Russians too

placed the greatest emphasis on firepower as a result of lessons learned when fighting German tanks in the Spanish Civil War. With hindsight, it would appear obvious that firepower should be the most important tank characteristic; after all, what is a tank other than a mobile chassis for a gun or guns, which provides at the same time some armour protection for the gun crew? Nevertheless, the British army continued to give priority to protection and mobility until well into the Second World War, partly because of a wrong appreciation of the tank's task and partly because, had they wanted more powerful guns, none suitable for tank mounting was available on the stocks in the artillery design establishment. The design of a more powerful gun, a 6-pdr (57-mm), had been initiated in 1938 but, due to understaffing in the design department and their preoccupation with other projects, no priority was given to this weapon and more than two years elapsed before a prototype was available for trials. It might well be asked why, when perfectly good 6-pdr guns, provided with both AP and HE ammunition, had been fitted to British tanks in World War I, the design was not modified for tanks in World War II. The answer probably lies in the fact that the earlier weapon had been a naval design, and interdepartmental rivalry precluded its modification and use by an army organization.

Thus, at the outbreak of war in 1939, British Cruiser and Infantry tanks were all armed with either a 2-pdr (40-mm) high velocity gun or, in the CS tanks, a 3-inch howitzer, while German medium tanks carried either a 37-mm high velocity gun or a 75-mm howitzer. It was not until 1942 that the 6-pdr (57-mm) began to be fitted in British tanks, and by this time the German tanks were mounting long-barrelled 50-mm or 75-mm guns, with 88-mm guns envisaged for the Tiger tanks then being designed.

The term 'tank firepower' includes all those items which together make up the armament of a tank. These include the main armament, together with its recoil gear, cradle and mounting, elevating and traverse mechanisms, sighting and fire control system and ammunition, the auxiliary armament, together with its mounting(s), ammunition and sights, and vision and target acquisition devices. The chapters that follow deal with developments in all these aspects of firepower by the main tank developing and producing countries (Britain, Germany, USSR and USA) in the Second World War. Another chapter covers general tank design parameters, the limitations they place upon tank armament and the effects of armament selection on vehicle design. The contribution of the other combatant tank-producing countries (France, Italy and Japan) to the development of tank firepower in the Second World War is of insufficient significance to warrant inclusion, and these countries are therefore omitted from consideration in these pages. Comparative weapon and ammunition dimensions and performance characteristics are given in the Appendices at the back of the book.

CHAPTER TWO

TANK DESIGN AND FIREPOWER

The firepower of a tank is its most important characteristic and its sole *raison d'être*. Armament selection will therefore play a large part in the tank's design; a large but not an overriding part, however, as there are many other factors, both physical and mechanical, which affect it and, like most things in life, the design of any tank represents a compromise between conflicting and sometimes mutually exclusive requirements.

A tank is designed by a team, made up of specialist designers of such aspects as armament, fire control, power plant, running gear and armour; the team must also concern itself with working within both the laws of physics and the constraints of the customer's outline specification. In addition, ergonomics and anthropometrics will be taken into account, with the aim of designing a viable machine that is easy to produce, easy to operate and maintain, is as cheap as possible, is reliable in operation and meets the customer's requirements. This is no easy task, as may be imagined, and many features which might be considered to be desirable have usually to be dropped in favour of those considered essential. This chapter is devoted to a consideration of some of the more important design constraints which affect and modify the selection of a tank's armament or firepower.

A tank design team will rarely, if ever, have an entirely free hand in the design of any armoured fighting vehicle (AFV). In the first place, the customer's requirements are paramount and these will be based upon the role that the projected vehicle will be required to fill. If, for example, the vehicle is intended for reconnaissance, priority in its design will be given to mobility. If, on the other hand, it will be used primarily to accompany and support infantry in attacks on fortifications or heavily defended positions, emphasis might well be placed on armour protection. Whatever the customer's requirements, however, there are certain fundamental parameters concerning overall vehicle height, width, length and weight within which, if the vehicle is to be sufficiently mobile, the design team must operate. These parameters are a combination of those imposed by the need for the vehicle to be strategically mobile (between and within theatres of war) and those imposed by the laws of physics if the vehicle is to be tactically mobile on the battlefield. A set of design formulae has gradually been built up by tank designers between the wars and during the Second World War, so that the viability of design proposals for a new tank can be quickly assessed.

For instance, if the projected vehicle is to be transportable by rail, the maximum permitted overall width and height are laid down by the loading gauges of the rail networks over which it is likely to be carried. Maximum width is also limited by the portable bridging and other river-crossing equipment in service with the army for which the vehicle is destined; maximum permissible vehicle weight and ground pressure are similarly limited by this equipment.

Once the maximum permissible width has been thus specified, the approximate length of the track on ground can be derived from the physical relationship between the length

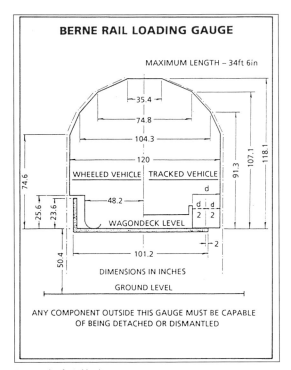

An example of a rail loading gauge.

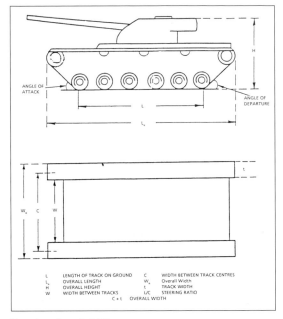

Dimensions of a tracked AFV.

of track on ground (L) and the width between track centres (C) – known as the the steering or L/C ratio – which must lie between 1.2 and 1.8 for maximum manoeuvrability. A vehicle too long in relation to its width will be difficult, if not impossible, to steer, while too short a vehicle will be directionally unstable.

The weight of a tracked vehicle is exerted on the ground through its tracks, and it was found from experience between the wars that, for reasonable performance on soft ground, a nominal ground pressure (NGP) beneath the tracks of between 6 and 12 lbs per square inch (psi) is necessary. If the NGP is greater than 12 psi, the vehicle will be liable to become bogged down in soft ground, while if it is lower than 6 psi it will lose adhesion in harder, hilly conditions. It is obvious that the NGP will be a function of both vehicle weight and the area of the track in contact with the ground. With the length of track on ground

(L) already derived from the steering (L/C) ratio, the area of track on the ground can only be varied by changing the width of the track.

The height of an AFV is affected not only by the rail loading gauge, in a conventional design of turreted tank, but also by the height of a standing man (the loader) in the turret; the recoil length of the gun in full depression; the loading length of the longest round of ammunition; the ground clearance specified by the customer and the height of the power plant. These then are some of the constraints placed upon the tank designers before detailed design can start. However, the customer will have specified the performance expected from the tank's main armament and, within these constraints, design effort will concentrate first on finding the armament to achieve this performance and then on fitting it into a tank whose overall dimensions will fall within the limits imposed by them. The armament selected will in turn impose certain dimensional constraints upon

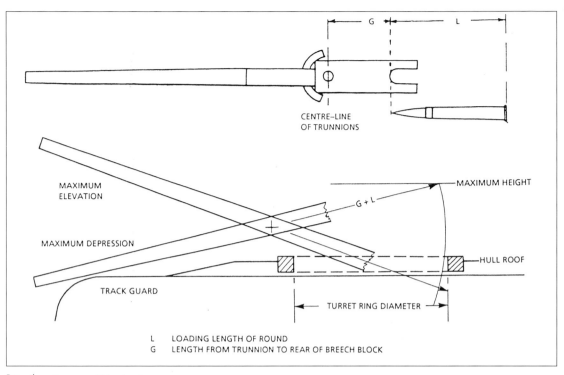

CENTRE–LINE
OF TRUNNIONS

MAXIMUM HEIGHT

G + L

MAXIMUM
ELEVATION

MAXIMUM DEPRESSION

HULL ROOF

TRACK GUARD

TURRET RING DIAMETER

L   LOADING LENGTH OF ROUND
G   LENGTH FROM TRUNNION TO REAR OF BREECH BLOCK

Fitting the main armament into a turret.

the designers, particularly if, as is likely, the main weapon is a high velocity gun with long recoil and long rounds of ammunition. The tank has over the years increasingly become an anti-tank weapon, so that its main armament has tended to be just such a gun, firing as its primary ammunition rounds which depend upon the projectile's kinetic energy to penetrate armour. High explosive anti-personnel ammunition, as well as smoke, can usually also be fired by such a gun (provided it is of a sufficiently large calibre for its HE projectile to be adequately lethal), but only in a secondary role and carried in correspondingly smaller quantities.

As can be seen from the diagram, in a turreted tank the minimum diameter of the turret ring, on which the turret rotates, is dictated by the gun's maximum recoil length as well as by the distance from the gun elevation trunnions to the rear of the gun breech block (G) added to the length of ammunition to be loaded (L). As the turret ring diameter cannot exceed the overall width of the tank, which has already been limited by rail loading gauge and portable bridging width limits, it is obvious that there is an upper limit to the size of gun which can be mounted in the projected tank. If the gun is to be able to clear external components of the tank, such as the track guards, engine decks, etc., at maximum depression, the angle of which will most probably have been defined by the customer, this will place a further limitation on the turret designer by defining a minimum height for the gun trunnions above the roof of the tank hull. This in turn will affect the minimum height of the turret roof above the trunnions.

Thus, by defining the degree of mobility,

both strategic and tactical, required of the projected vehicle, together with the performance expected of its main armament, the maximum weight, the size of the crew, the armour protection required and the tank's desired performance in terms of obstacle-crossing, road range and maximum speed, the customer has to a very great extent already designed the tank. The design team now has to examine the customer requirements in detail, to determine which of them can be met, which cannot and where compromises have to be made; as firepower is the most important of these requirements, every effort must be made to meet in full the customer's requirements regarding the armament of the projected vehicle. Since the early 1920s experience has shown that the most effective layout for a tank is one based on dividing the vehicle into three compartments:

1. The driving compartment at the front of the vehicle, containing the driver (and possibly also a co-driver/hull machine-gunner).
2. The fighting compartment in the centre, carrying the turret and main armament, turret crew and ammunition.
3. The engine compartment at the rear, containing the power plant and fuel tanks.

A tank's firepower is made up of offensive and defensive elements. Offensive firepower consists of the main and auxiliary armament, while the defensive aspect covers such close-in defence weapons as smoke projectors, anti-personnel grenade throwers and the personal weapons of the crew. Taking the offensive element first, the main armament is obviously the most important component and normally consists of:

1. A gun or howitzer. A gun is a high velocity weapon used for direct fire, the high projectile velocity ensuring that the projectile

has a low, flat trajectory. The howitzer is a low velocity weapon whose projectile has a high trajectory and is thus used for indirect fire on targets which are hidden behind obstacles or ground features. Both weapons consist of a rifled barrel, closed at one end by the breech ring and breech mechanism. At the breech end is the chamber, machined out to take the round of ammunition. The breech ring carries the lugs which connect it to the recoil mechanism as well as containing the cartridge case extractor levers. The breech mechanism comprises the breech block, with its firing mechanism, and the means of opening and closing it during the loading and firing cycle. In both the gun and howitzer firing fixed ammunition, the breech is sealed on firing by the expansion of the cartridge case in the chamber, in the process known as obturation. It contracts again after firing, so that it can be extracted when the breech is opened.

2. The cradle, in which the gun or howitzer is carried, pivoted on trunnions which enable it to be elevated or depressed in the vertical plane, and carrying the protective armoured gun mantlet. The cradle carries bearings, generally of phosphor-bronze, on which the gun/howitzer can slide when recoiling and running out.

3. The recoil gear connects the weapon to the cradle by means of the lugs on the breech ring. This consists of a buffer mechanism which absorbs the recoil of the gun/howitzer and a recuperator mechanism, which returns the weapon to its firing position (run-out).

4. The elevating mechanism connecting the weapon cradle to the turret.
5. The traverse system.
6. The fire control and sighting system.

7. The ammunition. In a low velocity weapon such as a howitzer the ammunition

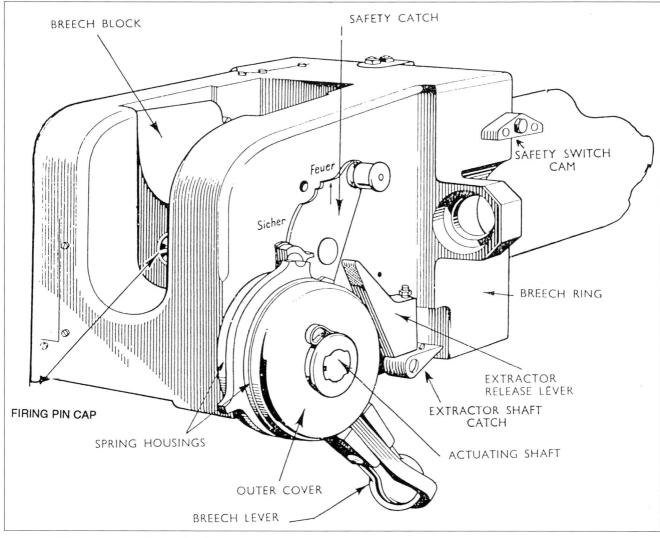

Typical gun components (German tank gun).

relies for its effect on the target upon the chemical energy (CE) of the explosive charge carried within the projectile. Types of CE projectile include High Explosive (HE) shell; Case (or canister) shot, filled with lead or steel balls which have a 'shot-gun' effect at the target on detonation; High Explosive, Anti-Tank (HEAT) shell which, on detonation at the target, burns its way through armour plate by means of the Munro Jet effect; and Smoke shell. A high velocity weapon's primary purpose, on the other hand, is to fire high velocity armour-defeating ammunition, which relies upon the projectile's kinetic energy (KE), resulting from its weight and velocity, to defeat the armour of opposing AFVs. Such weapons, provided that they are of sufficiently large calibre, can also fire CE ammunition. KE ammunition can include:

(i) Armour-piercing (AP), a solid steel shot.

(ii) Armour-piercing capped (APC), a solid steel shot with a nose cap fitted, to turn a striking projectile into the target plate and enable it to hit at 90°, or normal to the plate surface.

(iii) Armour-piercing capped, with ballistic cap (APCBC), as APC above, but with an added aero-dynamically-shaped cap to aid accuracy.

(iv) Hyper-velocity armour-piercing (AP/CR or APDS) shot, in which a small-calibre dense (e.g. tungsten-carbide) core is carried within a skeleton full-calibre projectile which disintegrates after leaving the gun barrel, leaving the core to carry on to the target at enhanced velocity.

Auxiliary armament consists of one or more machine-guns, one of which can often be used in the anti-aircraft role, firing AP and ball tracer ammunition.

Defensive firepower has a short range and is intended for the close defence of the tank, primarily against enemy infantry, artillery and tanks. It can include bomb-throwers, for throwing short-range anti-personnel grenades; smoke grenade dischargers, for discharging screening smoke to cover the tank's change of position or withdrawal; the auxiliary machine-gun armament and the crew's personal weapons (pistols or sub-machine-guns). In addition to the types of weapon already described, certain specialized armament for use against specific types of targets has also been mounted on tanks, including:

(i) Self-propelled anti-tank or artillery weapons, in limited traverse mountings, on turretless tank chassis. This is the largest category of specialized AFV weapons; it has the advantages of being cheaper to produce and simpler to maintain than a conventional turreted tank, as well as enabling a larger calibre of gun to be mounted than would be possible in a turret on any given tank. The lower silhouette also makes the turretless vehicle easier to conceal. The main disadvantages are lack of flexibility due to the gun's limited arc of traverse and limited mobility over rough ground if the gun barrel extends far beyond the front of the vehicle.

(ii) Anti-aircraft guns, single- or multi-barrelled.

(iii) Extra-large calibre mortars, for demolition of defence structures.

(iv) Flame-throwers.

(v) Rocket-propelled explosive hoses for mine-clearance.

The various components of firepower will be discussed in more detail, by country, in the succeeding chapters, but some generally applicable principles can be mentioned here. One of the cardinal rules of tank gunnery is to minimize the time between sighting a target and engaging it. As targets are usually identified by the tank commander, who has the best field of view, and transmitted verbally to the gunner by him in the form of a fire order, it helps if the commander has some means of traversing the turret so that the gunner has the target area in his sight. The commander's fire order will indicate the target and the ammunition to be used, so that the loader can load the correct round and the gunner can lay his sight on the target and, hopefully, hit it with his first shot.

To try to ensure that the gunner scores a first-round hit, the various factors which affect the flight of the projectile to the target have to be taken into account. These factors include range to the target – accurate range estimation is essential; target movement – the

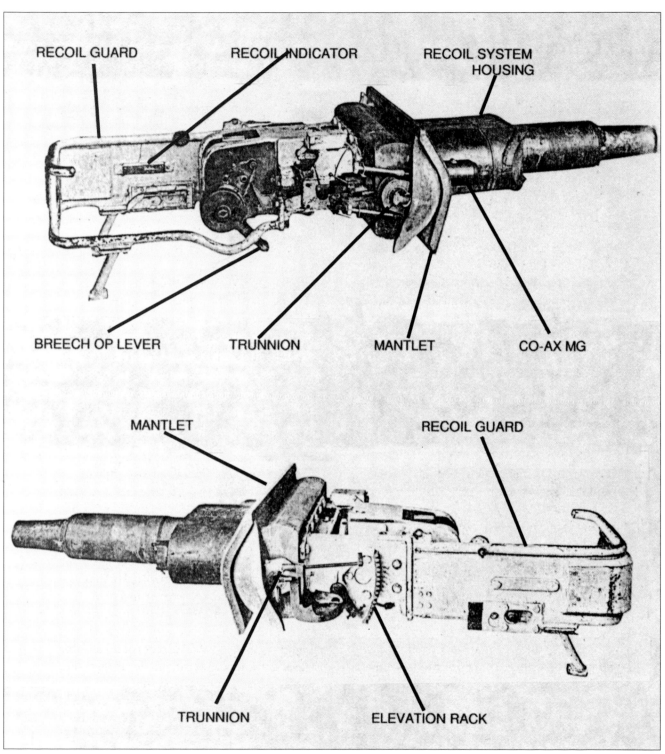

RECOIL GUARD   RECOIL INDICATOR   RECOIL SYSTEM HOUSING

BREECH OP LEVER   TRUNNION   MANTLET   CO-AX MG

MANTLET   RECOIL GUARD

TRUNNION   ELEVATION RACK

Typical tank main armament mounting (German 7.5-cm KwK L/24 from PzKpfw IV).

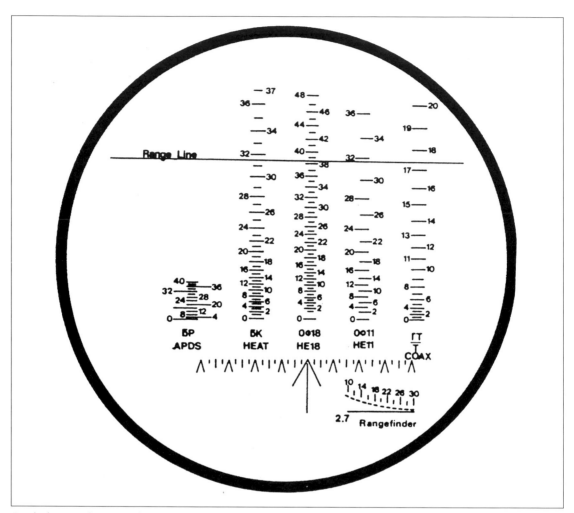

Typical sight range scale. (US Dept of Army)

gunner must be adept at 'aiming-off' the correct amount to compensate for this; cross wind – this applies more to low-velocity indirect fire as the effect on high velocity direct fire is minimal; accurate 'zeroing' of sight to gun, and elimination of any errors in the sight linkage (if any); minimising backlash in traverse and elevation systems; and rate of fire. This can also be a key factor, particularly when firing HE for effect; ammunition stowage must therefore be easily accessible and rounds easy to load.

Gun sights must be clearly marked with range scales and aiming marks, be easily replaced in case of damage and must give sufficient magnification to enable the gunner to distinguish targets at long range and in bad light. It is preferable that the sighting telescope should not allow bullets or shell fragments striking it to pass through into the gunner's eye. This can be achieved in a straight tube telescope by inserting an optical 'hinge' in the light path or by placing the sighting telescope in a periscope. For firing at night active near infrared (Near IR) light was used in conjunction with near IR sights towards the end of the Second World War. An IR searchlight was used to illuminate the target, which could then be seen by the commander through his IR sight. As this was an active system the IR searchlight on the tank tended to give away the tank's position to enemy gunners equipped with IR sights, so it was not much used. To ensure that the gunner's point of aim through his sight coincides with the axis of the gun bore, various means are used. The simplest involves placing a pair of cross-threads across the gun muzzle and laying these on a selected target at a suitable range by sighting through the firing pin hole in the breech block, using the traverse and elevating gear to do so. The gunner's sight aiming mark is then laid on the same target by means of the graticule adjusters in the sight. A more sophisticated method employs a special muzzle bore-sight, accurately machined to fit exactly in the gun muzzle, and this is used to lay the gun on to the target.

Traverse mechanisms can be either manually or power operated, the power in the latter case being provided either electrically or hydraulically, or a combination of both. Whichever method is selected, it should have a fast 'slew' rate and a smooth minimum tracking speed, and should incorporate an anti-backlash device. Obviously as turrets became heavier, as larger guns and thicker armour were used, power traverse became essential. Similarly elevation systems can employ manual or power-assisted mechanisms; as tank guns became longer either power assistance or a spring equilibrator became necessary. Early tanks employed shoulder control of the gun in elevation, even for firing on the move, but as guns increased in size this method became impracticable and was phased out during the Second World War. In its place, for firing on the move, an elementary system of power stabilization of the gun in elevation was introduced during that war and used with varying degrees of success.

Gun recoil mechanisms must incorporate some means of slowing down and stopping the gun as it recoils, and this is known as the buffer. The gun is returned to its pre-firing position by the recuperator. Both devices incorporate springs of one type or another, varying from simple coil springs to complicated hydro-pneumatic gas springs. The recoil system should also incorporate some method of indicating the length of recoil. This will also indicate the maximum permitted recoil length, so that the gunner can see when the recoil gear needs adjustment or topping up. As gun calibres and barrel lengths have increased, it has occasionally been found necessary to fit the gun with a muzzle-brake, a single- or multi-baffle device fitted to the gun muzzle to reduce recoil length.

Until 1945 at least, tank guns generally (although there were exceptions) were of the quick-firing (QF) type; that is, they fired fixed ammunition, in which the cartridge case and projectile were joined and loaded in one piece. Self-propelled artillery weapons, on the other hand, particularly the larger calibres, fired separate ammunition, in which, as the name implies, projectile and propellant charge were loaded separately. The charge could be contained either in a cartridge case (semi-fixed) or in bags (Bag-Loading or BL), which were consumed on firing and left little débris in the gun bore. With fixed and separate cased ammunition, the cartridge case is ejected from the breech into the fighting compartment after firing. Not only does this drag gun fumes with it into the fighting compartment but the fired cases also take up considerable space in the turret. They are normally ejected automatically by the gun into a bag or basket attached to the gun recoil guard and disposed of by the turret crew outside the tank at the first opportunity. Empty machine-gun cartridge cases pose

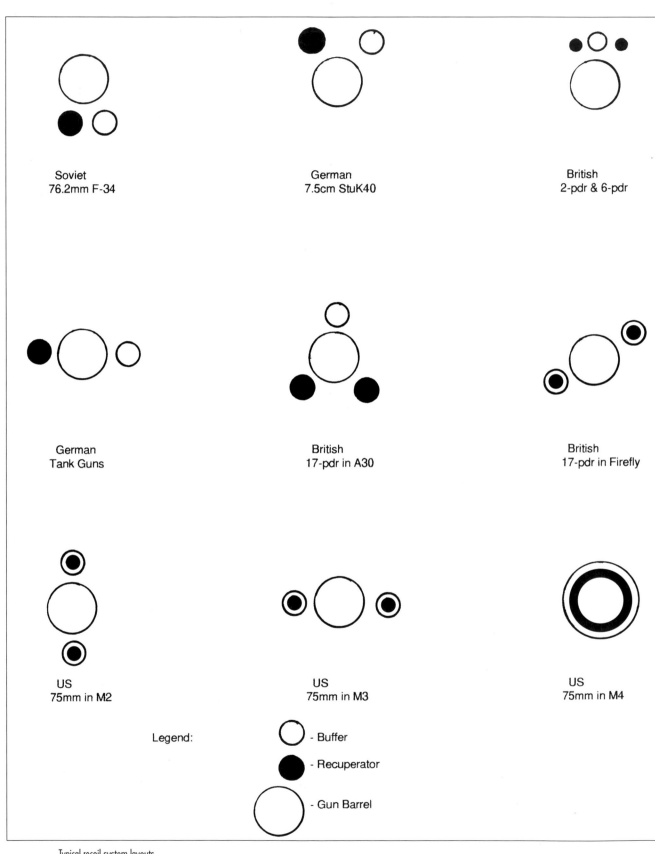

Soviet
76.2mm F-34

German
7.5cm StuK40

British
2-pdr & 6-pdr

German
Tank Guns

British
17-pdr in A30

British
17-pdr in Firefly

US
75mm in M2

US
75mm in M3

US
75mm in M4

Legend:

○ - Buffer

● - Recuperator

○ - Gun Barrel

Typical recoil system layouts.

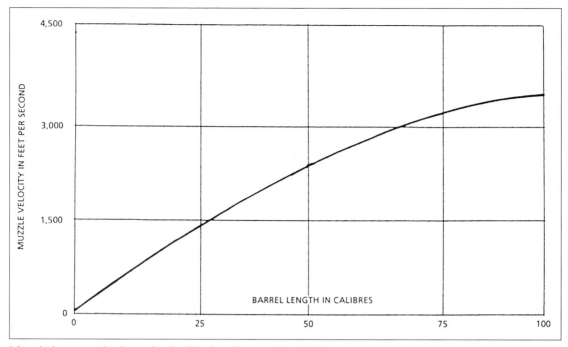

Relationship between muzzle velocity and gun barrel length in calibres. (Nachrichtenblatt der PzTruppen, Nov. 1944)

similar problems with regard to fumes and empty case disposal. To help with the fume problem, an extractor fan is often placed in the turret roof, as near to the machine-gun breech as possible, to aid in the dispersal of fumes from the interior of the turret.

With regard to auxiliary armament, it became the norm during the Second World War for one machine-gun to be mounted in the turret coaxially with the main armament, operated by the gunner and, in medium and heavy tanks particularly, for another to be hull-mounted beside the driver, operated by the co-driver. These were usually belt fed. Provision was also often made to mount a machine-gun on the turret roof. In some cases this was of a larger calibre than the normal tank machine-guns. Anti-personnel grenade dischargers were small single-load mortars disposed around the hull roof to give 360° coverage against infantry that was closing in, while smoke grenade launchers were mounted either in the turret roof, with independent traverse, or on either side of the turret to give the capacity for close smoke screening from any angle.

The following chapters show how the main combatant countries in the Second World War armed their tanks, how they developed their tanks' firepower as the war progressed and how they met and overcame the various design problems encountered in the process. It will be seen that some had a clearer idea of the relative importance of firepower than others, who tended to give greater priority to mobility and protection. Some countries too had a keener appreciation of the need to concentrate on quantity production of a few key types rather than producing small quantities of many different models. Similarly, one country, the USSR, had a very much clearer appreciation of the need for quantity rather than quality in the design and production of its AFVs.

CHAPTER THREE

BRITISH TANK ARMAMENT

As Great Britain had led the world in tank design and the tactical employment of tanks at the end of the First World War, it is therefore amazing that she entered the Second World War less well-prepared than Germany, France or the USSR in the types and quality of tanks in service or on the drawing-board. This had come about primarily because the War Office could not make up its mind about either the role to be filled by tanks in a future war or the types and quantities of tank or tanks required to fill it. It had equally failed to stand up sufficiently robustly to a parsimonious Treasury which allocated grossly insufficient funds for tank development and production. British industry, too, shared the blame, preoccupied as it was with recovery from the slump of the 1930s and coping with the business boom which followed it. Companies were unwilling to tool up for AFV orders too small to justify the capital investment involved, and only firms lacking full order books were at all interested in defence equipment contracts. These companies tended to be the more traditionalist and unimaginative, whose lack of orders tended to result from their preference for traditional manufacturing methods and their unwillingness to learn new techniques, such as the welding, rather than the traditional riveting, of armour plate.

The great exception to the lack of industry interest in tank production was Vickers-Armstrong, which had produced a multiplicity of tank designs in the pre-war years and which had, as a result, built a thriving tank export business. This had earned them a worldwide reputation as tank builders and went some way towards keeping the British flag flying in the tank field. Their plant in Newcastle was one of only two in the country specializing in tank production, the other being Nuffield Mechanisation & Aero in Birmingham, a plant built by Lord Nuffield in 1937 on modern production lines. The Royal Ordnance Factory at Woolwich also had some limited experience of tank design and production, but Vickers had the only design team with great experience in this field. Nuffield Mechanisation's designers had been drawn from its sister company, Morris Commercial Motors, and thus had experience of designing nothing heavier than a wheeled 8-ton truck.

While Vickers was perfectly able to survive on its tank export business, at least until the outbreak of war, it did its best to accommodate War Office requirements within the capacity of its plant. War Office patronage lent the cachet of official approval to its private venture designs, so their design team worked, where possible, to General Staff statements of requirements. They were thus privy to War Office thinking and enjoyed unprecedented access to officials and facilities, even establishing a branch of their drawing office in the Department of Tank Design, then at Woolwich.

By the time war broke out again in September 1939 the British War Office had finally made up its mind as to the categories of tank which it required for modern warfare. The Royal Armoured Corps was equipped with tanks of three categories, namely:

1. Light tanks: intended primarily for reconnaissance, thinly armoured, fast,

carried a crew of three men and were armed only with two machine-guns.

2. Cruiser (medium) tanks: intended for exploitation and rapid advance after a breakthrough, in the role traditionally fulfilled by the cavalry. They were armed with a 2-pdr high velocity anti-tank gun (or a 3-in howitzer for close support) and one or two machine-guns.

3. Infantry (heavy) tanks: designed for the support of infantry in the assault and thus heavily armoured. Apart from the Infantry Tank Mark I (Matilda), which was armed with only one 0.303-in machine-gun, they mounted the same armament as the cruisers.

LIGHT TANKS

Numerically, this was the largest category of tank in the RAC in 1939, and it was filled by a series of tanks of Vickers design, produced by Vickers, the Royal Ordnance Factory at Woolwich and other firms (in small numbers only) under Vickers' design parentage. Developed out of earlier Carden Loyd carriers, the light tank series had reached Mark VI by 1935, and it was this Mark, in various sub-Marks, that saw operational service in France in 1939–40 and in the Western Desert up to 1942. The various sub-Marks of the Light Tank Mark VI which entered service were:

Mark VI	80 produced, from July 1935 to September 1936.
Mark VIA	85 produced, from November 1936 to January 1937.
Mark VIB	850 produced, from April 1937 to January 1940. This may be described as the definitive version.
Mark VIC	130 produced from December 1939 to June 1940.

Light tank Mark VI. (Author's Collection)

All except the Mark VIC were armed with two Vickers water-cooled machine-guns, one of 0.303-in and the other of 0.5-in calibre; the Mark VIC substituted 7.92-mm and 15-mm BESA machine-guns for the Vickers. The BESA machine-gun was an adaptation by the Birmingham Small Arms Co. (BSA) of a Czech gun, the ZB 53. It had been selected as the standard British AFV machine-gun by the War Office when it had decided, in 1938, to replace the water-cooled machine-gun by an air-cooled gun in all British AFVs. Defensive armament on all Mark VI series light tanks consisted of a pair of single-shot 4-in smoke bomb-throwers.

Out of a total of some 1,100 light tanks Mark VI built, approximately 550 were shipped to France with the British Expeditionary Force and later with the 1st Armoured Division in 1939–40. There they were found to be both under-gunned and under-armoured against the German panzer units. There was little understanding in the British army, outside the Royal Tank Corps, of how light tanks were to be used in action. The possibility that light tanks might have to fight other tanks was outside the official view and therefore powerful anti-tank armament was not needed. The destruction of hostile tanks was considered to be primarily the task of the anti-tank gun. As regards armour protection, a War Office pamphlet published in 1931 (Modern Formations) stated that, for light tanks, speed was more important than firepower; weighing approximately 5 tons and with a maximum armour thickness of only 14 mm, the light tanks therefore relied upon speed for their protection, with a maximum speed on roads of some 35 m.p.h. In fact, against a well-equipped enemy the light tanks had proved useless. They were, however, excellent for training purposes and in overseas operations in India and Palestine before the Second World War against a lightly-armed enemy they had proved their

worth. They were withdrawn from active service as light tanks in 1942, as the US M3 Stuart light tanks, armed with a high velocity 37-mm anti-tank gun, had started to arrive in the Middle East from the USA, and were converted to anti-aircraft tanks, armed with either quadruple 7.92-mm BESA or two 15-mm BESA MGs.

This, however, was not the end of the British light tank. In 1937, Vickers had started the design of a private venture light tank intended to follow the Mark VI series, then in production. This vehicle was radically different from the Mark VI and its predecessors and was a notable advance over previous Vickers light tank designs. It had a more powerful armament, had a completely different running gear, was steered by 'bowing' the tracks in an arc and had thicker armour, welded rather than rivetted. An order for 120 vehicles, to be delivered in 1940, was placed by the War Office with Metropolitan-Cammell Carriage & Wagon Co. in November 1938 under the nomenclature of Light Tank Mark VII. In July 1940, as production was beginning, the General Staff reassessed tank requirements in the light of the BEF's withdrawal from France and reduced the ordered quantity to 70 tanks. The original quantity was reinstated later that month and, later still, increased by a further 120. A total of 177 Mark VIIs was eventually built, reduced from the planned total by extensive bombing of Metropolitan-Cammell's works in April 1941.

The Light Tank Mark VII was first issued to troops in November 1940 and its first operational use was in Operation Ironclad, the invasion of Madagascar in May 1942. Early that year, remaining Mark VIIs were earmarked for airborne use and at the same time the name Tetrarch, by which it is best known, was adopted for it.

The armament of Tetrarch consisted of the 2-pdr high velocity gun, with a coaxial 7.92-

Light tank Mark VII (Tetrarch). (Author's Collection)

mm BESA machine-gun, as with the cruiser and infantry tanks of the period. Some tanks, however, known as the Tetrarch CS (close support), mounted the 3-in howitzer in place of the 2-pdr gun. The difficulty in the Tetrarch, with its three man crew of which two were in the turret, was that the commander of the tank also had to load the main armament and the

MG. A few Tetrarchs were fitted with Littlejohn taper-bore adaptors on their 2-pdr guns. This was the invention of a Czech refugee, which 'squeezed' the diameter of the projectile in the bore and thus boosted the muzzle velocity and, as a result, its armour penetration performance.

The Tetrarch was not quite the last of the

Light tank Mark VIII (Harry Hopkins). (Author's Collection)

British light tanks. That honour goes to the Light Tank Mark VIII or Harry Hopkins, which first saw the light of day in 1941 as a prototype incorporating components surplus to requirements from the reduced Tetrarch order. Although incorporating many Tetrarch parts, Harry Hopkins had a completely redesigned hull with much thicker (38 mm) armour, more internal room and greater crew comfort. A Vickers design, it too was made by Metropolitan-Cammell, a total of 99 being built before the order was completed in 1944. Main armament of the Harry Hopkins was similar to that of Tetrarch, namely a 2-pdr gun with coaxial 7.92-mm BESA MG. Some Harry Hopkins chassis were used as self-propelled mountings for a 95-mm howitzer, the tank's turret being removed and the howitzer mounted, with limited traverse, in the hull glacis plate. This SP howitzer, originally known as the Harry Hopkins CS (close support), was later named Alecto. Alecto

carried a crew of five and up to forty-eight rounds of HE and smoke ammunition. Neither it nor the Harry Hopkins was used in action.

The complete list of British light tanks and their variants, together with their armament, in service in the Second World War, is as follows:

NOMENCLATURE	ARMAMENT
Mark VI	One Vickers water-cooled 0.303-in Medium MG. One Vickers water-cooled 0.5-in Heavy MG, coaxially mounted.
Mark VIA	As for Mark VI.
Mark VIB	As for Mark VI.
Mark VIC	One 15-mm BESA air-cooled Heavy MG. One 7.92-mm BESA

Light AA tank Mark I. (Author's Collection)

NOMENCLATURE	ARMAMENT
	air-cooled Medium MG, coaxially mounted.
AA Mark I	Four 7.92-mm BESA air-cooled AA MGs.
AA Mark II	Two 15-mm BESA air-cooled Heavy MGs.
Mark VII Tetrarch	One 2-pdr (40-mm) QF high velocity ATk gun or one 3-in Howitzer. One 7.92-mm BESA air-cooled Medium MG, coaxially mounted.
Mark VIII	As for Mark VII.
Mark VIII CS	One 95-mm Howitzer.

(N.B. *Full details of all the above weapons and their ammunition are given in Appendix A.*)

CRUISER TANKS

The second category of British tanks covered the Cruiser or, as it had been known until 1934, the Medium Tank. These were moderately fast and relatively lightly armoured 'cavalry' tanks, intended to be launched through the gaps punched in the enemy defences by the heavier infantry tanks and to penetrate far behind enemy lines in the exploitation role traditionally filled by the cavalry. The early tanks in this category were unnamed, being known only by their GS specification ('A') numbers. Thus the first to reach the army in 1938 in limited numbers were known as the A9, A10 and A13, respectively the Cruiser Tanks Mark I (A9), Mark II (A10) and Mark III (A13). The A9 and A10 shared the same Carden-designed running gear, engine, transmission and main

SP 25-pdr gun Alecto. (Tank Museum 863.02)

armament, the latter being the ubiquitous 2-pdr (40-mm) high velocity gun (or a 3.7-in (95-mm) breech-loading fixed charge mortar in the close-support versions) mounted in a turret with 360° traverse. Auxiliary armament consisted initially of a 0.303-in Vickers water-cooled MG mounted coaxially with the main armament and, in the case of the A9, two auxiliary turrets in the forward part of the hull roof, each mounting one 0.303-in Vickers MG. The A10 carried only one hull MG, a 7.92-mm BESA mounted in the hull front plate. The A10 was caught in the changeover from 0.303-in Vickers to the 7.92-mm BESA so in the original Cruiser Mark II version of the tank the hull MG was eliminated to simplify ammunition supply and stowage; the later Mark IIA had BESA MGs in both turret and hull mountings.

The A13 was itself produced in three Marks, all of which carried the same main armament as their predecessors, and all of which ran on a derivative of the revolutionary US Christie running gear. This used large diameter road wheels on a suspension system which gave a smoother ride than conventional systems and allowed very large vertical wheel movement, and thus high speed, across rough country. The decision to adopt this system led to the premature relegation of the A9 and A10 in favour of the A13 which, although having the same 14-mm armour basis as its predecessors, had a much higher maximum speed, in excess of 30 m.p.h. on roads. As with the A9 and A10, and indeed all cruiser tanks up to the A34 'Comet' of 1944, the hull consisted basically of an oblong box carried entirely

Cruiser tank Mark II (A10). (Author's Collection)

between the tracks. The width between the tracks thus limited the turret ring diameter and hence the maximum size of gun that could be mounted as main armament. This limitation should be borne in mind when the inferiority of British tanks' firepower compared to the German throughout the Second World War is discussed later. The A13 Mark I (Cruiser Tank Mark III) was built by Nuffield Mechanisation & Aero and carried a turret similar to that of the A9 but with a commander's cupola added. The A13 Mark II (Cruiser Tank Mark IV) was an up-armoured version of the Mark I with the extra armour bolted on, adding about 1 ton to the overall weight of the tank and very little to the protection. A later version, the Mark IVA, replaced the coaxial Vickers MG with the 7.92-mm BESA. The cruiser tanks Marks I to IV inclusive went to France with the BEF but did not perform well there. They were considered to be under-armoured, under-powered, unreliable and with tracks which

were too narrow and came off too easily, as a result of which they were taken out of production after the Dunkirk evacuation. However, the same tanks were represented in the Middle East, where there were no complaints and where they travelled hundreds of miles on their tracks without trouble. A better climate and better maintenance were probably the reason for the different reactions in the two theatres of war.

The Cruiser Tank Mark V (A13 Mark III) was the first cruiser tank to be named and was called 'Covenanter', thus starting the tradition of giving British tanks names beginning with the letter 'C'. It was a good-looking tank, designed by the London, Midland & Scottish Railway Co. before the Second World War, and it succeeded the A9, A10 and earlier Marks of A13, which had been taken out of production in 1939–40. Production started in April 1939 and continued until January 1943, but the Covenanter never saw action although large

Cruiser tank Mark III (A13). (Author's Collection)

Cruiser tank Mark IV (A13 Mark II). (Author's Collection)

Cruiser tank Mark V (A13 Mark III: Covenanter). (Author's Collection)

numbers were used for training. It was one of a series of fast cruiser tanks based upon the Christie suspension system. Like its predecessors it proved unreliable in service, suffering eternal cooling problems as well as track breakage and track throwing. Despite this, it was allowed, by a lack of firm control by the Ministry of Supply, to remain in production until 1943, for two years clogging up production lines, and using materials in short supply, which could have been better used for the production of superior cruiser tanks waiting in the pipeline. The main armament of Covenanter was the 2-pdr high velocity gun, the same as that of the A9, A10 and A13 Marks I and II; the auxiliary armament consisted of a 7.92-mm BESA MG mounted coaxially with the main gun. Having no other MG, the tank needed a crew of only four men, consisting of driver, gunner, loader/radio operator and commander.

Covenanter was succeeded by the Cruiser Tank Mark VI (A15), named 'Crusader' on its introduction into service and designed and built by Nuffield Mechanisation & Aero. It continued the use of the Christie suspension and in some other respects, such as the transmission, used Covenanter components. The original main armament was again the 2-pdr (40-mm) high velocity gun. Auxiliary armament consisted of two 7.92-mm BESA MGs, one mounted coaxially with the 2-pdr and the other in a sub-turret on the forward hull roof, next to the driver. At this time, the British army had six different Cruiser tanks and three Infantry tanks all armed with the 2-pdr, a gun which, in 1940, had out-performed its German 37-mm equivalent but which, by 1941, was clearly past its sell-by date. A replacement, the 57-mm calibre 6-pdr, was available, design having started in 1938 and a prototype ready for testing in early 1940, but shortages of staff and material, together with the unsuitability of the narrow British tank hulls then in service for adaptation to accept it, led to all the initial 6-pdr production being used for field anti-tank gun mountings. In the autumn of 1941, however, Nuffield Mech were asked to produce a scheme for modifying the Crusader to accept the 6-pdr in place of the 2-pdr, and a prototype for firing trials was completed and sent to Lulworth in the November. Production orders were placed as the result of the satisfactory completion of trials, and about 100 modified Crusaders, known as Crusader III, were available for the battle of Alamein in October 1942. Regiments of 6 Armoured Division were also equipped with 6-pdr tanks for the invasion of French north Africa (Operation Torch) the following month, and the Churchill infantry tanks of the 1st Army's two Army Tank Brigades in north Africa were also armed with the new gun.

By this time the Crusader was already considered obsolescent; like its predecessors, it too was very unreliable and the two-man turret, necessitated by the incursion of the 6-pdr into the turret, difficult and tiring to operate for the commander. It was succeeded temporarily by the Cruiser Tank Mark VII (A24), originally named Cromwell I and later renamed Cavalier, with a 6-pdr gun as main armament and auxiliary armament of two 7.92-mm BESA MGs, one coaxially mounted with the 6-pdr and the other in the hull. This had been on the stocks since mid-1941 and first entered service in July 1942. It was not a success and only fifty were built, most being converted to armoured observation posts for artillery and to armoured recovery vehicles. It was succeeded by two versions of the Cruiser Tank Mark VIII, one of which, the A27L (known in service as Centaur), was designed by Leyland Motors and was powered by the old Liberty engine (the 'L' after 'A27' stood for 'Liberty'), and the other, the A27M (Cromwell), designed by Birmingham Railway Carriage and Wagon Co. (BRC&W)

and powered by the new Rolls-Royce Meteor engine, developed from their Merlin aircraft engine, the 'M' in the A27 designation standing for 'Meteor'. Both versions had turrets designed round the 6-pdr/coaxial 7.92-mm BESA MG combination, as well as a ball-mounted 7.92-mm BESA auxiliary MG in the hull front vertical plate.

In external appearance, the A27L and M versions, as well as the A24, were almost indistinguishable. No use was made of sloped armour, the turrets in particular being square slab-sided affairs and the armour of both hull and turret of bolted and riveted rather than welded construction. It should be noted, however, that the outline design had been first drawn up in 1940, when the desert war was at a very early stage, which explains why some outmoded construction practices and design features were incorporated. For example, the main armament/coaxial MG had free elevation, shoulder-controlled by the gunner, rather than a mechanical geared system; shoulder-control of elevation had been introduced between the wars as a means of firing reasonably accurately on the move and, with the low speeds common to tanks of that period, it was a cheap and simple technique which gave reasonable results. With the advent of faster tanks with more flexible suspension systems, together with heavier main armament with greater barrel length, it became more difficult to maintain a consistent point of aim from a moving tank. In addition, a geared elevation system gives greater accuracy and stability over long ranges and also for indirect fire. Finally, in an attempt to keep the main armament in balance for shoulder control, a greater length of the gun had to protrude behind the trunnions into the turret, thus reducing crew space in the turret.

With the 6-pdr at this time, however, there was no call for indirect fire capability as there was no HE shell for this gun. The arrival of

Cruiser tank Mark VI (A15 Mark III: Crusader). (Author's Collection)

Crusader III (6-pdr). (Author's Collection)

the US M4 Medium Tank (Sherman) in British service in the Middle East theatre changed all that. The Sherman's 75-mm gun was a truly dual-purpose weapon, combining reasonable anti-tank performance with an excellent HE capacity, which enabled the tank to take on anti-tank gunners at ranges beyond the accurate reach of the machine-gun which was the British tanks' anti-personnel weapon. In addition, the Sherman not only had geared elevation which enabled accurate indirect fire but also included a rudimentary gyro-stabilizer in the elevation system which permitted reasonably accurate fire on the move. Although the stabilizer was not at first looked upon with favour by British tank gunners it gradually became not only accepted but essential, and provision

was made for its inclusion in the projected A41 'Universal Tank' (which later became the Centurion, prototypes of which were introduced just before the end of the war in Europe). Meanwhile, the provision of a high explosive round for the 6-pdr was being investigated with some urgency, together with schemes for this gun's replacement by a more powerful tank gun of at least 75-mm calibre with dual anti-tank and anti-personnel capability. While the search for a suitable dual-purpose tank weapon went on, the concept of separate gun and close-support tanks was also pursued. Again, a weapon of sufficiently large calibre to have a shell with a good high explosive performance was sought, and in 1942 a suitable weapon was formed by combining a shortened 3.7-in gun barrel

Crusader III AA Mark I. (Author's Collection)

Crusader III AA Mark II. (Author's Collection)

Cruiser tank Mark VIII Cromwell (A27). (Author's Collection)

with the breech ring of the 25-pdr field gun. This weapon was known as the 95-mm howitzer.

The fate of Centaur as a front-line tank was virtually sealed in 1943 by an exhaustive and detailed comparative automotive and gunnery trial, known as Exercise Dracula, between these two tanks and the petrol (M4A4) and diesel (M4A2) versions of the Sherman, in which both Shermans came out easily ahead of the British tanks in everything except maximum speed. As a result, production was sharply cut back and those tanks in service, apart from those in the training organization, were modified into anti-aircraft tanks, as the Centaur AA Mark I, armed with twin 20-mm Polsten cannon in a high angle mounting, carried in a well-armoured turret. Some chassis were also converted later into armoured bulldozers, known as the Centaur Dozer.

Cromwell was produced in large numbers, starting in February 1943; versions (Cromwell VI and VIII) armed with the 95-mm howitzer remained in service with armoured regiments until the 1950s. From the end of 1943 the 6-pdr of the Cromwell I, II and III was replaced by the British 75-mm tank gun in the Cromwell IV, V and VII. Versions with welded instead of riveted armour were the Cromwell Vw and VIIw. A further development of this tank, under GS Specification A30, was initiated in 1943, with a view to mounting the newly-developed 17-pdr (76.2-mm) high velocity anti-tank gun. The A30 was known in service as Challenger and it came into service in 1944, twelve (four per squadron) being provided in each armoured regiment. Only 200 had been ordered, but it was not a success, being under-armoured and difficult to steer because of its increased length, necessitated by the

Cruiser tank Challenger (A30). (Author's Collection)

SP tank destroyer Avenger (A30). (Author's Collection)

greater weight of the gun and turret. This had not been accompanied by a corresponding increase in width between track centres, increasing the L/C ratio to an unacceptable level. In case the A30 project did not prove successful, a parallel investigation into the possibility of mounting the 17-pdr gun in the Sherman had luckily, and unofficially, been undertaken at the RAC Gunnery School at Lulworth. This proved successful and a number of Shermans were so modified, the resulting tank being known as the Sherman Firefly. In December 1943 an order was placed on the Royal Ordnance Factory at Barnbow, Leeds, for the modification of 2,100 M4A4 tanks and so the best tank in the arsenal of the Western Allies came, almost by accident, into service.

Meanwhile in 1943, work had been progressing on a successor to Cromwell and Challenger, to General Staff specification A34. This tank, again based on Cromwell technology, was originally intended to mount a 75-mm gun of Vickers design but this was later changed, for reasons of commonality, to a 17-pdr (76.2-mm) gun modified by Vickers. To distinguish it clearly from other guns of this calibre it was designated as the 'Gun, QF, Tank 77mm' and it was only marginally less effective against tank targets than the 17-pdr. An order for 2,000 of the A34 was placed in 1944 and the prototype was completed in March of that year. Production started in the autumn, and by January 1945 143 had been built; the new tank was called Comet and it had an all-welded hull and a turret which was part cast and part rolled plate, again all-welded. Besides the 77-mm main armament, Comet had a coaxial 7.92-mm BESA MG and another in a ball mounting in the hull front

Cruiser tank Comet (A34). (Author's Collection)

vertical plate. Mechanically identical with the Cromwell, Comet was nevertheless a much better tank. Slightly slower (29 m.p.h.) and heavier (32.5 tons), it had a gun which far out-performed the 75-mm gun of the Cromwell, especially firing the new discarding sabot (APDS) ammunition at a muzzle velocity of some 3,600 ft/sec. It first saw action after the Rhine crossing but, despite its short war experience, was soon adjudged a success, proving reliable and far more effective than Challenger or Cromwell. It remained in service for almost fifteen years, the last being withdrawn from service in 1960.

Had it not been designed as a heavy cruiser, Comet might well have filled the role of the 'Universal Tank' so assiduously propounded by FM Montgomery. It was certainly well armoured and was armed with a very effective dual-purpose gun. To fill that role, however, GS specification A41 was written; it had first been mooted in August 1943 as a heavy cruiser tank able to defeat,

by the time it was in production, any German tank of its class. The aim was to have pilot and pre-production models ready by the end of 1944, with production starting on a small scale by the second quarter of 1945. The tank was to have the 17-pdr (76.2-mm) as main armament with a coaxial MG, with the possibility of up-gunning later to the 32-pdr (93.4-mm) gun. It was to weigh up to 45 tons, with frontal armour of 100 mm thickness. Production in fact started in May 1945, in the Royal Ordnance Factories at Woolwich and Nottingham, and the tank was named Centurion in service. It saw no action in the Second World War, but six prototypes were rushed out to Germany in Operation Sentry to be evaluated under combat conditions. Unfortunately, or fortunately, according to one's viewpoint, Germany surrendered before training could start. Automotive and gunnery trials were carried out and familiarization visits were made to other armoured regiments in Germany before the tanks returned to the UK in July 1945.

Cruiser tank Centurion (A41). (Author's Collection)

User opinion had been unanimously favourable; most crews who had tried them considered them to be 'the best I've ever seen'. However, two alternative auxiliary armament fits had been supplied in the coaxial position, one being the 20-mm Polsten drum-fed cannon and the other a conventional medium MG. The 20-mm Polsten was universally condemned as it and its ammunition took up more stowage space than the gun's effectiveness warranted. The Centurion remained in production for many years and in service with the British army and the armies of many overseas countries for many more; up-gunned and up-armoured several times, it was a very effective and reliable tank which re-established the British lead in tank design last seen at the end of the First World War. But it must not be thought that Centurion was ahead of its time. It was only approximately equivalent in firepower and armour protection to the German Panther, which had first appeared in quantity two years earlier, in 1943, while its firepower was inferior to those of the Tiger Models E and B. Where it scored over all its rivals, however, was in its combination of adequate firepower and protection with excellent mobility and reliability, both of these qualities being vastly superior to those of the Panther and both models of Tiger.

The British system of gun nomenclature was confusing to say the least. It was not until sometime after the Second World War that a more logical system of identifying a gun by its calibre and barrel length was introduced. Prior to and during the war, many guns were identified by the weight of the projectile fired, coupled often with the weight of the gun, for example, 'Gun, Tank, QF, 6-pdr 7 cwt'. Other weapons, such as the 3.7-in mortar, the 3-in howitzer and the 95-mm howitzer were identified by their calibre and also sometimes by their weight (for example, Howitzer, QF, 3 in 20 cwt).

'QF' stands for 'quick-firing', denoting that the projectile and propelling charge are fixed together and the fixed propelling charge is contained in a cartridge case. 'BL' stands for 'bag-loading' and is used to describe weapons the ammunition for which consists of separate projectile and propellant charge, the latter being variable and contained in bags.

The following is a list of cruiser tanks and their variants, together with their armament, which saw service in the Second World War. It excludes special adaptations such as dozers, bridgelayers, recovery vehicles and mine-clearance devices based on cruiser tank chassis which were not fighting tanks.

NOMENCLATURE	ARMAMENT
Mark I (A9)	One 2-pdr (40-mm) high velocity gun. One coaxial 0.303-in water-cooled Vickers MG. Two hull-mounted 0.303-in water-cooled Vickers MGs.
Mark I (CS)	One 3.7-in breech-loaded mortar. Aux. armament as for Cruiser Mark I.
Mark II (A10)	Main armt as for Cruiser Mark I. One hull-mounted 0.303-in water-cooled Vickers MG.
Mark II (CS)	Main armt as for Cruiser Mark I (CS). Aux. armt as for Cruiser Mark II.
Mark III (A13 Mark I)	Main armt as for Cruiser Mark I. One coaxial 0.303-in water-cooled Vickers MG.

NOMENCLATURE	ARMAMENT	NOMENCLATURE	ARMAMENT
Mark IV (A13 Mark II)	Main armt as for Cruiser Mark I. Aux. armt as for Cruiser Mark II or two 7.92-mm BESA MGs.	Mk III	Twin 20-mm Oerlikon cannon only.
		Mark VII (A24L) (Cavalier)	Main armt as for Crusader Mark III. One coaxial 7.92-mm BESA MG. One hull-mounted ditto.
Mark V (A13 Mark III) (Covenanter)	Main armt as for Cruiser Mark I. One coaxial 7.92-mm BESA MG.	Mark VIII (A27L) (Centaur)	Main and aux. armt as for Cavalier.
Mark V (CS)	One 3-in howitzer. Aux. armt as for Cruiser Mark V.	Centaur Mark IV (CS)	One 95-mm howitzer. Aux. armament as for Cavalier.
Mark VI (A15 Mark I) (Crusader)	Main armt as for Cruiser Mark I. One coaxial 7.92-mm BESA MG. One hull-mounted 7.92-mm BESA MG.	Centaur AA Mark I	Twin 20-mm Polsten cannon, no hull MG.
		Mark VIII (A27M) (Cromwell Marks I, II &III)	Main and aux. armt as for Cavalier.
Ditto (Mark II)	Main armt as for Cruiser Mark I. One coaxial 7.92-mm BESA MG.	(Marks IV, V & VII)	One 75-mm gun. Aux. armt as for Cavalier
Ditto (Mark III)	One 6-pdr (57-mm) 7 cwt gun. One coaxial 7.92-mm BESA MG.	Cromwell CS (Marks VI & VIII)	One 95-mm Howitzer. Aux. armt as for Cavalier.
Mark VI (CS)	One 3-in howitzer. Aux. armt as for Cruiser Mark V.	Challenger (A30)	One 17-pdr (76.2-mm) gun. One coaxial 7.92-mm BESA MG.
Crusader Command tank	6-pdr and coaxial MG replaced by dummy gun.	Comet (A34)	One 77-mm gun. Aux. armt as for Cavalier.
Crusader OP tank	Ditto, coaxial BESA MG retained.	Centurion (A41) Mark I gun.	One 17-pdr (76.2-mm) One 20-mm Polsten cannon or one coaxial 7.92-mm BESA MG in turret.
Crusader AA tank Mark I	One 40-mm Bofors AA gun.		
Crusader AA tank Mk II	Twin 20-mm Oerlikon cannon and coaxial Vickers gas-operated MG.		

(N.B. *Full details of the above weapons and their ammunition are given in Appendix A.*)

INFANTRY TANKS

The British were almost alone before the Second World War in requiring a category of tank devoted to supporting the infantry soldier on foot in the frontal assault of defended positions. Tanks in this category were more heavily armoured (60–80 mm on the front) and slower, with a maximum speed of 15 m.p.h., than the cruisers. Firepower of the Infantry tanks was in most cases inferior or identical to that of the Cruiser tanks already described, consisting generally of a 2-pdr, 6-pdr or 3-in howitzer as main armament with either 0.303-in Vickers or 7.92-mm BESA machine-guns as coaxial and hull auxiliary armament. As with the Cruisers, firepower was relegated, top priority in this case being given to protection where with the Cruisers it had been given to mobility.

For such a task, the Infantry tanks' firepower until 1944 was pathetically inadequate; only the Close Support (CS) tanks had main armament with an anti-personnel capability for firing high explosive shell, and the 2-pdr high velocity gun firing only armour-piercing shot was of no use against defences, infantry in the open or artillery gun crews, although its penetrative performance against enemy armour was better than its equivalent German weapon, the 37-mm tank and anti-tank gun. The need for a specialized infantry support tank was always questionable but was perpetuated by the unfortunate combination in the War Office in 1935 of a cautious Master General of the Ordnance (MGO) (General Sir Hugh Elles, the Tank Corps commander in France in the First World War), who questioned the tactical side, and a highly-qualified engineer as Director of Mechanisation (Major-General Davidson), who questioned the technical side of the fast cruiser tank armed with a high velocity gun. Elles still saw tank warfare in terms of his experience in 1917–18, as a result of which he favoured tanks with thick armour and anti-personnel, rather than anti-tank, armament, supporting infantry on to their objectives rather than operating on their own looking for enemy tanks to engage; he does not seem to have considered what would happen to such tanks if they encountered enemy tanks looking for them. To Elles, speed and anti-tank firepower were of little importance, although to the Royal Tank Corps (RTC) at that time it had long been held that every tank should have a gun.

On Elles, therefore, must fall a large part of the blame for the first Infantry tank, built to General Staff specification A11 by Vickers under their codename Matilda in 1935–6. This ridiculous vehicle came into service as the Infantry Tank Mark I (Matilda) in February 1939. Designed down to a price (it cost only some £5,000 per tank, and that included development costs), it had the three advantages of thick (70 mm) armour, light weight (11 tons) and cheapness; these advantages were easily outweighed, however, by its inadequate armament of one 0.303-in Vickers machine-gun, its low maximum speed of 8 m.p.h. and small crew of only two men. It was immediately criticized by the RTC as being no faster than the Mark V of the First World War and powerless against other tanks. In extenuation it must be said that the German PzKpfw I, the first tank produced in Germany after Hitler's accession to power and first used in the Spanish Civil War in 1936, was lighter and had thinner armour than the Matilda, although it was armed with two 7.92-mm machine-guns as against the one Vickers MG of the British vehicle and had a three man crew. A total of 140 'I' Tanks Mark I was nevertheless produced, as an interim measure pending the introduction of a better vehicle. The majority were sent to France with the BEF in 1939–40 and left there after the evacuation.

Infantry tank Mark I Matilda (A11). (Author's Collection)

Within the RTC, demand grew for a bigger Matilda, faster and armed with a gun, so the General Staff issued their specification A12, calling for a tank armed with the 2-pdr (40-mm) high velocity gun, protected by armour with a maximum thickness of 70 mm and with a crew of four men. The firm charged with its development was the Vulcan Foundry, and their solution involved a cast turret and a hull fabricated from castings and rolled plate, giving much cleaner lines than had previously been seen in British tanks. The prototype reached the military testing establishment in April 1938 and the trials officers were highly pleased with its performance. There is no doubt that it was not only the best British tank but also one of the best in the world at that time. It was only unfortunate that its turret ring diameter would not permit the mounting of a larger gun. Production orders were soon placed, but it was a complicated tank to produce and not

one suited to mass production, so that, by the outbreak of war in September 1939, only two were in service. It became the Infantry Tank Mark II (A12) in service, and inherited the name Matilda from its predecessor when the latter went out of service after Dunkirk. In addition to the 2-pdr main armament, auxiliary armament consisted of one coaxial machine-gun (0.303-in Vickers in the Matilda I, 7.92-mm BESA in later Marks) and two single-shot 4-in smoke bomb-throwers mounted externally on the turret side but operable by cable from within the turret. In the close support version of the Matilda, the Infantry Tank Mark II (Matilda) CS, a 3-in (76.2-mm) howitzer was substituted for the 2-pdr gun.

A total of 2,987 Matildas was produced and the tank saw service in the Middle East, Australia and the Soviet Union, production ceasing in August 1943. Matilda was used as the basis for a series of mine-clearing tanks

Infantry tank Mark II Matilda (A12). (Author's Collection)

mounting rotary flails; the first version was known as Scorpion and retained the Matilda's turret and armament, the second as Baron, from which the turret was removed. Both these versions, as well as one with an anti-mine roller device (AMRA: Anti-Mine Roller Attachment), were used in the Western Desert campaign. The other device which used the Matilda as a basis was the Matilda CDL (Canal Defence Light). This consisted of a special turret containing a searchlight with a 'flickering' device shining through a narrow slit and intended to give light for night action and to dazzle the enemy. Some 300 of these devices were ordered in 1940 but, although available in the UK and the Middle East, they were never used in action.

The successor to the Matilda, the Infantry Tank Mark III or Valentine, was not designed to meet a General Staff specification but was a private venture by Vickers Armstrong; it

thus had no 'A' number. It seems odd to say the least that in time of war, and with tank design and building capacity in short supply, one of the key producers of tanks in the UK could find the time and the design capacity to produce a private venture tank. It was typical of the lack of firm control exerted by the Ministry of Supply over tank manufacturers such as Vickers and Nuffield Mechanisation during the Second World War, one of the reasons for the multiplicity of tank types of inferior design and firepower with which the long-suffering Royal Armoured Corps was inflicted. The name 'Valentine' reflects its Vickers parentage, as Vickers always liked to give its aircraft and tank products names beginning with the letter 'V'.

In fact, Vickers' proposals for the new tank had been first presented to, and turned down by, the War Office in February 1938; revised proposals were accepted, however, and a

Infantry tank Mark III Valentine (Author's Collection)

production order placed in July 1939, with deliveries to start in May 1940. Production was shared between Vickers at Newcastle-on-Tyne, Metropolitan-Cammell at Wednesbury, Staffs., and Birmingham Railway Carriage and Wagon Co. By June 1940 10 had been delivered and production increased until a total of 6,855 Valentines had been built in England by the time production ceased in 1945. In addition to these, a further 1,420 were built in Canada by the Canadian Pacific Railway in Montreal between June 1941 and mid-1943, when Canadian production terminated. The combined total of 8,275 vehicles was far greater than that of any other British tank produced in the Second World War, the British-built total alone exceeding that for the Churchill, the next most popular British tank.

The Valentine was quite different in appearance and construction from its predecessor. Where the Matilda employed gently curved or sloped castings the Valentine used flat rolled plate in a rivetted and bolted construction of mainly vertical armour. A much simpler tank to build and maintain than Matilda, the Valentine was 10 tons lighter, shorter and lower, with armour protection some 10 mm thinner but with the same main armament (the 2-pdr (40-mm) and coaxial 7.92-mm BESA machine-gun) and a crew of only three men. It was later up-gunned, substituting first the 6-pdr (57-mm) and later the British 75-mm gun for the 2-pdr of the original version, which was called the Valentine I after June 1941. The up-gunned versions became, respectively, the Valentine VIII and IX (6-pdr) and the Valentine XI

(British 75-mm). The two-man turret of the Valentine I, II and IV was replaced by a three-man version in the Valentine III and V. A turret crew of only two men meant that the tank commander had not only to command the vehicle and operate the radio but also to load the gun, and this was found to be too much for one man to do adequately, particularly under the stress of battle. The problem was exacerbated for the troop commander who had, in addition to his duties in his own tank, to command the tanks of his troop. With the advent of the 6-pdr, turret space was limited and a two-man turret crew was again forced on the user in the Valentine VIII and IX; not only that, but there was no space in the mantlet for a coaxial machine-gun, another serious drawback. The 75-mm gun Valentine was known as the Valentine XI, while the Canadian-built vehicles were the Valentine VI and VII. The latter substituted the 0.30 calibre Browning air-cooled machine-gun for the 7.92-mm BESA coaxial MG.

As with most British Infantry and Cruiser tanks, the Valentine chassis was used as the basis for self-propelled anti-tank and field guns, as well as for several 'special devices' such as bridge-laying tanks and mine-clearing tanks with rollers, rakes or flails. Only the self-propelled guns will be listed here, armed as they were with significantly larger weapons, albeit with only limited traverse; the 'special devices' carried only defensive weapons in the shape of machine-guns or the personal weapons of the crew. Other variants of Valentine were produced, including a New Zealand version mounting the 3-in howitzer from the Matilda CS tank, an artillery observation post (OP) tank with a dummy gun and a dozer vehicle known as the Valentine Dozer.

The first SP weapon was the 6-pdr (57-mm) anti-tank gun, mounted behind a shield in the fighting compartment of a turretless tank. It was not proceeded with as it was overtaken by the Valentine VIII and IX, mounting the 6-pdr tank gun in a turret with 360° traverse and greater armour protection. The second SP version mounted the 25-pdr (88-mm) field gun in an urgent modification programme in 1942. The gun was mounted in a simple armoured box on a turretless Valentine II chassis, the ammunition being towed in a limber behind the tank. The vehicle was known in service as the Bishop; some 100 were built and they saw service in the Western Desert, Tunisia and Sicily. The 17-pdr (76.2-mm) SP gun was known as the Archer and was developed in 1943. It eventually succeeded the Valentine in production, and remained in service in the British Army of the Rhine until the 1950s. Archer mounted a rearward facing 17-pdr in an open-topped armoured superstructure on a Valentine chassis. It was a successful modification, largely due to its low silhouette and rear-facing gun, allowing of easy concealment and fast forward exit from fire positions. A total of 665 Archers was built; they saw service in Italy and north-west Europe during the Second World War.

The successor to the Valentine stemmed from General Staff specification A20. This specification had been issued in late September 1939 for a slow (10 m.p.h.), heavily armoured (proof against a 37-mm anti-tank gun) Infantry tank, able to negotiate waterlogged ground cratered by shell fire, somewhat on the lines of the Mark VIII tank of 1918. The first prototypes, produced by Harland and Wolff, were unsatisfactory and a revised GS specification A22 for the Infantry Tank Mark IV was issued in July 1940, with Vauxhall Motors Ltd being invited to undertake the design. It was originally envisaged as having a more powerful gun than the ever-present 2-pdr (40-mm), but none was available at that time. The 2-pdr was therefore selected as the main

SP 25-pdr gun Bishop. (Author's Collection)

SP 17-pdr gun Archer. (Author's Collection)

Infantry tank Mark IV Churchill I (A22). (Author's Collection)

armament, the auxiliary armament consisting of a 7.92-mm BESA machine-gun mounted coaxially with the main armament, a 3-in howitzer mounted in the hull front vertical plate beside the driver and a 2-in bomb thrower in the turret roof for close smoke screening. By the end of 1940 the first Infantry Tank Mark IV prototype was undergoing trials and the first production tanks appeared in June of the following year; it was named Churchill after the prime minister. This initial version was known as the Churchill I; the Churchill II substituted a 7.92-mm BESA MG for the 3-in howitzer. With such a short development time and with the tank put into production virtually off the drawing board it is not surprising that many design faults needed to be corrected. Vauxhall supplied teams of engineers to user units, however, and after the completion of an urgent rectification programme the Churchill proved to be a very reliable tank.

The 2-pdr was soon to be replaced by the 6-pdr (57-mm) gun and two types of redesigned turret, one cast and the other welded from flat plate, were introduced to accept it. The version with the welded turret was known as the Churchill III while that with the cast turret was the Churchill IV. The Churchill I remained in service with front-line tank battalions as a close support tank, but the Churchill II was relegated to training; both vehicles were used in action for the first time by the Canadians in the abortive Dieppe raid on 19 August 1942. Other versions of the Churchill followed the Churchill IV; one, known as the Churchill IV (NA 75) was converted in North Africa to take the 75-mm gun, 0.30 calibre Browning MG, mantlet and mounting of the US Sherman tank, thus giving the Churchill a larger gun and the capacity to fire a high explosive shell which the 6-pdr at that time lacked. The Churchill V substituted the 95-mm howitzer for the

6-pdr of the Churchill IV as a close support tank, while the Churchill VI mounted the British 75-mm gun as main armament, together with geared elevation instead of the shoulder-control used for both the 2-pdr and 6-pdr. The Churchill VII, which also mounted the British 75-mm gun, was an altogether better protected version, with 6 inches of frontal armour. The close support version of this tank, the Churchill VIII, was armed with the 95-mm howitzer and was the final version of the Churchill to enter production. Further Marks, IX, X and XI, were allotted before the end of the Second World War but these were Churchill III, IV, V and VI reworked with appliqué armour but retaining their original armament. Production of the Churchill finally ceased in October 1945 after some 5,640 had been built. It was the second most popular British tank of the Second World War after the Valentine and was certainly one of the most successful British tanks in that war. It was the last manifestation of the pre-war policy of separate Cruiser and Infantry tanks and thus the last British Infantry tank to enter service with the British army. Some versions, such as the Churchill Bridgelayer and the Armoured Vehicle Royal Engineers (AVRE), remained in service well after the end of Second World War, while the Churchill VII served in the Korean War until replaced by the Centurion. Other vehicles based on the Churchill chassis which saw service included the Armoured Recovery Vehicle (ARV) and various special devices such as the armoured ramp carrier (ARK) and sundry mine-clearing devices such as the flail (Toad).

Although no more Infantry tanks entered British army service after the Churchill, two related projects which reached the prototype stage before the end of the Second World War are worthy of mention when cataloguing developments in British tank armament during that war. Various GS specifications for

so-called heavy assault tanks had been issued in 1942/3 under the numbers A31, A32 and A33 without any worthwhile designs resulting. Nuffield Mechanisation submitted a series of proposals between May 1943 and February 1944 under the generic heading of Assault Tank (AT), but it was not until their proposal AT16 arrived at the War Office on 5 February 1944 that one was accepted. The proposal was in answer to GS specification A39, and was for a vehicle weighing some 72 tons, armed with a modified 3.7-in heavy AA gun (known as the 37-pdr), mounted in a limited traverse ball mounting in the 9-in thick cast front plate, and three machine-guns, two in a twin mounting in a sub-turret on the superstructure roof and one in the front plate. The proposal was accepted and the tank (for such it was classified, although in reality a self-propelled gun) given the name Tortoise. An order for 25 vehicles was placed in February and confirmed in May 1944, with delivery required from September 1945. The long lead time resulted in the build programme being overtaken by the cessation of hostilities, and only six pilot vehicles were completed, in 1946. As finally built, Tortoise weighed 78 tons and the gun was modified to fire a 32-lb projectile, thus becoming known as the 32-pdr (93.4-mm). The design had broken all the rules previously imposed by rail loading gauges and military bridging and was a nightmare to move. Under its own power, however, it proved surprisingly reliable and an excellent gun platform for its supremely accurate main armament. Although seemingly an anachronism and something of a white elephant, the thinking behind it was not just a British mental aberration. The Germans had long had in service a series of SP assault guns ranging in weight up to 75 tons in the case of the Jagdtiger, as well as heavy tanks such as the Tiger and Königstiger, weighing 56 and 68 tons respectively, with high velocity guns

Infantry tank Mark IV Churchill IV (6-pdr). (Tank Museum 357-30)

Infantry tank Mark IV Churchill VIII (95-mm howitzer). (Tank Museum 1774/A3)

Heavy assault tank Tortoise (A39). (Tank Museum 3024/E1)

ranging in calibre from 7.5 cm to 12.8 cm, and it was to counter these that Tortoise was originally envisaged. The Soviet army had also made great use of heavy SP assault weapons, and it was largely in the hope of helping to dissuade them from continuing their conquests westwards that it was decided to tour BAOR in 1948 with two Tortoises as ostentatiously as possible, while seeming to keep the vehicle under tight security. Whether or not this had the desired effect we shall probably never know, but the project was dropped without ever going into production.

The other related project was the Black Prince, designed in response to GS specification A43, issued in December 1943. It had been inspired by the inability of Challenger and the Sherman Firefly to engage the German Panther and Tiger on equal terms and the Churchill's inability to accept the 17-pdr (76.2-mm) gun. The latter tank was too narrow to permit the turret ring diameter

necessary for the 17-pdr, so a redesign was necessary, based on the Churchill VII and using as many of its components as possible. It was hoped that it might also be possible to substitute the 32-pdr gun for the 17-pdr. A full-scale mock-up was inspected at Vauxhall's Luton plant in August 1944 and the first prototype completed in the following January. Obviously based on the Churchill, in beefed-up form, it mounted the 17-pdr as main armament, with a coaxial 7.92-mm BESA MG, in a turret modified from that of the Comet and another mounted in the hull front vertical plate. A combination of factors, however, caused the project to be dropped. The standard 350 h.p. Bedford engine of the Churchill was not powerful enough for the Black Prince's 52 tons and, by the time plans had been made to replace it with the 600 h.p. Rolls-Royce Meteor engine, the decision to concentrate the future tank programme on only one class of tank, the 'Universal', was

Infantry tank Black Prince (A43). (Tank Museum 1773/B5)

about to be made. In the event, the A41 Centurion, being developed in parallel, became the selected Universal tank.

The table which follows lists the Infantry tanks and their variants that saw service in the British army between 1939 and 1945, together with their armament. It excludes special adaptations which were not fighting tanks, such as bridgelayers, mine-clearance and other special devices, dozers and recovery vehicles, but does include the AVRE.

NOMENCLATURE	ARMAMENT
Mark I (A11) (Matilda)	One 0.303-in water-cooled Vickers MG.
Mark II (A12) (Matilda I)	One 2-pdr (40-mm) high velocity gun with coaxial 0.303-in water-cooled Vickers MG. Two 4-in single-shot smoke bomb throwers on RH turret side.
Ditto (Matilda II to V)	As for Matilda I except 7.92-mm air-cooled BESA MG.
Ditto (Matilda CS)	One 3-in (76.2-mm) howitzer. Aux. armt as for Matilda II.
Mark III (Valentine I to V)	As for Matilda II to V except 2-in bomb thrower vice twin 4-in.
Ditto (Valentine VI & VII)	As for Valentine I to V except coaxial MG was 0.303-in Browning.
Ditto (Valentine VIII & IX)	One 6-pdr gun and no coaxial MG. Otherwise as for Valentine I to V.
Ditto (Valentine X)	As for Valentine VIII and IX but with

NOMENCLATURE	ARMAMENT
	coaxial 7.92-mm BESA MG added.
Ditto (Valentine XI)	One 75-mm (British) gun and coaxial 7.92-mm BESA MG.
Carrier, Valentine, 25-pdr Gun, Mark I (Bishop)	One 25-pdr (88-mm) gun.
Valentine SP 17-pdr gun (Archer)	One 17-pdr (76.2-mm) anti-tank gun.
Mark IV (A22) (Churchill I)	One 2-pdr in turret, with coaxial 7.92-mm BESA MG. One 3-in howitzer in hull front.
Ditto (Churchill II)	Turret armt as for Churchill I. One 7.92-mm BESA MG in place of 3-in howitzer in hull.
Ditto (Churchill III & IV)	One 6-pdr (57-mm) gun in place of 2-pdr. Otherwise as for Churchill II.
Ditto (Churchill IV (NA 75))	One US 75-mm gun and coaxial 0.30 cal Browning MG in turret. Otherwise as for Churchill II.
Ditto (Churchill V)	One 95-mm howitzer. Otherwise as for Churchill II.
Ditto (Churchill VI)	One British 75-mm gun. Otherwise as for Churchill II.
Ditto (Churchill VII)	As for Churchill VI.
Ditto (Churchill VIII)	As for Churchill V.
Ditto (Churchill IX, X & XI)	As for Churchill IV, V and VI, respectively.

NOMENCLATURE	ARMAMENT
Churchill AVRE	One 290-mm Spigot Mortar.
Heavy Assault Tank (A39) (Tortoise)	One 32-pdr (93.4 mm) gun. Three 7.92-mm BESA MGs, two in twin mounting in sub-turret, one in hull front.
Heavy Infantry Tank (A43) (Black Prince)	One 17-pdr (76.2 mm) gun and coaxial 7.92-mm BESA MG in turret. One hull-mounted 7.92-mm BESA MG.

(N.B. *Details of the above weapons and their ammunition are given in Appendix A.*)

BRITISH TANK ARMAMENT DEVELOPMENT SUMMARIZED

The story of the development of British tank armament in the Second World War is one of too little, too late. A fundamentally wrong appreciation, prior to the outbreak of war, of how tanks would be employed in a future war, coupled with poor intelligence on Germany's tanks and their employment, led to late development of adequate armament and ammunition through the early years of the Second World War. Britain having entered the war with an adequate high velocity anti-armour weapon in the 40-mm calibre 2-pdr gun, the introduction of more powerful weapons to take on the heavier German armour was precluded for too long by:

1. A shortage of gun design and production facilities. After the evacuation of the BEF in 1940, the threat of imminent invasion required the maximum possible production of existing weapons to make good the losses sustained in France.

2. Tanks so designed as to be incapable of being up-gunned. The narrow hulls of British tanks, carried entirely between the tracks, meant that no larger diameter turret ring could be fitted and thus no larger turret suitable for a gun of larger calibre.

3. The multiplicity of tank types being produced, consequent upon the decision to have three categories of tank, with resulting pressure on limited tank design and production facilities.

For the above reasons, all British gun tanks produced from 1940 until 1942 were armed with the 2-pdr, which proved increasingly inadequate in the Western Desert campaign against the German PzKpfw IIIs and IVs with their high velocity 5-cm and 7.5-cm guns. Apart from its poor armour penetration performance compared to these weapons, the 2-pdr had no HE capability; the only anti-personnel capability of a gun tank armed with the 2-pdr came from its limited range machine-guns, whereas both the German weapons fired HE ammunition. For longer range engagement of infantry, gun crews and defences it was necessary to provide close support tanks, armed at first with a 3.7-inch breech-loading mortar which was replaced by the 3-inch (76.2-mm) howitzer. There were, however, never enough of these tanks, which were usually kept in squadron headquarters, and their indirect fire capability was limited.

The 2-pdr began to be replaced by the 6-pdr (57-mm) in 1942, Valentines, Churchills and Crusaders being adapted to take it. It had a good anti-tank performance, although less good than the German long-barrelled 7.5-cm gun, but again no HE shell. In addition, crew space in the modified Valentine and Crusader turrets was cramped and the Valentine had to dispense with its coaxial machine-gun to accommodate the 6-pdr. The arrival in the Middle East of the US Lee/Grant and Sherman with their dual-purpose 75-mm guns increased the demand for a high explosive shell for the 6-pdr and for the provision of a British 75-mm tank gun. In the meantime, 120 Churchill IV tanks in North Africa were fitted in 1943 with the 75-mm gun, 0.30 calibre Browning coaxial MG, mounting and mantlet from the M-4 Sherman in a conversion named 'Churchill IV (NA75)'. By the time that a high explosive shell for the 6-pdr was ready for issue, the 6-pdr was in the process of being replaced by the British 75-mm, 77-mm and 17-pdr (76.2-mm) tank guns, and the 3-in howitzer by the 95-mm howitzer in close support tanks.

The advent of the 77-mm and 17-pdr guns at last put the British tank on an almost equal footing with its German counterpart, particularly from 1944 in the anti-tank role, using hyper-velocity APDS ammunition, while the tanks armed with them (Comet and Centurion) were increasingly well-armoured and reliable. Had the war continued, it had been planned to modify the 3.7-in anti-aircraft gun for tank mounting, firing a 32-lb projectile, and prototypes of the Tortoise, a heavy assault tank mounting this gun, were in fact produced before the war's end.

Other, more specialized, weapons and mountings were used to arm tanks in the anti-aircraft and AVRE roles. Anti-aircraft light tanks mounted quadruple 7.92-mm BESA MGs in a power-operated turret, while Cruiser tanks carried AA guns of larger calibre. One version was fitted with twin-

Churchill AVRE. (Tank Museum 357.81)

mounted 20-mm Oerlikon or Polsten cannon and the other mounted a single 40-mm Bofors light AA gun. The Armoured Vehicle Royal Engineers or AVRE was a highly specialized Churchill Infantry tank conversion employed in the assault on fixed defences, and was armed with a 290-mm spigot mortar firing a 40-lb Petard round, known as a 'Flying Dustbin', to a maximum range of 80 yards. Another Churchill tank conversion was the Crocodile, a flame-throwing tank based on the Churchill VII.

Although not a weapon in the conventional sense it was nevertheless highly effective in the assault on prepared defences in Italy and north-west Europe in the closing stages of the war and is included here for that reason.

With regard to auxiliary tank armament, British tanks employed three types of medium machine-gun during the Second World War. The first was the water-cooled Vickers in 0.303-in and 0.5-in calibre, replaced from 1940 onwards by the air-cooled BESA in calibres of 7.92 mm and 15 mm. The third

Infantry tank Mark IV Churchill IV (NA 75). (Tank Museum 1778/B1)

gun, in calibres of 0.30 in and 0.5 in, was the air-cooled Browning, fitted in US tanks supplied under Lend-Lease as well as in the Churchill IV (NA75). Of the three types, the Browning occupied the least mantlet and turret space and was selected as the preferred fit in postwar tanks such as Centurion for this reason.

For close-range defensive armament, early British tanks carried twin single-shot 4-in bomb-throwers, mounted externally on the turret side. They were loaded externally but fired by cable from the inside of the vehicle, and were used for firing close-range smoke bombs. They were later replaced by a 2-in bomb-thrower mounted in the turret roof, loaded and fired internally. In addition to the personal weapons of the crew, consisting of pistols, sub-machine-guns and grenades, a Bren light machine-gun was also carried for anti-aircraft defence. For this purpose, a light mounting was often provided on the turret roof.

CHAPTER FOUR

GERMAN TANK ARMAMENT

The introduction of the tank by the Allies in the First World War and the successes that they achieved were not lost on the defeated German army, and those in positions of influence in post-war Germany were quick to appreciate how essential to the renaissance of the German army a healthy tank design and manufacturing base would be. They were helped in assessing their tank requirements by the writings of such British proponents of the tank as Major-General J.F.C. Fuller and Captain Basil Liddell Hart and in the design and testing of their early prototypes by the cooperation of Landsverk in 'neutral' Sweden and the Vickers tanks supplied to Communist Russia. The latter country permitted the Germans to assemble and test their 'agricultural tractors' at the Kazan proving ground. In addition, a competent and active military intelligence network kept the German General Staff well informed regarding tank development in other countries, particularly in the UK, which was seen by them as the world leader in the design and employment of tanks.

Prevented by the terms of the Treaty of Versailles from developing or producing armoured fighting vehicles, Germany nevertheless began their development in great secrecy in 1926. In fact, it is believed that some firms began preliminary design work in 1921, only three years after the end of the war. The early tanks, light vehicles which later became the Panzerkampfwagen (abbreviated to PzKpfw, meaning 'AFV') I and II but which were at that time disguised under the title of 'Landwirtschaftlicher Schlepper' (La.S: agricultural tractor), were

assembled and tested at Kazan between 1926 and 1932. With Hitler's accession to power in 1933, however, the organization of AFV design and manufacture was brought into the open. The equivalent of General Staff specifications were drawn up and issued by a branch of the Heereswaffenamt (HWA, or Army Weapons Office) known as Waffen Prüfungsamt 6 (Wa Prüf 6: Weapon Testing Office 6), various companies with related experience were selected as potential AFV manufacturers, and gunnery test ranges and automotive proving grounds were built. Prominent among the firms selected as both tank and gun manufacturers were Friedrich Krupp AG of Essen and Rheinmetall Borsig of Düsseldorf; others selected for tank design and assembly included Henschel und Sohn of Kassel, Maschinenfabrik Augsburg-Nürnberg (MAN) of Nürnberg and Daimler Benz AG of Berlin/Marienfelde. Automotive proving grounds were located at Ulm (near Münsingen), Sennelager (Haustenbeck), Kummersdorf and Döllersheim, while gunnery trials took place at Meppen.

From the start the Germans, unlike the British, showed a clear-headed appreciation of the overiding importance of firepower in tank design, and to that end they developed early a series of tank guns of increasing calibre and calibre length, together with a clear system of identifying them. All tank guns were known as Kampfwagenkanonen (abbreviated to KwK), and were designated by their calibre in centimetres and the barrel length in calibres. For example, 5-cm KwK39 (L/60) indicated a 5-cm tank gun, designed in 1939, with a barrel length of 60 calibres. Together with a range of suitable tank guns, the German tanks were designed, unlike those of the British, so that they could easily be up-gunned when necessary and, when turret size limited the size of weapon, they removed the turret and mounted the larger weapon on the turretless tank chassis as a self-propelled weapon. In the case of field guns and howitzers, the gun retained its original field-version designation with the abbreviation (Sf) after it, to indicate Selbstfahrlafette (self-propelled mount). In other cases, guns and howitzers so mounted included Panzerabwehrkanonen (Pak: anti-tank guns), anti-aircraft guns (Flugabwehrkanonen, abbreviated to Flak), assault guns (Sturmgeschütze or Sturmkanonen, abbreviated to Stu.G. or Stu.K), assault howitzers (Sturmhaubitzen, abbreviated to Stu.H. and tank destroyers (Panzerjäger abbreviated to Pz.Jäg.))

To match this range of weapons, the Germans simultaneously developed a series of four tanks in the light (5-ton and 10-ton) and medium (15-ton and 20-ton) categories before the Second World War, most of which remained in service, in up-dated form, throughout the war. Heavy tanks were developed from 1942 onwards, largely to counter the threat of the Soviet tanks and self-propelled weapons which were appearing in increasing numbers. German tanks, as they were taken into service, were identified by a Roman number equivalent to the British Mark number, starting at 'I' in 1935 and ending at 'VI' by the end of the war. The different models of each tank were identified by a Model (Ausführung, abbreviated to Ausf.) letter after the tank designation. All AFVs taken into service were also allotted an Ordnance Vocabulary Number (Sonder Kraftfahrzeug Nummer, abbreviated to Sd Kfz, meaning 'Special Motor Vehicle Number').

Wa Prüf 6 issued their first specification, for a light tank in the 5-ton weight class, in 1933, immediately following the accession to power of Hitler and the National Socialist party. Henschel und Sohn, whose proposal was accepted, produced three prototypes by the end of December that year; the first vehicle ran in February 1934 and all three were inspected in April, leading to the placing of a production order for 150 vehicles three months later. As these came into service they took the official title of Panzerkampfwagen I (PzKpfw I), the Ordnance Vocabulary Number allocated to the PzKpfw I being Sd Kfz 101. The PzKpfw I was in the same weight class as the British Light Tank Mark VI series, with armour protection of the same order. It too carried a crew of two men, a commander/gunner and a driver/radio operator, and was armed with two Dreyse MG 13K magazine-fed machine-guns of 7.92-mm calibre, where the equivalent British machines had one medium and one heavy machine-gun, both belt-fed. The German tank had a significantly lower maximum speed (24 m.p.h.) than the British Mark VI's 35 m.p.h. The first Model of the PzKpfw I was known as Ausf.A and was used primarily for driving and tactical training, being open-topped and without a turret. The next model, the Ausf.B, was produced in larger numbers in 1935, and was first used operationally in the Spanish Civil War. The PzKpfw I was also used as the basis for a command vehicle (Kl.Pz.Bef.Wg, Sd Kfz 265), with a fixed turret armed with one ball-mounted MG, as well as for a self-propelled tank destroyer, mounting the Czech 4.7-cm anti-tank gun, in which form it was known as the Panzerjäger I (Pz.Jäg. I), and a 15-cm heavy infantry gun (S.I.G.33).

In July 1934, the HWA issued a specification for a tank in the 10-ton weight class, the LaS 100, to Henschel, MAN and Krupp, each of whom designed and produced prototypes. Comparative trials of these prototypes, under the supervision of WaPrüf 6, took

Light tank PzKpfw I (SdKfz 101). (Author's Collection)

place at the Ulm proving ground throughout 1935, as a result of which the MAN version was accepted for production and taken into service as the PzKpfw II (Sd Kfz 121). With a crew of three men and armed with a 2-cm KwK 30 with coaxial 7.92-mm MG34 machine-gun, the early models (a1, a2, a3, b and c) of the PzKpfw II weighed some 7 tons and had a maximum road speed of 25 m.p.h. These models were followed in 1937 by the Ausf.A and in 1938 by Ausführungen B and C, differing in only minor details. Models D and E, however, designed by Daimler Benz, differed radically in armour thickness and suspension, and appeared in 1939. By 1940, however, all had been converted to flame-thrower tanks, designated as the PzKpfw II (F). The Ausf.F, incorporating much thicker armour and leaf-spring suspension, was in production by June 1941

and was the last direct development of the LaS 100. The total production of PzKpfw I and II tank chassis, of which many were used as mountings for SP guns, from 1940 to January 1944 was only 632, with a maximum monthly output of 25 in 1942. One final version of the PzKpfw II is worth a mention; rather as the British with the Tetrarch and Harry Hopkins, the Germans produced, in 1942, a small number of an updated light tank with thicker armour and a redesigned turret, known as the PzKpfw II Ausf. L (Luchs: Lynx) (SdKfz 123). With a weight in action of nearly 12 tons and a crew of four, it had a maximum road speed of 40 m.p.h., although still armed with the same weapons as the earlier models. As was the case with the PzKpfw I, the PzKpfw II chassis was later used as the basis for various SP guns such as the 7.5-cm Pak 40 (L/46),

Light tank PzKpfw II (SdKfz 121). (Author's Collection)

Light tank PzKpfw II, Ausf. L (Luchs, SdKfz 123). (Author's Collection)

known as the Pz.Jäg. II (Sd Kfz 131 and 132), the captured Soviet 7.62-cm Pak 36(r) and the 10.5-cm light field howitzer le.FH 18, known as the Geschützwagen (GW) II Wespe (Wasp) (Sd Kfz 124).

The specification for the 15-ton tank was issued by the HWA in 1936 to MAN, Daimler Benz and Rheinmetall Borsig and the three resulting prototypes were tested at Kummersdorf from late 1936 to the end of 1937. The Daimler Benz version was accepted by Wa Prüf 6 and production of the Zugführerwagen (ZW: troop commander's vehicle) was entrusted to Henschel, MAN and Daimler Benz. There followed a period of continuous development; five models, the Ausf.A, B, C, D and E, of which only a small number of each were made, appeared by 1939. Production of the Ausf.F, of which some 450 were built, started in 1939. Models G and H appeared in 1941, Models J, L and M in 1942 and Model N (mounting the 7.5-cm KwK L/24) in 1943. The ZW was first used operationally in Poland in 1939 and in service was designated PzKpfw III (Sd Kfz 141). It was a highly successful and reliable tank, of which some 5,650 were built between 1940 and August 1943; the highest monthly production figure was 213, in 1942. The tank weighed some 22 tons in action, 7 tons more than the weight specified by the HWA. It carried a crew of five and had a maximum road speed of 28 m.p.h. Its armament varied according to the model, Ausf. A, B and C mounting the 3.7-cm KwK (L/45) with two coaxial 7.92-mm MG 34 machine-guns and another mounted in the hull front vertical plate, while Ausf.E, F, G, H and early J substituted the 5-cm KwK (L/42) for the 3.7-cm gun and omitted one of the coaxial MG 34 MGs. Later Ausf.J, L and M substituted the longer 5-cm KwK 39 (L/60) for the (L/42) gun; all models retained the hull-mounted MG 34. The Ausf.N replaced the 5-cm main armament with the 7.5-cm

howitzer (7.5-cm KwK L/24) of the PzKpfw IV. This vehicle was used to give local protection fire support to the heavy tanks of the heavy tank battalions, introduced later in the war. In addition to the machine-guns and the crew's personal weapons, auxiliary armament of the later models (Ausf.M and N) included two sets of three smoke bomb projectors, one set mounted on each side of the turret at the front, to give a local smoke screen; although having to be loaded externally they could be fired electrically, together or individually, from inside the vehicle. As with the earlier tanks, the PzKpfw III chassis was used as the basis for a number of self-propelled guns, the most numerous of which was the Sturmgeschütz III (Sd Kfz 142) (Stu.G.III: assault gun) mounting the 7.5-cm K (L/24) in a limited traverse mounting in the front of a heavily armoured susperstructure. Another version mounted the 10.5-cm Stu.H. 42 (L/28) and was known as the Sd Kfz 142/2. A further SP variant mounted the 7.5-cm Stu.K. 40 (L/48) anti-tank gun.

In the spring of 1935, Krupp, Rheinmetall Borsig and MAN were asked to submit proposals for a tank in the 20-ton weight class, the BW (Bataillonsführerwagen: battalion commander's vehicle). Of these, the Krupp proposal was accepted by the HWA and their prototype underwent trials at Uln and Kummersdorf throughout 1937. A production order was placed on Krupp the same year and, by 1939, three Models (Ausführungen A, B and C) had been produced, of which Ausf.B and C were battle-tested in the Polish campaign. Modifications resulting from experience gained in this campaign were incorporated in the Ausf.D, which appeared in late 1940; Models E and F1 followed in the following year. All Models of the BW, known in service as the PzKpfw IV (Sd Kfz 161), up to and including the F1, were armed with the short 7.5-cm KwK (L/24) howitzer and two 7.92-mm MG34

Medium tank PzKpfw III, Ausf. F, G and H (SdKfz 141). (Author's Collection)

Medium tank PzKpfw III, Ausf. L (SdKfz 141). (Author's Collection)

Medium tank PzKpfw III, Ausf. N (SdKfz 141). (Author's Collection)

Medium tank PzKpfw IV, Ausf.D, E and F1 (SdKfz 161) (7.5-cm L/24). (Author's Collection)

machine-guns, one coaxial with the main armament and the other ball-mounted in the superstructure front vertical plate. In 1942 the PzKpfw IV was up-gunned, in the Ausf. F2 and G the low velocity 7.5-cm L/24 gun being replaced by the high velocity 7.5-cm KwK 40 (L/43). This was the tank known by British troops in the Western Desert campaign as the 'Mark IV Special'. This gun in turn was replaced in 1943/4 by a lengthened version, the 7.5-cm KwK 40 (L/48), in Ausf. H and J. Both the L/40 and L/48 guns were fitted with double-baffle muzzle brakes to reduce recoil. Machine-gun armament remained the same in all models of the PzKpfw IV except the last two; these carried an anti-aircraft 7.92-mm MG 34 on a ring mounting on the commander's cupola, a modification necessitated by the over-whelming Allied air superiority towards the end of the war. The PzKpfw IV was a good all-round medium tank, well-armed and

reliable; however, it was so similar in weight and mobility to the PzKpfw III that it is puzzling to know why the HWA kept both tanks in production throughout the war. Although similar in general performance, each tank used different components and assemblies, making logistics in the field unnecessarily complicated; a sensible solution would have been to have combined the two into a PzKpfw III/IV, using the best components from each to ease production and logistics in the field. In fact, there was a proposal to do this at the end of the war, and prototypes of a PzKpfw III/IV chassis were built as the Geschützwagen (GW) III/IV, but by this time it was too late. A total of 8,506 of all models of the PzKpfw IV was produced between 1940 and February 1945, with a maximum monthly production of 334, attained in June 1944. A considerable proportion of this total was converted to self-propelled chassis for assault guns, field and

Medium tank PzKpfw IV, Ausf.F2 and G (SdKfz 161) (7.5-cm L/43). (Author's Collection)

Medium tank PzKpfw IV, Ausf.H and J (SdKfz 161) (7.5-cm L/48). (Author's Collection)

medium artillery and AA guns, too numerous to enumerate here, and ranging in calibre from 15-mm AA cannon to 15-cm medium guns and assault howitzers.

The next tank to be developed was out of the range of weight classes envisaged prior to the Second World War, and represented a return to the heavy tank concept favoured by the Germans in the previous conflict. The specification, issued in late 1941 by the HWA to both Henschel and the Dr.h.c.F. Porsche KG organization in Stuttgart, called for each company to design, and supply a prototype of, a tank in the 45-ton weight class mounting a tank version of the famed '88' AA/anti-tank gun, the 8.8-cm KwK 36 (L/56). The need for such a tank was a result of the German encounter with the Soviet T34 medium and the KV heavy tank in 1941, which had caused as great a shock to the German panzer troops as had the British introduction of tanks on the Western Front to the German infantry in September 1916. Hitler personally took a great interest in the

development of this tank, and insisted on having a demonstration of both prototypes at his Rastenburg HQ on his birthday, 20 April 1942. As a result of this and later trials, the Henschel vehicle was adjudged to be the better and an order for Henschel to start production in August 1942 was issued. However, Porsche had already received an order, thanks to Hitler's personal interest in Ferdinand Porsche, for 90 vehicles, and it was decided to complete these as SP mountings for an 8.8-cm (L/71) high velocity anti-tank gun, the 50 turrets already ordered for these vehicles being allocated to Henschel production. The Porsche vehicle, on being taken into service, became known initially as the Ferdinand (after Dr Ferdinand Porsche) and, later, as Elefant (Elephant) Pz.Jäg. Tiger (P) (Sd Kfz 184) (Elefant).

The Henschel vehicle, which in action weighed 56 tons, entered production as planned in August 1942. It carried a crew of five men and, in addition to its 8.8-cm main armament, carried the standard coaxial and

8.8-cm tank destroyer Elefant (SdKfz 184). (Author's Collection)

Heavy tank PzKpfw Tiger, Ausf.E (SdKfz 181). (Author's Collection)

hull-mounted 7.92-mm MG34 machine-guns. Its defensive armament consisted of five anti-personnel S-Mine throwers, distributed round the hull roof and specifically provided to combat Red Army tank hunters, and two sets of three smoke grenade dischargers, one mounted forward on each turret side, to give local smoke protection. In service, this tank was known initially as PzKpfw VI, Ausf.E (Sd Kfz 181) and later as the PzKpfw Tiger Ausf.E. It had a maximum speed on roads of 23 m.p.h. and could be sealed and driven underwater to a depth of 13 feet, air for engines and crew being drawn from the surface by means of a schnorkel device. This feature again was designed for the Russian front, with its many rivers crossing the line of advance, and was included in the first 495 tanks only. Despite its impressive size, armament which easily outperformed that of any Allied tank of its period and armour

thickness equalled only by the Churchill, the Tiger was not reliable and had a very short range of action of only about 40 miles across country; it was also too complicated for mass production in wartime. With the wide cross-country tracks necessitated by its weight, Tiger was outside the rail loading gauge and had to be provided with a second set of narrow tracks for rail transport. A total of 1,350 tanks out of 1,376 ordered was produced between August 1942 and August 1944, the maximum number built in any one month being 104, in April 1944; all were built by Henschel at their Kassel plant. Ten Tigers were converted in 1944 into self-propelled mountings for the 38-cm naval rocket launcher (Raketenwerfer) RW 61; designated as an assault mortar, this vehicle was officially known as the Sturmmörser (Stu.Mrs) Tiger.

The next tank to be introduced had

Assault mortar Tiger. (Author's Collection)

originally been intended to replace the PzKpfw IV in the 30-ton weight class. Two prototypes were produced, by Daimler Benz and MAN, in 1941, both mounting the 7.5-cm (L/48) gun and with armour arrangement based on the sloping plate layout of the Soviet T34. Wa Prüf 6 decided, however, that the 7.5-cm (L/71) gun was required, so MAN were asked to redesign their vehicle to carry this gun. The resulting vehicle was accepted and put into production by MAN at the end of 1942; in action it weighed 45 tons, carried a crew of five and had a maximum road speed of 34 m.p.h. In service it was known as the PzKpfw V Panther (Sd Kfz 171) and it ran to three models, Ausf. D, A and G; all mounted the same main armament and coaxial MG34, but the hull machine-gun was omitted on the Ausf D. Altogether 4,814 Panthers

were produced, between November 1942 and February 1945, at first only by Daimler Benz and MAN but from January 1943 also by Henschel and Maschinenfabrik Niederasachsen-Hannover (MNH). The Panther was arguably the best tank produced by any of the combatants in the Second World War; there would have been no argument had the Germans had sufficient time to engineer out the 'bugs' in the vehicle but, as it was, Panther turned out to be almost as unreliable in service as the Tiger.

Several variants of the Panther were produced. The most numerous was the Jagdpanther or Pz.Jäg. Panther (Sd Kfz 173), which mounted the 8.8-cm Pak 43 (L/71) high velocity gun in a limited traverse mounting in the highly-sloped front glacis plate, which was extended up to the superstructure roof,

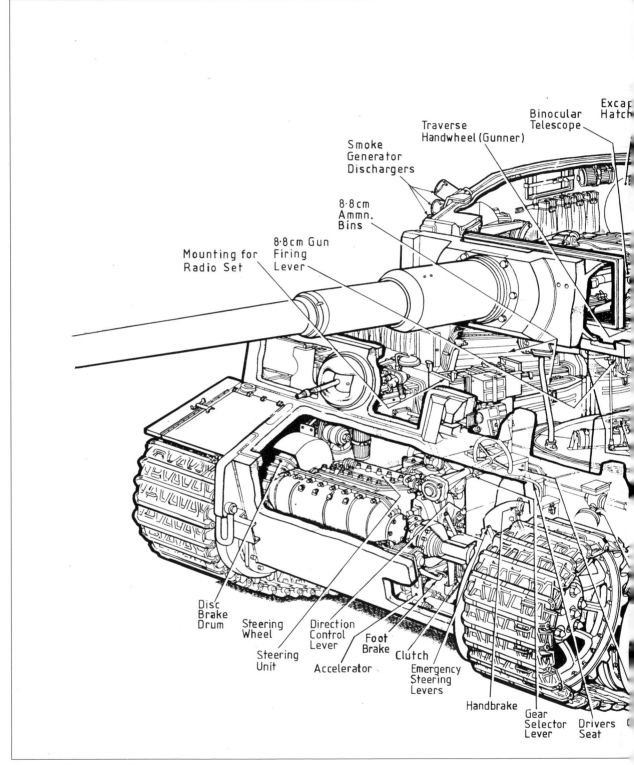

Ghosted view of PzKpfw Tiger Ausf.E. (Author's Collection)

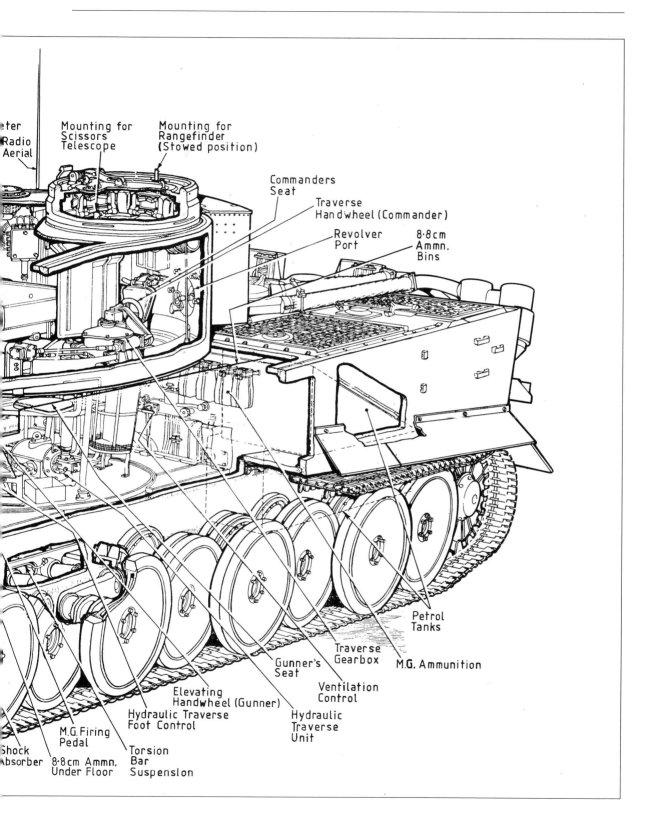

ter
Radio
Aerial

Mounting for
Scissors
Telescope

Mounting for
Rangefinder
(Stowed position)

Commanders
Seat

Traverse
Handwheel (Commander)

Revolver
Port

8·8cm
Ammn.
Bins

Petrol
Tanks

Traverse
Gearbox

M.G. Ammunition

Gunner's
Seat

Ventilation
Control

Elevating
Handwheel (Gunner)

Hydraulic Traverse
Foot Control

Hydraulic
Traverse
Unit

M.G. Firing
Pedal

Torsion
Bar
Suspension

Shock
Absorber

8·8cm Ammn.
Under Floor

Medium tank PzKpfw Panther (SdKfz 171). (Author's Collection)

8.8-cm tank destroyer Jagdpanther (SdKfz 173). (Author's Collection)

together with a ball-mounted 7.92-mm MG34. The other variant, armed only with a hull MG and a 2-cm KwK, was an armoured recovery vehicle on the Panther chassis, known as the Panzerbergewagen (Pz.Berge.Wg) Panther (Sd Kfz 179).

As if there were not already enough (and adequate) different types of tank in the German inventory, Hitler's desire for bigger and better tanks caused further frittering away of valuable materials and design and production capacity towards the war's end by calling for a tank even heavier than the Tiger, to mount the 8.8-cm (L/71) gun in a turret. In the autumn of 1942, Wa Prüf 6 had given Henschel the order to design a heavier development of the PzKpfw Tiger Ausf. E, to incorporate thicker armour, sloped as on the Panther and Soviet T34, and the 8.8-cm (L/71) gun as main armament. Porsche also redesigned his Tiger to conform to this new specification but history repeated itself. As with the earlier Pzkpfw VI Tiger the Porsche design was rejected in favour of that of Henschel, but the fifty turrets already ordered by Porsche for the Porsche vehicle were again allotted to the Henschel production. Henschel completed the first prototype of what became known in service as the PzKpfw Tiger Ausf.B (Sd Kfz 182) in October 1943. Production started in December of that year, the first 50 tanks having the Porsche turret and the remainder a simpler design of turret with

thicker armour which eliminated the vulnerable re-entrant angle beneath the gun mantlet of the Porsche design. The PzKpfw Tiger Ausf.B was armed with the 8.8-cm KwK 43 (L/71) gun with one 7.92-mm MG34 machine-gun coaxially mounted with it and another MG34 in a ball mounting in the front glacis plate. The external multiple smoke bomb dischargers of the Tiger Model E were replaced by a single discharger, loadable from inside the turret and with 360° of independent traverse, mounted in the turret roof. Manned by a crew of five, the Tiger Model B weighed some 68 tons in action and had a maximum road speed of approximately 21 m.p.h. Like its immediate predecessors, the Tiger Model E and the Panther, the Tiger Model B (also known as Königstiger (King Tiger or Royal Tiger)) was

Heavy tank PzKpfw Tiger, Ausf.B (SdKfz 182). (Author's Collection)

12.8-cm tank destroyer Jagdtiger (SdKfz 186). (Author's Collection)

unreliable; like the Tiger Model E its width exceeded the rail loading gauge when fitted with its battle tracks, so that a set of narrower tracks for rail travel had to be provided. Production of this tank by Henschel continued right up to the time of the German surrender; by the 31 March 1945, 485 vehicles had been completed as against 512 scheduled. The greatest number built in any one month was 84, in August 1944. The total order for the PzKpfw Tiger Ausf.B called for 950 vehicles to have been completed by September 1945, and to meet this target Henschel had to subcontract the construction of 100 tanks to Nibelungenwerke of St Valentin in Austria, to commence in May 1945.

One variant of the PzKpw Tiger Ausf.B was developed as a self-propelled tank destroyer. This was known as the Jagdtiger (Hunting Tiger) (Sd Kfz 186) and was the heaviest AFV in service with any army during the Second World War, weighing in at 70 tons and carrying a crew of six. It was armed with the 12.8-cm Pak 44 (L/55) or Pak 80 (L/55) mounted in the slab-like superstructure front plate and a ball-mounted 7.92-mm MG34 in the hull front glacis plate. Production took place at Henschel's Kassel plant and at Nibelungenwerke in Austria; two of those built by the latter firm had the suspension designed by Porsche for his version of the Tiger Model B, while those built by Henschel had the suspension of the PzKpfw Tiger Ausf. B. Production started in July 1944 and, of the 150 ordered, 77 had been completed by the end of the war.

Hitler's search for ever bigger and heavier tanks was not satisfied by the Tiger Model B, however, and two projects for super-heavy tanks were in progress at the war's end. These were the 180-ton Maus (Mouse), a private venture being designed by the Porsche organization (an amusing contrast to their earlier design of the Volkswagen or People's Car!) and backed personally by Hitler, and the E-100, a 140-ton tank forming part of a HWA plan for a whole range of 'E' tanks to replace all existing types and intended for introduction in 1945/6. Prototypes of both had been built by the end of the war but neither had progressed beyond that stage; the main armament of both was to have been a 12.8-cm tank gun.

In addition to tanks of native German design, built in Germany and Austria, the German army made great use of foreign vehicles and guns, both captured British, French and Soviet and those designed and built in countries under German occupation. Tanks taken into German army service were generally those to which no equivalent existed in the German army. On being taken into German service the nomenclature of the country of origin was dropped in favour of a German nomenclature allotted by the HWA according to their own system, in which all foreign equipments (Fremden Geräte) were

given a Fremden Gerät number, followed by the initial letter of the country of origin in brackets. The foreign tank most used by the German Army was the Czech LTH light tank, known by the Germans as the PzKpfw 38(t); this vehicle, modified in various forms, was used throughout the Second World War either as a tank (in the early campaigns in France and the Low Countries) or as the basis for a series of SP guns, with Sd Kfz numbers in the 130 series. All production took place at the Skoda works in Pilsen. No other foreign tank was employed on such a scale, but limited use was made of certain French vehicles such as the Char B2, Hotchkiss H35 and H39, Renault AMC35 and R35 and the Somua S35 and S40, both as tanks (chiefly in the Balkans and Norway) and as SP artillery carriages.

German ideas and methods with regard to self-propelled artillery underwent considerable modification between the introduction of the first assault equipment (the Sturmgeschütz 7.5 cm K (L/24) on Stu.G.III) in 1940 and the end of the Second World

7.5-cm assault gun Stu.G.III (SdKfz 142). (Author's Collection)

War. Those changes can be directly traced to the German war situation at the time and the changes in the tactical roles of such equipments dictated thereby. Apart from the one specifically designed equipment mentioned above, the chassis of the then obsolete PzKpfw I was utilized for the improvized mounting of the 15-cm heavy infantry gun (15-cm s.I.G.33) and the 4.7-cm Czech anti-tank gun (4.7-cm Pak (t). From this period almost to the end of the war, self-propelled equipments were of two main types, those specifically designed for the purpose or those improvized to make possible the SP mounting of as many guns as possible in the shortest possible time. Both types were based on existing tank chassis, the first on current designs and the second on obsolescent designs of chassis. The 7.5-cm K (L/24) on Stu.G.III falls into the first category and remained in service (apart from modifications in the armament) until the end of the war; into the second category fall all the equipments introduced up to December 1942, many of which were based on the chassis of the French 'Loraine' tractor, the Czech PzKpfw 38(t) and various half-tracked vehicles. These latter equipments are characterized by their slightly or unmodified tank chassis, their light, bullet-proof, open-topped superstructures and the armament, practically unmodified from the field mounting version. The specifically designed equipments, on the other hand, are characterized by their thick armour and roofed-in fighting compartments, low silhouettes and the modified or redesigned tank chassis upon which they were based. From January 1943, equipments introduced into service were divided fairly evenly between the first and second categories, the latter however, coming well to the fore in the latter part of 1944/early 1945 as the need for as many mobile, heavily-armoured anti-tank guns as possible became more urgent.

In addition to their classification by their overall general design, German SP artillery can also be classified according to the type of armament, whether low velocity HE firing, high velocity anti-tank or high-angle, anti-aircraft weapons. In the period from September 1939 to December 1943, when the war situation was more favourable to them, the German need for the first two types was approximately equal and that for the last type almost non-existent. Approximately equal proportions of the first two types and a very small number of the third were therefore employed. In the subsequent phase up to the end of the war, however, the emphasis was placed more and more upon anti-tank and anti-aircraft equipments, with a consequent falling off in the number of low velocity HE firing types.

It is impossible to attempt to cover the wartime history of German self-propelled artillery equipments in any more detail in this brief space, as there was a total of at least sixty-six such equipments in service during the war. Those based on tank chassis are listed at Appendix B. Listed below, however, are the tanks of German design, which were in German Army service from 1939 to 1945, together with their armament.

NOMENCLATURE	ARMAMENT
PzKpfw I Ausf.B (Sd Kfz 101)	Two 7.92-mm Dreyse MG13K machine-guns.
PzKpfw II Ausf.a, b, c, A, B, C, D, E and F (Sd Kfz 121)	One 2-cm KwK 30 (L/55). One coaxial 7.92-mm MG34.
PzKpfw II Ausf.L (Pz.Sp.Wg.Luchs)	One 2-cm KwK38 (L/55). One coaxial MG34.

7.5 cm assault gun Stu.K.40 (SdKfz 142/1). (Author's Collection)

7.5-cm tank destroyer PzJäg IV (SdKfz 162). (Author's Collection)

NOMENCLATURE	ARMAMENT	NOMENCLATURE	ARMAMENT
(Sd Kfz 123) PzKpfw III Ausf.A, B, C, D, E and F, (Sd Kfz 141)	One 3.7-cm KwK (L/46.5). Two coaxial 7.92-mm MG34. One hull-mounted MG34.	H and J (Sd Kfz 161/2)	(L/48) Aux. armt as for Ausf. A. PzKpfw V Panther One 7.5-cm KwK42
PzKpfw III Ausf.G, H and J (Sd Kfz 141)	One 5-cm KwK (L/42). One coaxial MG34. One hull-mounted MG34.	Ausf.D (Sd Kfz 171)	(L/70) One coaxial 7.92-mm MG34. Six smoke bomb-throwers, three each side of turret.
PzKpfw III Ausf.J, L and M (Sd Kfz 141/1)	One 5-cm KwK39 (L/60). Aux. armt as for Ausf. G, H and J, plus three smoke bomb throwers each side of turret on Ausf.M.	PzKpfw Panther Ausf.A and G (Sd Kfz 171) MG34.	As for Ausf.D plus one hull-mounted External smoke bomb-throwers replaced by one in turret roof. One AA MG34 on cupola ring mounting.
PzKpfw III Ausf.N (Sd Kfz 141/2)	One 7.5-cm Kwk (L/24) Aux. armt as for Ausf.J, L and M.	PzKpfw VI Tiger Ausf.E (Sd Kfz 181) MG34.	One 8.8-cm KwK36 One coaxial 7.92-mm (L/56). One hull-mounted MG34.
PzKpfw IV Ausf.A (Sd Kfz 161)	One 7.5-cm KwK37 (L/24) Aux. armt as for PzKpfw III Ausf.G, H and J.		Six external smoke bomb-throwers, three per turret side. Five 'S' mine throwers on hull roof.
PzKpfw IV Ausf.B and C (Sd Kfz 161)	As for Ausf.A but hull MG omitted.	PzKpfw Tiger Ausf.B (Königstiger) (SdKfz 182) (L/71). MG on cupola.	One 8.8-cm KwK43 Three MG34, one coaxial, one hull-mounted and one AA One smoke bomb-thrower in turret roof.
PzKpfw IV Ausf.D, E and F1 (Sd Ktz 161)	As for Ausf.A.		
PzKpfw IV Ausf.F2 (Sd Kfz 161/1)	One 7.5-cm KwK40 (L/43) Aux. armt as for Ausf. A.		
PzKpfw IV Ausf.G,	One 7.5-cm KwK40		

(N.B. *Details of the above weapons and their ammunition are given in Appendix C.*)

German Tank Armament Development Summarized

The makers of German tank policy, both before and during the Second World War, were quite clear that a tank's firepower is its most important characteristic. High priority was given to the development of a range of weapons around which suitable tanks could be designed and this policy succeeded brilliantly; the tank weapons with which Germany entered hostilities in 1939 were equal or superior to any which were then aligned against them. This superiority was maintained throughout the war by a judicious and far-sighted policy of development, whereby a new gun, or an improved version of an existing weapon, was always available when required. Briefly, the story of German tank armament development during the war is one of continuous increases in gun calibre, barrel length (and consequently, muzzle velocity) and weight of projectile; existing tanks were up-gunned with the improved version or, if this were not possible, a new tank was designed to receive it.

Apart from the two light tanks, the PzKpfw I and II, which were armed only with machine-guns, German tank main armament consisted generally of a high velocity gun mounted in a turret with 360° traverse, although some (the PzKpfw IV and the PzKpfw III Model N) were armed with a 7.5-cm low velocity close-support weapon. A 7.92-mm machine-gun (or, sometimes, two) was mounted coaxially with the main armament and an additional 7.92-mm machine-gun was often mounted in the hull front. On later tanks, as air superiority was gained by the Allies, a third 7.92-mm machine-gun in the anti-aircraft role was carried on a ring mounting around the commander's cupola. Additional defensive armament was also carried on later tanks in the shape of three single-shot smoke bomb-throwers mounted externally on each side of the turret, which could be fired from inside the turret to give a quick defensive screen of smoke. On the last tanks to be introduced before the end of the war, these smoke bomb-throwers were replaced by a single projector mounted in the turret roof with 360° independent traverse and loaded and fired from within the turret. Early versions of the Tiger Model E also carried five 'S' Mine dischargers on the superstructure roof to deter ambitious tank hunters.

German tank guns were all similar in basic design, and all were provided with QF fixed HE and AP ammunition. A novel standard feature was the electric primer and firing gear, which had the advantage of eliminating the firing delay characteristic of the mechanical firing systems and percussion primers found in Allied tank guns and ammunition. Breech blocks were of the vertical sliding wedge type with spring opening and closing, and incorporated a semi-automatic system for opening the breech and ejecting the empty cartridge case after firing. Recoil systems consisted of an hydraulic buffer and hydro-pneumatic recuperator; a recoil indicator was incorporated into the recoil guard, to indicate when the system needed topping-up. Those 7.5-cm tank guns with a calibre length of 48 or more were provided with a double-baffle muzzle brake to absorb some of the recoil energy, while the breech ring of the 7.5-cm KwK42 (L/70) gun of the Panther was fitted with an air-blast gear operated automatically by the gun's recoil to blow out the barrel after firing and prevent fumes entering the turret. The sequence of tank gun development was:

NOMENCLATURE	ARMAMENT
PzKpfw III	3.7-cm KwK (L/46.5), replaced by 5-cm KwK (L/42), replaced by

Assault tank StuPz IV (Brummbär) (SdKfz 166). (Author's Collection)

NOMENCLATURE	ARMAMENT
PzKpfw IV	5-cm KwK39 (L/60), replaced by 7.5-cm KwK (L/24). 7.5-cm KwK (L/24), replaced by 7.5-cm KwK40 (L/43), replaced by 7.5-cm KwK40 (L/48).
PzKpfw Panther	7.5-cm KwK42 (L/70).
PzKpfw Tiger Ausf E	8.8-cm KwK36 (L.56).
PzKpfw Tiger Ausf B	8.8-cm KwK43 (L/71).

With regard to machine-guns the standard medium machine-gun calibre was 7.92 mm – all were air-cooled. At the outbreak of war, the MG13 (Dreyse) gun was being replaced by the MG34 and was fitted only to the PzKpfw I Ausf.B. The MG34 was some 2 lb heavier and 15 in shorter than the MG13 and had a rate of fire nearly twice as high. It had the further advantage of being belt-fed, with disintegrating link belts, whereas the MG13 was fed by box (25 or 100 rounds) or drum magazines (50 rounds). Both types were recoil-operated and fired the same ammunition at the same muzzle velocity of 2,525 feet/sec.

The 2-cm machine guns KwK30 and KwK38 carried by the PzKpfw II were also air-cooled and recoil-operated, and fired same HE and AP ammunition. The KwK38 was, however, some 16 lbs lighter than the KwK30 and had a rate of fire of 480 rounds/minutes compared to the latter's 280 rounds/minute. Both were magazine-fed, the magazines holding 10 rounds; both had an overall length of more than 6 feet.

CHAPTER FIVE

SOVIET TANK ARMAMENT

Prior to and during the First World War, the Russian army had little experience of armoured vehicles. Apart from the armouring, at the Putilov factory, of some Austin chassis purchased from Britain at the outbreak of war in 1914, and a few Peerless armoured cars from the same source, there was no organized armoured force in Russia. After the Revolution, AFVs made little impression on the Revolutionary Government, apart from a few armoured cars and Renault light tanks (M17), the latter acquired in 1920. The only AFVs in Russia were the British Mark Vs and Whippets left behind (but immobilized through lack of spares) when the British tank detachments sent to bolster the White Russian army were withdrawn in 1920.

Russian interest in AFVs was aroused by the German tank centre established with Russian connivance but contrary to the terms of the Treaty of Versailles, at Kazan in 1921. As described in the previous chapter, it was at this centre that all the preliminary assembly and testing of the German La.S. and La.S.100 took place in the late 1920s. By this time, Soviet heavy industry, which had been decimated by the Revolution, had been resuscitated to the extent that, in 1927/8, the Soviets were able to build a number of copies of the Renault FT light tank, known in Soviet Russia as the MS1 or T-18. This represented a considerable technical advance for the USSR. From this position they progressed to the building of a medium tank, the T-24, which was the first of a number of different tank designs produced in the absence of a clear idea as to what role the tank was required to fill. Between 1930 and 1932 the Soviet authorities shopped around for

AFVs among foreign tank producers and bought a number from Vickers; these included medium tanks, fifteen 6-ton light tanks and some Carden Loyd Mark VI machine-gun carriers. The carriers were successfully copied by the Soviets, their version being called the T-27 tankette, carrying two men and a machine-gun, and used by frontier protection battalions. The Vickers 6-ton light tank, a most successful private venture design, was also built in the Soviet Union as the T-26. Both the single- and twin-turreted versions were produced at first but the latter was soon dropped. The version with the single turret was armed with a 45-mm (1.77-in) L/46 high velocity gun. This was a larger calibre than was used by any other contemporary light tank and was an early indicator of the importance which the Red Army and its successor, the Soviet army, would always attach to tank firepower.

With so many rivers running across the grain of their country, the Soviet military foresaw a need for amphibious tanks and again turned to Vickers for their first purchases. Thereafter they again built their own copies under the nomenclature of T-37 and T-38 but, although these vehicles performed reasonably well in the water, they had to be so lightly built (to gain the necessary buoyancy) as to be virtually worthless as tanks. Soviet tank theorists were almost as interested in the mobility of tanks as in their firepower and, in their search for cross-country speed, they, like the British, showed interest in the American Christie high speed tracked vehicle, of which they bought some samples. Soviet designers then developed the Christie tank into their own version, the

Light tank T-26. (Author's Collection)

BT (Bystrokhodnii Tahk or 'fast tank'), so successfully that they were able to up-gun it three times before it was rendered obsolete by its successor, the T-34 medium tank.

Like most countries in the mid-1930s, Soviet tank theory envisaged three categories of tank; a light tank for reconnaissance (the T-26), a fast medium tank for exploitation (the BT) and a heavy tank for breaking through enemy defences in support of infantry. The latter category was again filled by tanks based on Vickers designs, the T-28 (based on the Vickers 16-tonner) and the T-35 (based on the Vickers 'Independent'). In all cases, however, the Soviet preoccupation with tank firepower was evident as, in their domestically produced versions, they consistently mounted guns of larger calibre than were fitted in the foreign originals. Thus the T-35, for example, was armed with a low

Medium tank T-28 (top) and heavy tank T-35. (Author's Collection)

velocity L/16.5 gun of 76.2-mm (3-in) calibre in the main turret and two 45-mm (1.77-in) L/46 high velocity guns in sub-turrets, whereas the 'Independent' carried only a 3-pdr (47-mm) as main armament.

The series of Five-Year Plans initiated by the Soviet Union in 1928 changed the tank picture dramatically. In that year the Red Army had possessed only 92 tanks; the Siberian Military District, for example, which stretched from the Urals to the Pacific Ocean, had only 30 light tanks and 21 armoured cars. By 1935 Soviet stocks of tanks had increased to over 10,000, with production increasing each year. When the Germans invaded the USSR in June 1941, they estimated the Red Army's tank force to comprise 24,000 tanks, outnumbering those of the invading force by about seven to one. But while the technical advances made so rapidly by Soviet heavy industry had been dramatic, armoured doctrine had not kept pace, being repeatedly frustrated by political interference and the inexperience of military commanders. The chief exception to the latter weakness was a former Czarist officer named M.N. Tukhachevsky, later to be a Marshal of the Soviet Union and often regarded as the Soviet Union's equivalent to the German General Guderian. It was he who, from 1930 onwards, concentrated on the establishment of mechanized formations of up to corps strength, and the development of the Soviet armoured force would undoubtedly have been more effective in both the Finnish War (the Winter War) and the Great Patriotic War (the Second World War) had Tukhachevsky and his supporters not been arrested in June 1937 on Stalin's orders, court-martialled and shot. Stalin had seen him and the armoured corps as a threat, and followed up his court-martial with a wholesale purge of the Soviet officer corps, in which some 35,000 officers were shot, imprisoned or dismissed. The mechanized corps were also disbanded and

tank elements were re-allocated to infantry formations for the direct support of infantry, based on recommendations by the commander of the Soviet tank force sent to assist the Republicans in the Spanish Civil War, General D.G. Pavlov. It was this political interference, together with the poor secondary technical education of tank personnel and the shortage of tank radios, which reduced the efficacy of the Soviet tank corps and offset their superiority in tank numbers over the Germans in June 1941. The T-26 and BT tanks commanded by Pavlov in Spain had, however, proved markedly superior to the German PzKpfw I and Italian tankettes fielded by the German Condor Legion supporting Franco's forces, and made such a deep impression on the Germans that their commander, von Thoma, offered a reward for the capture of one intact.

With Hitler's accession to power in Germany in 1933, the earlier Soviet cooperation with the Reichswehr was broken, but by now Soviet tank technology was growing apace and independently of its former foreign advisers. The new German threat increased the priority given to the Red Army and, by 1935, now with 10,000 tanks, it possessed easily the largest armoured force in the world. The very magnitude of the Soviet tank production effort meant that, as in the Second World War with the US Sherman and its 75-mm gun, many of their tanks were obsolete by the time they went into action; this was certainly true of the T-26 light tank, BT and T-28 medium tanks and the T-35 heavy tank with which the Red Army initially met the German invasion. By 1941 the medium tank which was to revolutionize tank design worldwide and defeat the German invaders by the sheer numbers in which it was produced, namely the T-34, was in production to replace the BT, although not yet in service in any numbers.

Like the Germans, the Red Army placed

more stress on firepower than on either of the other two tank characteristics, and to that end developed a range of high velocity guns and low velocity howitzers of standard calibres, suitable both for turret mounting and for limited traverse mounting as self-propelled weapons on tank chassis. All AFV main armament weapons were characterized, as was so much of Soviet tank design, by mechanical simplicity, a design facilitating quantity production with limited resources in machine tools and skilled labour, and by use of fine finish only where essential: where a fine finish was not essential to the correct functioning of an assembly or component, surfaces were left with a comparatively rough finish. Soviet tank guns in the Second World War ranged in calibre from 45-mm (1.77-in) through 76.2-mm (3-in), 85-mm (3.35-in), 100-mm (4-in) and 122-mm (4.8-in) to 152-mm (6-in); self-propelled weapons were of the same calibres. Soviet tanks of the Second World War were designed with a realistic outlook and a practical approach to the requirements of an armoured fighting vehicle; they showed a clear-headed appreciation of the essentials of an effective tank and the requirements of war, duly adjusted to the particular characteristics of the Soviet soldier, the terrain over which they were likely to fight and the manufacturing facilities available. In particular, and as the Germans had done with their tanks, Soviet tanks introduced into service during the Second World War were all capable of being up-gunned as the need arose, while the basic running gear and power plants were retained throughout the war and through the various vehicle modification and improvement programmes, thus simplifying production and logistics.

The tanks with which the Red Army met the initial German onslaught of Operation Barbarossa in June 1941 were mainly the T-26 light, the BT medium and the T-35 heavy; none was a match for the German panzers, being under-armoured and under-gunned. Although it fielded some 24,000 tanks against the German invaders, outnumbering their panzer forces by some 7:1, the Red Army, and in particular its mechanized force, was badly trained and badly led by officers the majority of whom were scared to use personal initiative in the aftermath of the terror of the Great Purge for fear of losing their jobs or worse. The Germans scented an early and easy victory as their forces advanced rapidly (the Red Army losing some 20,000 of its tanks in the process) until halted by a combination of the worst winter in living memory and a counter-offensive by some tough Siberian divisions. The Soviets had, however, managed to dismantle their vital tank manufacturing plants and remove them, lock, stock and barrel, to the east, out of range of the Luftwaffe bombers, where they were soon resuming manufacture in quantities that the Germans could not hope to match. Manufacture was initially concentrated on production of the new medium tank, the T-34, and a new heavy tank, the KV-1. The T-34 was first produced in 1940 and was a development of, and replacement for, the BT fast tank, armed with a 76.2-mm (3-in) gun; some 1,000 had been built by the time of the German invasion. It was soon followed by two new heavy tanks, both named after Soviet Marshal Klimenti Voroshilov, the KV-1 (armed with the same 76.2-mm (3-in) dual-purpose gun as the T-34) and the KV-2 (mounting a 152-mm (6-in) howitzer).

Soviet AFV nomenclature has varied; for light and medium tanks before and during the Second World War it consisted of the letter 'T' (for TAHK: Tank) followed by a two-digit number. For heavy tanks the system was less consistent. Prior and subsequent to the Second World War it was similar to that for medium tanks, but during that war heavy tanks were named after Soviet personalities such as Klimenti Voroshilov (KV) and Iosef Stalin (IS). The different 'Marks' of heavy tank were distinguished by a number after the name as, for example, 'KV-1', 'IS-3'. After the war, when the medium and heavy weight classes were merged into a 'universal tank' class, nomenclature reverted to the 'T' system. When a weapon was mounted with limited traverse on a self-propelled mounting based on a tank chassis, it was designated as 'SU' (Samokhodnaya Ustanovka: self-propelled mounting), followed by the calibre of the weapon in millimetres. As the Germans did, the Soviet army made great use of self-propelled guns and howitzers, on light, medium and heavy tank chassis, in the Second World War.

LIGHT TANKS

Soviet production of light tanks was on a very much smaller scale than that of their medium and heavy tanks but, nevertheless, by comparison with British and German production quantities, the numbers produced were large. The T-26 series was very numerous, some 4,500 of all models being produced from 1931 to 1941. The original twin-turreted version, generally known as the T-26A, mounted a 7.62-mm (0.3-in) DT machine-gun in each turret but was very soon considered to be under-gunned. Accordingly, a 37-mm (1.45-in) high velocity gun was mounted, initially in the left-hand turret with the right-hand one removed, but later in a redesigned turret, offset to the left, this version being known as the T-26B. Both versions carried a crew of three men. An improved T-26B with thicker, welded armour and mounting the 45-mm (L/46) gun with coaxial 7.62-mm machine-gun was introduced in 1937, known as the T-26B-2, but after combat experience in Spain and Manchuria was found to be under-armoured. The final version of the

T-26, the T-26S (T-25C in Cyrillic script), incorporating the improvements dictated by combat experience, appeared in 1938 armed with the same 45-mm main armament as the T-26B but in a redesigned, centrally-mounted turret; the T-26S had an all-welded hull and turret of improved shape and thicker armour. The T-26 was finally taken out of front line service in 1942, although it was still better armed than the contemporary British (2-pdr) and US (37-mm) light tanks and the German PzKpfw I and II.

A series of light amphibious tanks, loosely based upon the Vickers A4E11, was also produced between 1931 and 1941 in addition to the T-26 series. These comprised the T-37, T-38 and T-40, of which the most significant was the T-40. All were armed only with machine-guns, and all remained in service until 1942 in reconnaissance and air landing units. However, the Finnish campaign had made clear that more armour protection was needed, so amphibious capability was sacrificed to a greater weight of armour in a non-amphibious modification of the T-38 known as the T-60. The T-60 was armed with a 20-mm (0.78-in) ShVAK automatic gun, mounted with a coaxial 7.62-mm (0.3-in) DT machine-gun in an offset turret, and its armour protection was increased to 20-mm. Production started in December 1941 and some 6,000 were built, a later version known as the T-60A having increased armour protection of 35 mm on the hull and 25 mm on the turret.

The T-60 also proved inadequate in combat, so a new tank with thicker armour and heavier armament was introduced early in 1942. This vehicle, known as the T-70, was armed with the 45-mm (1.77-in) L/46 high velocity gun and coaxial 7.62-mm (0.3-in) machine-gun. It still had a crew of only two men, which meant that the overworked commander/gunner/loader was unable to make the maximum use of the heavier

Light tank T-60. (Author's Collection)

armament with which the tank had been provided. The T-60 and T-70 were used alongside heavier tanks in the tank brigades and regiments, as well as in reconnaissance units, and in 1942/3 made up a fifth of the armoured force. By 1945 their shortcomings led to their withdrawal from front line service and their use as light artillery tractors and improvised mounts for artillery rocket launchers and various anti-aircraft weapons. The T-70 chassis was also used as the basis for the first Soviet purpose-built self-propelled gun, the SU-76. This mounted the 76.2-mm (3-in) L/41.5 gun in a fixed, open-topped superstructure at the rear of a lengthened T-70 hull, the gun being provided with a double-baffle muzzle brake to reduce recoil to an acceptable level. This equipment carried a crew of four.

The complete list of Soviet light tanks in service with the Red Army in the Second World War, together with their armament, is as follows:

NOMENCLATURE	ARMAMENT
T-26A	Two 7.62-mm DT MGs, one in each turret.
T-26B	One 37-mm (1.46-in) high velocity gun and coaxial 7.62-mm DT MG in offset turret, on early versions. In later models, 37-mm gun replaced by 45-mm (1.77-in) L/46 weapon.
T-37A	One 7.62-mm DT MG in one-man turret.
T-38	As for T-37A.

Light tank T-40. (Author's Collection)

Light tank T-70. (Tank Museum 3213/E6)

NOMENCLATURE	ARMAMENT
T-40	One 12.7-mm (0.5-in) MG with coaxial 7.62-mm DT MG in one-man turret.
T-60	One 20-mm ShVAK automatic gun and one 7.62-mm DT MG in one-man turret.
T-70	One 45-mm (1.77-in) (L/46) high velocity gun and coaxial 7.62-mm DT MG in one-man turret.
SU-76	One 76.2-mm (3-in) L/41.5 high velocity gun in limited traverse mounting in fixed, turret-like superstructure.

MEDIUM TANKS

As already described, between 1927 and 1939, Soviet tank design was considerably influenced by then-current practice in other countries and especially in Britain. Various prototype medium tanks were designed and built in the USSR in this period, most owing much of their appearance to foreign designs, if carrying heavier armament than their foreign originals. None reached the production stage until the T-28, a multi-turreted tank weighing some 28 tons and carrying a crew of six men. The T-28 owed much to the British Vickers A1E1 Independent in its appearance and the first of its various versions, the Model A, appeared in 1933. Its armament consisted of a 76.2-mm (3-in) L/16 howitzer mounted in the main central turret and one 7.62-mm (0.3-in) machine-gun in each of two forward sub-turrets. The T-28B, which appeared in 1938, replaced the 76.2-mm howitzer with the L/26 gun of the same calibre. A few T-28s were sent to Spain, but its first real experience of combat was against the Mannerheim Line in the Finnish War of 1939–40; there it was found to be inadequately armoured, and the attempt to remedy this defect resulted in the vehicle being too slow and unwieldy for its role. It nevertheless remained in production until 1940, and was still in service when Germany invaded the USSR in 1941.

The lessons learned in the invaluable testing ground of the Spanish Civil War led the Soviet tank designers to go back to the drawing board while development of the T-28 continued, and a series of designs, developed one from the other, was begun in 1937 leading first to the T-46. This was an attractive tank, armed with a 45-mm high velocity gun and two 7.62-mm (0.3-in) machine-guns, one mounted coaxially with the main gun and the other in the rear of the turret. It was, however, not put into production, being followed in 1939 by the A-20, a development from it carrying similar armament. The A-20 led in turn to the A-30, which also appeared in 1939. This was armed with a 76.2-mm (3-in) gun, in response to a requirement for the tank to be able to penetrate 60 mm of armour at a range of 1,300 metres. The A-20 in its turn was followed in the same year by the T-32, but it is not easy to set out these prototypes in chronological order. All, however, bore a resemblance to the T-34 in their outward appearance and obviously played important parts in the development of this tank.

A parallel development in the medium weight class was that of the BT fast tank, intended for exploitation in the traditional cavalry role. Arising out of the Soviet purchase of two US Christie M1930 convertible tanks (known in the USSR as the BT-1) in December 1930, the BT was accepted for service in the Red Army in May 1931 before any Soviet prototypes had been built or tested. The first Soviet-built unarmed prototypes (known as BT-2) were completed in October of that year and took part in the Moscow parade on 7 November. Production of the BT-2, armed with a 37-mm (1.46-in) gun and a ball-mounted 7.62-mm (0.3-in) MG in the turret, began in 1932 and ended the following year after some 400 vehicles had been built. The BT-2, while appreciated for its speed by the Red Army, was unreliable and the turret too cramped for its two-man crew. In the November 1932 Moscow parade, two of the ten participating BT-2 tanks broke down. In efforts to improve the tank's reliability and fightability two modified designs (the BT-3 and BT-4) were proposed and rejected, but the BT-5, which was armed with the 45-mm (1.77-in) tank gun mounted in the larger turret of the T-26 light tank, was put into production in 1934. An artillery version, the BT-5A, mounting the 76.2-mm (3-in) Model 27/32 howitzer in the T-28 turret, was also produced in small quantities. The problems with the engine and transmission experienced in the BT-2 persisted in the BT-5 so a further redesign, involving power plant, transmission and hull, was undertaken in 1935, resulting in the BT-7, of which an artillery version, known as the BT-7A and mounting the same turret and armament as the BT-5A, was also built. Despite these changes the engine problems remained, so that a new version, the BT-8, powered by a new V-2 diesel engine of Soviet design, which was also to power the T-34 medium and KV heavy tanks, was introduced in 1939. Some 750 were produced before production ceased to make way for the new T-34 in 1941. A total of 7,000 BT tanks was produced, of which about 1,000 were BT-8; some 65 BT-5s saw combat in Spain in the Spanish Civil War, where it was found to be clearly superior to the PzKpfw I and Italian tankettes of the Nationalist forces. When the

Light SP gun SU-76. (Tank Museum 2949/B1)

Fast tank BT-7 (nearest camera) and medium tank T-46. (Author's Collection)

German army invaded the USSR in 1941 in Operation Barbarossa, about one third of the total Red Army tank strength was composed of BT tanks of various models. The BT was replaced by the T-34 in service units in 1941–2.

While it is no part of this book's purpose to describe in detail any of the tanks engaged in the Second World War, the T-34 deserves a special mention in view of the influence which it exerted on tank design worldwide during and since the war. It had a profound effect on the panzer troops who first encountered it in action in July 1941, so much so that a party of high level German tank designers and manufacturers was flown to Orel in Hitler's personal aircraft in October 1941 at the behest of General Guderian, to examine captured specimens of the tank with a view to producing a German version. The T-34 was a mould-breaking design, particularly with regard to its armour protection and layout. The great majority of tanks hitherto had frontal hull armour stepped to follow the outline of a seated driver, and hull, superstructure and turret sides and rear composed of vertical or near-vertical plates, whereas the T-34 armour was well sloped all round, using only three thicknesses of plate. Armour was welded rolled plate except for the cast turret. The designers had been quick to appreciate that not only were sloped plates more difficult to penetrate than vertical armour of the same thickness but also that sloping the armour saved weight. This simple but highly efficient hull was carried on an improved Christie-type suspension whose greater wheel movement gave improved cross-country performance, especially when combined with an advanced diesel power plant, modified from an aero engine, with an output of some 500 b.h.p. This gave the 28-ton tank a power/weight ratio of nearly 18 h.p./ton. Combined with a simple but wide track, giving the vehicle a

nominal ground pressure of some 11.3 lb/in², these features gave the T-34 excellent cross-country mobility combined with very good armour protection. The armour layout, high power/weight ratio and low ground pressure have formed the basis for most postwar tank designs worldwide. In particular, the armour layout was copied in the German Panther and Tiger Model B tanks introduced later in the Second World War.

If the T-34 was so advanced in its armour protection and mobility characteristics, what about its firepower, the characteristic given top priority in tank design by the Soviet tank designers? This was the weakest aspect of the tank. Its main armament was the 76.2-mm (3-in) F-34 dual-purpose gun of only 30.5 calibres in length, carried in a cast turret with 360° traverse and firing a 14-lb projectile. While this gun compared favourably with contemporary British, American and German tank guns, it was soon to be outclassed by the 7.5-cm KwK40 (L/43) and (L/48) guns of the German PzKpfw IV. Secondary armament comprised a 7.62-mm (0.3-in) DT (Degtyarev) machine-gun (fed by 63-round drum magazines) ball-mounted coaxially with the main armament, but capable of independent traverse and elevation, in the turret and another, operated by the wireless operator, ball-mounted in the front hull glacis plate. The main armament, while adequate when the tank was first introduced, did not have a long enough barrel or a high enough muzzle velocity to give it an effective anti-tank performance as thicker enemy tank armour was introduced. It did have a reasonable anti-personnel performance when firing lower velocity shrapnel and HE shell. However, it was not only the main armament capability that weakened the firepower of the T-34 but also the fact that it had a turret crew of only two men (commander/gunner and loader) and that there was no turret floor to revolve with the turret, the crewmen having

Medium tank T-34/76. (Author's Collection)

to walk around on the top of the ammunition boxes as the turret traversed. This was particularly difficult in action, when the turret floor consisted of opened and unopened boxes, as well as being littered with empty cartridge cases due to the lack of an empty cartridge bag. These weaknesses detracted little, however, from an outstanding and robust medium tank which, despite a rough external finish from which all unnecessary machining had been eliminated, was well armoured, highly mobile and adequately armed. Three models of the T-34/76 were produced, the T-34/76A (described above), the T-34/76B, which was up-armoured, mounted a slightly longer (41.2 calibres) 76.2-mm gun and appeared in 1941, and the T-34/76C, distinguishable by having a commander's cupola, which appeared towards the end of 1942.

One further development of the T-34 was introduced in 1943, largely as a result of encountering the German PzKpfw IV with the long-barrelled 7.5-cm (L/43) and (L/48) guns and the PzKpfw Tiger Model E with its 8.8-cm main armament. This was the T-34/85, in which the hull frontal armour thickness was increased to 100-mm (4-in) and the main armament up-gunned to a long-barrelled 85-mm (3.35-in) L/51.5 gun, mounted in an enlarged, three-man, turret. The 85-mm gun fired an anti-tank projectile weighing 20.4 lbs. The T-34/85 entered service in early 1944 and was approximately the equal of the German PzKpfw Panther.

The T-34 chassis was used as the basis for several self-propelled assault and anti-tank guns, all mounted in a limited traverse mounting in the hull front plate, extended upward to accommodate the gun mounting.

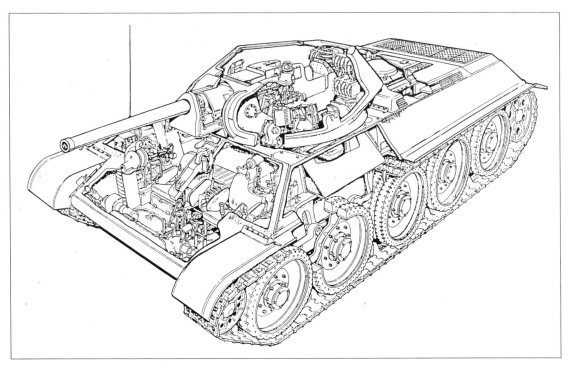

Medium tank T-34/76 — ghosted view. (Author's Collection)

Medium tank T-34/85. (Tank Museum 340/G1)

These included:

SU-122	The 122-mm (4.8-in) M-38 assault howitzer, produced in answer to the German Stu.G.III.
SU-85	The 85-mm (3.35-in) D-5S L/51.5 anti-tank gun, produced to augment the T-34/85 in a cheaper and less-complicated AFV with a lower silhouette.
SU-100	An up-gunned version of the SU-85, armed with the 100-mm (3.9-in) D-10S L/54 anti-tank gun in place of the 85-mm and produced to augment the T-44 medium tank, intended to be armed with the tank version (D-10T) of the same 100-mm weapon. Introduced in early 1945.

Between 1940 and 1945, a total of some 40,000 T-34 tanks of all models was produced, a total equalled in the Second World War only by the US medium tank M4 Sherman.

By 1943, however, even the T-34/85 was being outclassed by the German PzKpfw Tiger and the various 8.8-cm SP anti-tank guns such as the Elefant and Hornisse then being encountered. In addition, POW and other Intelligence reports suggested that even more powerful anti-tank weapons were on the German stocks. It was decided to design a more powerfully-armed replacement for the T-34, taking advantage of the redesign to replace the Christie suspension, with its internal hull width penalty, by a horizontal transverse torsion bar system and using the additional internal width thereby gained to accommodate a larger turret ring and a transversely-mounted engine. The new tank was known as the T-44 and it was to mount the 100-mm (3.9-in) D-10T (L/54) tank gun. Due to the temporary shortage of the 100-mm gun, however, early production vehicles mounted the 85-mm gun of the T-34/85. The T-44 made its first appearance in 1945 but, rushed into service as it was, it was found to have serious faults and it was taken out of production before many had been produced.

Soviet medium tanks and their variants which saw action in the Second World War, together with their armaments, are listed below:

NOMENCLATURE	ARMAMENT
T-28	One 76.2-mm (3-in) L/16.5 gun and coaxial 7.62-mm DT MG in main turret. One 7.62-mm DT MG in each of two sub-turrets, one replaced in some vehicles by 45-mm (1.77-in) M-32 (L/46) high velocity gun.
BT-2	One 37-mm (1.46-in) M-30 high velocity gun and one ball-mounted 7.62-mm MG beside it in turret.
BT-5	One 45-mm (1.77-in) M-32 (L/46) gun and coaxial 7.62-mm MG in turret.
BT-5A	One 76.2-mm M-27/32 (L/16.5) howitzer.
BT-7	As for BT-5.
BT-7A	As for BT-5A.

85-mm tank destroyer SU-85. (Tank Museum 2457/E3)

Medium tank T-44. (Tank Museum 698/A2)

NOMENCLATURE	ARMAMENT	NOMENCLATURE	ARMAMENT
BT-8	As for BT-5, plus additional 7.62-mm DT MG in rear turret wall.		mounted 7.62-mm DT MG in front hull glacis plate.
T-34/76A	One 76.2-mm (3-in) L/30.5 gun and one 7.62-mm DT coaxial MG in turret. One ball-mounted 7.62-mm DT MG in hull front glacis plate.	SU-122	One 122-mm M-38 field howitzer, mounted in extended front hull glacis plate, with limited traverse.
T-34/76B	One 76.2-mm F-34 (L/41.2) gun. Aux. armament as for T-34/76A.	SU-85	One 85-mm (3.35-in) D-5S (M-43) L/51.5 high velocity gun mounted in extended front hull glacis plate, with limited traverse.
T-34/76C	As for T-34/76B.	SU-100	One 100-mm (3.9-in) D-10S (L/54) high velocity gun mounted in extended front hull glacis plate, with limited traverse.
T-34/85	One 85-mm (3.35-in) D-5T (L/51.5) high velocity gun, with coaxial 7.62-mm DT MG in enlarged three-man turret. One ball-	T-44	One 85-mm (3.35-in)

NOMENCLATURE   ARMAMENT

D-5T (L/51.5) tank gun in early vehicles, replaced by 100-mm (3.9-in) D-10T (L/54) gun in later production. Aux. armt as for T-34/85.

In addition to the above listed tanks and SP guns, the various medium tank chassis were used as the basis for many special devices, such as bridge-layers, dozers, flame-thrower tanks, armoured recovery vehicles, mine-ploughs and rollers and fascine carriers. Many of these were ad hoc field conversions of standard gun tanks, but virtually all were armed only with one 7.62-mm machine-gun apart from the crew's individual weapons.

HEAVY TANKS

The third tank category favoured by the Red Army both before and during the Great Patriotic War was that of heavy tanks. Initially inspired by the need to counter such foreign tanks as the French Char 2C and the British Independent, designed by Vickers, a demand arose in 1932 for a heavy assault tank able to deal both with enemy infantry and with hostile anti-tank weapons, as well as giving greater strength to breakthrough formations than the medium T-28 tank could give. In response to this demand the T-35 was designed. First appearing in 1932 it was a vast tank weighing some 45 tons; its hull bears a striking resemblance to that of the British Churchill, which was not to appear for another ten years. In general appearance too it bore more than a passing resemblance

100-mm tank destroyer SU-100. (Tank Museum 2455/D4)

Medium SP howitzer SU-122. (Tank Museum 2455/A1)

to the Independent, although better armed. With five turrets, it carried a variety of weapons; a 76.2-mm (3-in) L/16.5 howitzer was mounted, with a coaxial 7.62-mm MG, in the main turret, round which were grouped four subsidiary turrets, the off-side front and near-side rear each mounting a 37-mm gun in early production and a 45-mm gun from 1935, and the other two sub-turrets each with one 7.62-mm machine-gun. The early version with the two 37-mm guns was known as the T-35A, that with the 45-mm guns as the T-35B. The T-35 proved mechanically troublesome, however, and only about thirty were produced. These were fielded in the Red Army's attempt to repel the German onslaught in 1941, the majority captured by the Germans in their advance had broken down or run out of fuel rather than being knocked out by enemy action.

Work on a replacement for the T-35 began in 1938 at the Kirov plant in Leningrad. As the requirement was for a vehicle with 60-mm (2.4-in) armour to keep out 37-mm anti-tank gun projectiles, and as an adequate anti-tank performance could now be obtained

from the longer, higher velocity 76.2-mm (3-in) tank gun, it was decided to dispense with the sub-turrets originally proposed in the intermediate designs SMK and T-100, thus saving weight, and to make do with one turret mounting the new gun. The new tank resulting from this requirement emerged in prototype form in September 1939 and was named Klimenti Voroshilov (shortened to KV) after the Soviet People's Commissar for Defence. It had a maximum frontal armour thickness on hull and turret of 75 mm, weighed about 47 tons in action and carried a crew of five, two in the hull and three in the turret. The original KV-1 tank was armed with a 76.2-mm (3-in) gun, 30.5 calibres in length. In the KV-1A which succeeded it, this gun was replaced by a longer one (the M-40) with a barrel length of 41.5 calibres. Both the KV-1 and 1A had the same auxiliary armament of three 7.62-mm (0.3-in) DT machine-guns, one being mounted coaxially with the main armament, a second on a ball mounting in the rear turret wall and the third in a ball mounting in the front hull vertical plate. Another version, known as the KV-2

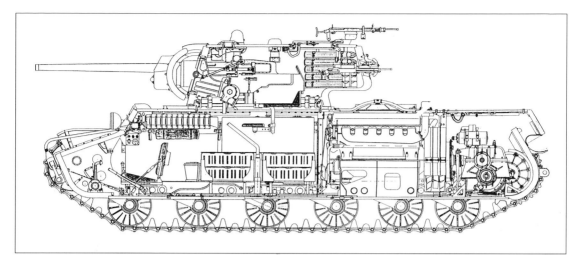

Heavy tank KV-1 – sectioned view. (Author's Collection)

Heavy assault tank KV-2. (Author's Collection)

and mounting a 152-mm (6-in) L/20 howitzer in a massive slab-sided turret, was produced at the same time, although in smaller numbers. Both KV-1 and KV-2 took part in the Finnish campaign, in which their heavy armour and armament proved their worth against the Mannerheim Line. By the time of the German invasion in June 1941 some 500 of both types of KV tank were available. As a result of lessons learned at this time, an up-armoured version of the KV-1, the KV-1B, was produced. This had frontal and side armour of 100-mm (4-in) thickness, but this was again found to be inadequate and further

Heavy tank KV-85. (Tank Museum 2443/C3)

up-armouring to 120-mm took place on the KV-1C in 1942. The KV-2, however, was found to be too conspicuous and clumsy and it was phased out in the same year. The appearance of the German PzKpfw Tiger on the Leningrad front in August 1942 emphasized to the Red Army the need for a heavy tank with more powerful anti-tank armament with which to combat it, and the modification of the KV-1 to fulfil this need was put in hand. The resulting tank, the KV-85, consisted of a modified KV-1 hull with the driver repositioned to the centre of the hull front and no hull machine-gunner. On the hull was mounted an enlarged, cast turret, similar to that of the T-34/85, mounting the 85-mm (3.35-in) D-5T (L/51.5) tank gun and carrying a turret crew of three men. There were thus now three AFVs armed with this development of the M-39 anti-aircraft gun, namely the T-34/85, the SU-85 and the KV-85. The latter vehicle was only an interim solution to the heavy tank requirement, soon to be replaced by a further development of the basic KV heavy tank, the Iosef Stalin or IS. The Red Army desired not just parity with, but technological superiority to, enemy tanks, particularly in firepower. Some 10,000 KV tanks of all models were produced before production switched to the IS series.

Two self-propelled weapons were mounted on KV chassis, the first being the SU-152, a modified KV tank chassis mounting a 152-mm (6-in) L/29 howitzer with limited traverse in a fixed superstructure, designed and a prototype built in twenty-five days. Another version of this vehicle was completed with the 122-mm A-19S high velocity gun in place of the 152-mm howitzer and was known as SU-122 – not to be confused with the other SU-122, consisting of a 122-mm howitzer on T-34 chassis.

The Iosef Stalin was based on a modification of the original KV tank. The same engine was employed, but with a synchromesh transmission and regenerative steering to simplify driving and increase manoeuvrability. The hull was improved in shape and protection by the use of cast armour, and the KV torsion bar suspension and steel-tyred road wheels were retained in the interests of standardization. As originally produced, the IS-1 mounted the 85-mm tank gun in a three-man turret similar to that of the KV-85, this version being known as the IS-1A. It appeared in small numbers only in 1943, being soon supplanted by the IS-1B which substituted the 100-mm (3.9-in) D-10T tank gun for the 85-mm. This too was very shortly superseded in early 1944 by the IS-2, which was armed with the 122-mm (4.8-in) tank gun D-25 (L/43). At that time, this was the most powerful gun ever to have been mounted in a tank and, with its double-baffle muzzle brake, bore a striking resemblance to the larger German tank guns. It was a modification of a field artillery piece, the M-43, and guns fitted to early production IS-2s retained the interrupted screw breech mechanism of the field piece. Later guns were modified to the standard type of tank gun falling-wedge breech block, which was simpler and quicker to use. The ammunition was separate rather than the more common fixed ammunition of previous tank guns, on account of its size. This meant that projectile and charge had to be loaded separately, thus further slowing a rate of fire already adversely affected by the screw breech mechanism. The armour-piercing round could penetrate 185 mm (7.3 in) of armour at 1,000 metres. Auxiliary armament in the IS-1A, IS-1B and IS-2 consisted of three 7.62-mm (0.3-in) DT machine-guns, one mounted coaxially with the main armament, one in the rear wall of the turret and one in a fixed mounting in the upper hull front. The IS-2 weighed 45 tons in action, carried a crew of four and could attain a maximum road speed of 23 m.p.h.

Heavy tank IS-1. (Tank Museum 2449/A1)

Heavy tank IS-2. (Tank Museum 2947/E1)

The IS-3, the final Soviet heavy tank development of the Second World War, caused almost as much of a sensation as had the T-34 when first introduced. It was a development of the Iosef Stalin with drastically redesigned turret and hull armour, which influenced postwar tank design almost as much as the T-34 had influenced it in the Second World War. The design arose from the Soviet requirement to combine the 122-mm tank gun with improved armour protection with no increase in weight, and it succeeded brilliantly. Both hull and turret were reshaped drastically, the hull front being welded from flat plates into a sloped and pointed configuration making a difficult ballistic target and one which gave rise to its Red Army nickname of 'Shchuka' ('Pike', or 'Hecht' as the Germans called it). The turret

was lowered and rounded into a turtleshell shape, eliminating the shot-traps which characterized the design of earlier heavy tank turrets. The volume and weight saved by this redesign enabled the weight of the IS-3 to be kept just below that of the IS-2 despite a 40 mm increase in armour thickness (to 200 mm on the front of the turret), while the vehicle height was lower by one foot. The prototype was produced in November 1944 and incorporated the same armament as the IS-2 except that the 7.62-mm MG in the rear wall of the turret was sensibly eliminated and a 12.7-mm (0.5-in) AA MG was mounted on the commander's cupola. Although some 500 IS-3s had been produced by the war's end only very few saw action, as issue to units had only just started. Its appearance in the Berlin Victory Parade in September 1945, however, caused

Heavy tank destroyer ISU-122. (Tank Museum 2456/C1)

considerable shock to Western observers who knew that nothing as powerfully-armed or well-armoured existed in the inventories of their own armies.

As with other Soviet tanks in the Second World War, the IS tank chassis served as the basis for self-propelled guns; these were known as 'ISU', a combination of 'IS' and 'SU', to distinguish them from earlier SUs on T-34 and KV chassis. One was an update of the earlier SU-152, known as the ISU-152. It consisted of the 152-mm (6-in) M-37 (L/29) gun/howitzer mounted in a limited traverse mounting in the front plate of a fixed superstructure on a modified IS-2 tank chassis. The other was the ISU-122 tank destroyer, in which the 122-mm (4.8-in) A-19S (L/43) or D-25S (L/45) gun of the IS-2 tank was similarly mounted on a modified IS-2 chassis. The L/45 gun was distinguished externally from the A-19S by its double-baffle muzzle brake. The advantages of such SP guns over their tank equivalents were threefold: firstly they could carry very much more ammunition, secondly, they had a much lower silhouette, making concealment easier, and thirdly, they were cheaper, quicker and easier to produce. Their main disadvantage was the limited independent traverse, while the long-barrelled guns of the tank destroyers imposed limitations on cross-country travel in undulating or hilly country.

Below are tabled the Soviet heavy tanks which saw action in the Second World War, together with the SP guns based on them:

NOMENCLATURE	ARMAMENT
T-35A	One 76.2-mm (3-in) L/16.5 howitzer and coaxial 7.62-mm

NOMENCLATURE	ARMAMENT	NOMENCLATURE	ARMAMENT
	(0.3-in) DT MG in main turret. One 37-mm (1.46-in) high velocity gun in each of two sub-turrets. One 7.62-mm DT MG in each of the other two sub-turrets.	SU-152	(L/45) anti-tank gun, mounted as for SU-152. One 152-mm (6-in) ML-20 (M-37) gun/howitzer (L/29) with multi-baffle muzzle brake, mounted with limited traverse in fixed superstructure.
T-35B	As for T-35A except for two 45-mm (1.77-in) high velocity guns in place of two 37-mm.	IS-1	One 85-mm (3.35-in) D-5T (L/51.5) or 100-mm D-10T (L/54) anti-tank gun with coaxial 7.62-mm DT MG in turret front. One ball-mounted 7.62-mm DT MG in turret rear wall and one fixed DT MG in hull front plate.
KV-1	One 76.2-mm (3-in) L/30.5 gun with one 7.62-mm DT MG coaxially mounted in turret. One 7.62-mm DT MG in ball mounting in rear wall of turret and one in hull front vertical plate.		
KV-1A	As for KV-1 except 76.2-mm M-40 (L/41.5) gun replaced the L/30.5 gun.	IS-2	One 122-mm (4.8-in) D-25 (L/43) anti-tank gun and coaxial 7.62-mm DT MG in turret front. One ball-mounted 7.62-mm DT MG in turret rear wall and one fixed DT MG in hull front.
KV-1B	As for KV-1A.		
KV-1C	As for KV-1A.		
KV-2	One 152-mm (6-in) L/20 howitzer and co-axial 7.62-mm DT MG in turret. One 7.62-mm DT MG in hull front plate.	IS-3	One 122mm (4.8in) D-25 (L/43) anti-tank gun and coaxial 7.62mm DT MG in turret. One fixed DT MG in hull front. One 12.7-mm (0.5in) DShK AA MG on commander's cupola.
KV-85	One 85-mm (3.35-in) D-5T (L/51.5) tank gun and coaxially mounted 7.62-mm DT MG in turret. One fixed 7.62-mm DT MG in hull front.		
		ISU-122	As for SU-122.
SU-122	One 122-mm A-19S	ISU-152	As for SU-152.

SOVIET TANK ARMAMENT DEVELOPMENT SUMMARIZED

Like their German equivalents, Soviet tank policy-makers were quite clear from the start of Soviet interest in tanks that firepower was the most important of a tank's characteristics, with mobility second and armour protection third in importance. At the same time it was considered highly desirable, if not essential, that the firepower of Soviet tanks should be greater in each category of light, medium and heavy than any equivalent foreign vehicle. Equally, it was considered that a tank gun's primary function should be the penetration of armour, although it should also have the capability of firing HE anti-personnel ammunition. Thus from the 37-mm and 45-mm high velocity tank guns with which the Red Army entered the Great Patriotic War, all Soviet tank guns were provided with both armour-piercing and high explosive rounds, and the story of Soviet tank firepower development in that War was one of constantly increasing calibre, muzzle velocity and weight of projectile.

Soviet tank designers were equally clear-headed about the need for having as few tank designs as possible compatible with their tasks, and for keeping designs as simple to operate and to manufacture as possible. Except where absolutely essential, such as in gun sights, engine components, bearings and gun bores, finish did not matter as long as the component could be easily assembled and functioned satisfactorily. By these means, the Soviets were able, despite the disruption to their industries caused by the German invasion, to produce a range of efficient fighting tanks in quantities matched only by the USA.

This clear-headed appreciation of requirements meant that the Soviets really produced only one basic chassis in each category of light, medium and heavy tanks which they were able consistently to up-gun and up-armour, and with which they were consistently able to match and outnumber their German opponents, throughout the war. These basic chassis were:

T-60   Developed into the T-70
T-34   Developed into the T-44
KV   Developed into the IS

All had been designed before the Soviet Union entered the war, but proved capable of modification to equal the best available in any other of the industrialized countries of the West – a tribute indeed to those who set out the Soviet requirements and to the designers who satisfied them.

As the Germans had done, the Soviets also used their basic tank chassis as mounts for self-propelled guns with equal success. In most cases, the guns so mounted were tank guns of either the same or a larger calibre than the guns mounted in the tanks themselves, giving the same or greater firepower but in a cheaper vehicle with a lower silhouette and carrying more ammunition than the tank mounting the same gun.

The general layout of Soviet tanks conformed to those of other countries, being made up of three compartments, namely the driver's compartment at the front, fighting compartment in the centre and the engine/transmission compartment at the rear. The fighting compartment contained the turret, capable of 360° traverse and mounting the main armament and, usually, a coaxial 7.62-mm (0.3-in) DT machine-gun, and the turret crew of sometimes two (commander/gunner and loader) and sometimes three (commander, gunner and loader) men.

The range of Soviet tank guns in the Second World War consisted of:

37-mm (1.46-in), replaced by the 45-mm (1.77-in) L/46 gun
76.2-mm (3-in) L/30.5, replaced by the

Heavy SP assault howitzer ISU-152. (Tank Museum 946.10)

longer L/41 version, in turn replaced by 85-mm (3.35-in) L/51.5, replaced by 100-mm (3.99-in) L/54 in medium tanks and SPs.

122-mm (4.8-in) L/43 or L/45 in heavy tanks and SPs.

152-mm (6-in) L/20 howitzer (in KV-2) or L/29 gun/howitzer in SU-152 and ISU-152.

All except the 122-mm and 152-mm weapons employed fixed ammunition and were provided with manual or semi-automatic breech opening and cartridge ejection, with a vertically sliding wedge breech block; the exceptions employed separate projectile and charge and had manually-opened interrupted screw breech mechanisms giving a slower rate of fire. Gun and howitzer recoil mechanisms consisted of an hydraulic buffer and a hydro-pneumatic recuperator. Elevation of both tank and SP guns was by handwheel, as was the traverse of SP weapons. Tank turret traverse mechanisms, on the other hand, provided both hand and power option through the same epicyclic gearbox, power operation being electric. Locks were provided in both traverse and elevation systems for locking the gun and turret when travelling out of action.

Gun sights were an exception to the general rough finish of Soviet tank components and assemblies, and were designed and finished to a high standard. In both the T-34 and KV series, the gunner was provided with both telescopic and periscopic

Heavy tank IS-3. (Tank Museum 2448/D5)

sights and the commander with a panoramic sight of unnecessary complication and sophistication. Gunner's telescopes for use with the 76.2-mm and 85-mm weapons were cranked instruments (TMFD) of moving eyepiece type with an illuminated graticule for use in poor light. The graticule carried range scales for both main armament and coaxial machine-gun. With later weapons, such as the 100-mm and 122-mm tank guns, a stationary eyepiece telescope copied from the German design was employed. This incorporated an optical hinge so that the gunner's eye could remain stationary when elevating the gun, and an armour plate in the hinge to prevent fragments entering the gunner's eye. The periscopic dial sight (PT) was a periscopic telescope with a rotating head and an elevating top prism, also with an illuminated graticule and containing range scales for both main armament and coaxial MG.

Auxiliary armament was limited on all tanks prior to the introduction of the IS-3, to 7.62-mm (0.3-in) Degtyarev (DT) machine-guns. The DT was a gas-operated light MG, magazine fed from drum magazines holding 63 rounds, which could be dismounted from the tank and used as a ground LMG in conjunction with the bipod, butt strap and pistol grip provided. DT MGs were mounted coaxially with the main armament, in ball or fixed mountings in the hull front and, in the KV-1 and IS-1 and IS-2, in the rear wall of the turret. On the IS-3 and later tanks and SP guns, AA protection was given by a 12.7-mm (0.5-in) DShK MG mounted on the commander's cupola. No provision for firing close-range or main armament smoke was made, but smoke screens were generated by injecting fuel from special external auxiliary tanks into the engine exhaust system. Similarly there was no provision, apart from the crew's personal weapons, for close-range anti-personnel protection. Anti-aircraft protection on the earlier tanks was by firing one or more of the tank's DT MGs from the hip or shoulder, not a very accurate or comfortable method!

To sum up the Soviet development of tank armament in the Second World War, it consisted of a limited range of weapons, used in both field, tank and SP roles, in which calibres were standardized and regularly increased as the need arose. The tanks on which they were to be mounted were so designed as to be simple to manufacture and operate, and capable of being up-gunned to take the next size of weapon when required. Two of their tank designs, the T-34 and the IS-3, were of such revolutionary armour layout as to have influenced the designs of tanks worldwide both during and after the war, while the 122-mm gun of the IS series was the biggest gun to have been mounted on a tank up to, and for some time after, that tank's introduction.

CHAPTER SIX

AMERICAN TANK ARMAMENT

As explained in chapter one, the Americans were late entrants to the First World War and even later converts to the idea of the tank. Their tank force at the end of the war was small and equipped with Renault light tanks of French design and heavy tanks of British design and manufacture; had the war been prolonged, the United States were scheduled to produce large numbers of both Renault light tanks (under licence) and Mark VIII heavy tanks of British design (under a joint manufacture agreement), and the experience of large-scale tank manufacture and operation so gained would have clarified in the mind of the US army how tanks should be employed and designed. As events turned out, however, the Armistice signalled the cancellation of these production orders and the US army failed to gain experience of the large-scale employment of tanks in battle which would undoubtedly have influenced their later thoughts on the roles of armour and the designs of tank required to fulfil them.

Rather as Britain had done between the wars, only more so because of their distance from Europe and the isolationism that set in after 1919, the United States saw little need for land forces, and even less for expensive mechanized units in a peacetime in which the security of the United States was not thought likely to be under threat. The result was that they neglected the development of armour more than any other of the major powers, which therefore proceeded slowly, in fits and starts. The American Tank Corps, only founded in 1918, was abolished by the National Defense Act of 1920, which declared that tanks would henceforth be part of the Infantry branch, with the result that US tank doctrine, such as it was, was biased towards the support of infantry. The thousand or so US-built Renault light tanks and British Mark VIII heavy tanks which had survived the cancellation of the massive tank build programme of the First World War were organized into four tank battalions distributed to infantry formations, a situation broadly similar to that of the Soviet tank force after the Stalin purge of the 1930s, mentioned in chapter five.

In 1922, the US War Department published its policy on tank development over the next ten years, stating, among other things, that: 'As a matter of economy and simplicity in organization, the number of types of tanks should be kept to a minimum. Reliance cannot be placed on a single type of tank, but two types, a light and a medium, should be capable of fulfilling all assigned missions.' The light tank was not to exceed 5 (short) tons and the medium 15 (short) tons in weight, the US short ton containing 2,000 lbs. Armament of the medium tank was to consist of machine-guns and guns of larger calibre, capable of engaging enemy tanks on a basis of equality; no requirement for high angle (i.e. indirect) fire was foreseen. Funds and effort were to be applied principally to development rather than to the building of complete tanks.

Influenced by the British mechanized force exercises of 1927, the US Army formed in 1930 a full-time mechanized force of regimental size, composed of cavalry, infantry and artillery, but the move towards a specialized armoured force was halted in its tracks by the new Chief of Staff, General

Douglas MacArthur, in the following year, when he laid down that all arms were to be mechanized and that the cavalry would assume the armoured role. To circumvent the 1920 Congressional Act, which had specified that tanks would be the responsibility of the Infantry, light tanks were designated as 'combat cars'. By 1939 a mechanized cavalry brigade (the 7th) had been equipped with 112 'combat cars' and there was some pressure for it to be expanded into a division on German Panzerdivision lines. Following the outbreak of the Second World War in that year there was some expansion of tank production, but it was the German victories of 1940 in Europe which proved decisive in the development of armoured forces in the US Army. Congress was now willing to fund massive increases in armoured strength, which was just as well as, like the Red Army ten years earlier, the US army was perilously short of armoured vehicles and could boast only 464 tanks/combat cars in the whole of the United States.

After 1940, in which only 330 new tanks had been built, there was a phenomenal increase in production; 4,052 were built in 1941, 24,997 (more than the entire German tank production from 1939 to 1945) in 1942 and 29,487 in 1943. The only other country to approach these figures in the Second World War was the USSR and, again like the USSR, such quantities could only be attained by the mass production of a few tried types, especially the M4 medium tank. Unlike the other combatant countries, the US army initially favoured only two categories of tank, namely light and medium. During the war, however, the need for a heavy tank was finally recognized. From July 1940 to the end of the war, the Americans produced 28,919 light, 57,027 medium and 2,330 heavy tanks, a total of 88,276. In addition, they built a total of 43,481 self-propelled guns, of which a large proportion was composed of tank destroyers. These were used to equip the separate tank destroyer force which, at its peak, comprised 106 battalions, each equipped with 36 SP anti-tank guns.

Although conforming in general layout to tank design practice in the rest of the world, that is with a driver's compartment in front, a fighting compartment (carrying a turret with 360° traverse, mounting the main armament and turret crew) in the centre and an engine/transmission compartment at the rear, US tanks were characterized by a completely different external appearance from tanks of other countries, being much higher in silhouette, with slab sides and an unusual volute spring suspension of the road wheels. The extra height was largely due to a transmission tunnel down the centre of the vehicle necessitated by the combination of a rear engine with a front sprocket drive to the track. Tracks were rubber-padded where those of all other countries were made up of studded steel links; the US tracks were kind to metalled roads but gave reduced grip in mud across country or in icy conditions. Roomy inside, especially compared to Soviet tanks, the extra internal volume thus requiring to be armoured added unnecessarily to the weight of the vehicle. However, roominess made for ease of access to internal components for maintenance while the US practice of replacing faulty components by complete assemblies instead of repairing in situ with spare components also made repair simpler.

The greatest contribution made to Allied tank design in the Second World War by the United States was their insistence on the need for a dual-purpose weapon as main armament and their adoption of the 75-mm (2.95-in) gun. However, the 75-mm had a relatively poor armour-piercing performance despite a useful HE shell, and it would undoubtedly have been better if they had realized the need for up-gunning as enemy tanks continually increased their armour protection. This they steadfastly ignored, despite having had a suitable 76-mm (3-in) tank gun in 1942, preferring to rely for tank destruction on the tank destroyer battalions with their 76-mm (3-in) and 90-mm (3.5-in) guns. Another valuable contribution, although it was not fully appreciated when first encountered by British tank crews, was the gyroscopic gun stabilization system fitted to the majority of US light and medium tanks. This stabilized the gun in elevation and enabled firing on the move with reasonable accuracy where conventionally-equipped tanks with geared manual elevation had to halt to aim and fire. Such systems, stabilizing both the gun in elevation and the turret in azimuth, became standard on main battle tanks after the war. Turrets were provided with hydraulic power traverse systems.

The Americans preferred periscopic tank gun sights to the straight tube telescopic sights used by the British and Germans and used in addition to periscopic sights by the Red Army in their earlier tanks. The periscopic sight incorporated the sighting telescope in a periscope connected by linkage to the gun mounting and positioned in the turret roof. This type of sight had the advantages of needing no weakening hole in the gun mantlet, of easing the gunner's problem of keeping his eye to the sight when elevating or depressing the gun (requiring only a small backwards and forwards movement of the head compared to the difficult up and down movement required by a telescope) and of eliminating the gunner's vulnerability to fragments penetrating the telescope down the line of sight to the gunner's eye. It did pose parallax problems when adjusting the sight to the gun as well as backlash problems in the linkage to the gun mounting. Auxiliary armament consisted of air-cooled Browning machine-guns of .30 calibre (7.62-mm) and .50 calibre (12.7-mm).

American tanks were shipped in large quantities to the UK and the Middle East and issued to many British armoured units. They were reliable, effective and popular with their crews, despite the Stuart's tendency occasionally to catch fire when starting and the Sherman's propensity for catching fire when hit by the enemy, leading to its being nicknamed the 'tommy-cooker' by the Germans. The 75-mm gun of the medium tanks M3 and M4 was particularly appreciated for its high explosive capability, at a time when neither the British 2-pdr nor 6-pdr tank gun was issued with a high explosive round.

United States tank nomenclature is basically simple once the principles have been clearly understood. Model numbers are distinguished by the letter 'T' (for 'Test') in prototype and experimental vehicles and by the letter 'M' for tanks accepted for service. These letters are followed by one or more digits, allocated in sequence in each category of light, medium or heavy, to indicate the model of tank. Subsequent modifications are indicated by the letter 'A', followed by the number of the modification, e.g. Medium Tank M4A3 is the fourth model of medium tank to be accepted into service in the A3 modification. Minor modifications are distinguished by the letter 'E' followed by a digit indicating the modification. The 'T' number rarely coincides with the 'M' number, however, just to confuse matters. To confuse them even further, it is possible to have tanks of different categories, light, medium or heavy, with the same 'M' numbers in service at the same time, for which reason the tank category is always stated in the title: e.g. Medium Tank M3, Light Tank M3, etc. The naming of US tanks after US army generals was a practice started by the British in the Second World War, for example, with the Stuart (M3/M5) light tank, the Lee/Grant (M3) and Sherman (M4) medium, but the practice has since been continued by the US army.

Light tank M3 (Stuart). (Tank Museum 2877/A4)

LIGHT TANKS

The development of combat cars in the light tank category started in desultory fashion in the 1920s, limited by severe fiscal restraints imposed throughout the decade. It culminated in the T1E4 in 1931, which established the rear engine/front sprocket layout adopted for nearly all subsequent US light and medium tanks. This was followed in the early 1930s by three more prototypes in the T2 series, inspired by, and with several features of, the Vickers 6-ton light tank which, it will be remembered, had also served as the prototype for the Soviet T-26 light tank. Concurrently with the T2, Rock Island Arsenal produced, for cavalry use, the T5 combat car, which differed from the T2 primarily in having the twin bogie volute spring suspension which characterized all subsequent US light and medium tanks until the M22 and M24 light tanks, rather than the

Vickers type of leaf spring suspension. The T5 entered US army service as the Combat Car M1 in 1938. An improved version with modified turret and trailing idler wheel to increase the length of track on ground and improve the L/C ratio was introduced as the M2 in 1939. This was designated the Light Tank M1A1 in 1940 upon the formation of General MacArthur's Armored Force, and was armed with one .50 cal and one .30 cal Browning MG in the turret and one .30 cal MG in the hull. Meanwhile, the infantry in 1939 had upgraded their M1 Light Tank into the M2, armed with a 37-mm (1.46-in) L/50 gun and coaxial .30-in (7.62-mm) Browning MG in a turret with 360° traverse, as well as a hull-mounted machine-gun. Although only some 50 Combat Cars M2 and Light Tanks M2 had been produced by September 1939, the outbreak of the Second World War in Europe led to quantity production of the Light Tank M2A4 with an order for 329

Light tank M22 (Locust) leaving a Hamilcar glider. (Tank Museum 165-782)

vehicles. This version had an increased auxiliary armament of two fixed .30 cal MG's mounted in the hull and one .30 cal MG in an AA mount on the turret roof. The turret was provided with hand traverse only. A few M2A4 light tanks were delivered to the British army in 1941 but were used by them only for training. Some were used by the US army in the early Pacific campaigns, but again most were used for training.

In July 1940 an improved version of the light tank, known as the Light Tank M3, was approved for service, and entered production in March 1941. This tank had thicker armour (38 mm on the front) and reinforced suspension to take the greater weight, a welded rather than a riveted turret and, from mid-1941, a gyro stabilization system in elevation for the main armament and two jettisonable external fuel tanks to give the vehicle greater range. In August 1941 further improvements were incorporated in the M3A1, consisting of power traverse for the turret, the provision of a turret basket, and the elimination of the commander's cupola, to reduce height, and the two sponson-mounted fixed hull machine-guns.

With the passing of the Lend-Lease Act in 1941 M3s began to enter British army service, known as the Stuart light tank, petrol-engined versions as the Stuart I and diesel models as the Stuart II. Some 4,600 M3A1s were produced by American Car & Foundry. Most were known as Stuart III in British service except for some 210 with Guiberson diesel engines, known as Stuart IV. In British service the Stuart was fitted with twin external smoke bomb dischargers on the turret side.

Shortage of the Wright Continental radial aero engine which powered the majority of the M3s led to the development of the Light Tank M5, originally scheduled to be designated M4 but changed to avoid confusion with the Medium Tank M4

(Sherman) then entering service. The M5 was powered by twin Cadillac V-8 car engines combined with a Hydra-Matic transmission, retaining the turret and running gear of the M3A1 but with a redesigned and all-welded hull. The M3A3, the final version of the Light Tank M3 series, incorporated most of the improvements of the Light Tank M5 but retained the Continental power plant. Both the M3A3 and the M5A1 entered production in December 1942. In British service the M3A3 became the Stuart V and the M5A1 the Stuart VI. Total production for the M3 numbered 13,859 vehicles and for the M5, 8,884. Production of the M3A3 was terminated in August 1943 after 3,427 vehicles had been built. The M5A1 continued in production until June 1944 and was the major type in US army service in 1944–5.

Although increasingly replaced by medium tanks as the war progressed, the M3 and M5 light tanks served in the US army and Marine Corps with distinction throughout the war. They saw action in the Pacific, Mediterranean and north-west Europe theatres, in north Africa with British units even before the United States entered the war. In British service in the desert campaign the Stuart was a popular tank, the equal of the British cruiser tank in firepower and protection and its superior in terms of ease of handling, maintenance and manoeuvrability. Its ease of handling and reliability earned it the nickname of 'Honey' from the British crews.

By now, of course, the upper light tank weight limit of 5 short tons, set by the War Department back in 1922, had been greatly exceeded, the M3A3 weighing some 14 tons in action and the M5A1 15 tons, exceeding the upper limit for medium tanks set at the same time. This merely illustrates the difficulty of quantifying the weight limits in the various categories of tank at a time of constant up-gunning and up-armouring, always a misleading and inaccurate method

Light tank M24 (Chaffee). (Tank Museum 3014/A1)

of classifying tanks. It is preferable to categorize them by the role which they are intended to fill. This is illustrated even more strikingly by the 'light' tank M24 (Chaffee) which replaced the M3/M5 series.

In 1943, the Ordnance Department, in conjunction with Cadillac, the builders of the M5 series, began design work on a replacement for the M5 incorporating a 75-mm gun as main armament as well as improved armour protection. A prototype, the T24, ran successfully in October 1943 as a result of which production orders were placed and the first production vehicle, taken into US army service in May as the Light Tank M24, was delivered in April 1944. The M24, although employing the Cadillac power plant and Hydra-Matic transmission of the M5 series, was a radically redesigned vehicle of more conventional appearance than its light or

medium tank predecessors: gone was the high silhouette, slab-sided appearance and awkward bogie suspension of the earlier designs, to be replaced by a low, sleek vehicle with well-sloped armour and large diameter road wheels sprung on transverse torsion bars, in the manner of the German tanks and the Soviet KV and IS series. It was armed with a turret-mounted lightweight 75-mm (2.95-in) M6 (L/39) gun developed from an aircraft weapon. This gun had a similar performance to that of the old M3 gun of the M4 (Sherman) medium tank but weighed considerably less, and employed a space-saving concentric recoil mechanism. The main armament was stabilized in elevation and the turret provided with hydraulic power and manual traverse. Auxiliary armament consisted of two .30 calibre Browning MGs, one mounted coaxially with the main armament and the other in the right hull front, and a .5-in (12.7-mm) Browning AA MG mounted on the turret roof. With 28-mm thick hull armour and a mantlet 38 mm thick, the M24 weighed some 18 tons in action and was manned by a crew of five. It was built by two manufacturers, Cadillac and, from July 1944, Massey Harris. By the end of the war, when production ceased, Cadillac had built some 3,300 and Massey Harris 770 vehicles. Some were shipped to the UK, and in British service it was known as the 'Chaffee', a name adopted also by the US army after the war. The M24 saw service in the Italian, north-west Europe and Pacific theatres from late 1944, where it proved a good reconnaissance vehicle with enough firepower to inflict damage on the enemy and whose manoeuvrability and agility enabled it to survive on the battlefield.

As with so many other tanks of both sides in the Second World War, the M24 was used as the basis for several self-propelled weapons, and this point might be the right place at which to mention and describe the unusual nomenclature used by the US Army to distinguish its self-propelled artillery. Instead of the more customary abbreviations 'SP', 'Sf' or 'SU', used by the British, German and Soviet Armies to denote self-propelled weapons, the Americans went into more detail. The basic tank chassis was called a 'Motor Carriage', abbreviated to 'MC' and was preceded by a letter denoting whether it was carrying a mortar ('M'), gun ('G') or howitzer ('H'). Generally speaking, Gun Motor Carriages mounted the gun in an open-topped turret with 360° traverse, while MMCs and HMCs mounted their weapons with limited independent traverse in open-topped fixed superstructures. The Light Tank M24 was to form part of a family of AFVs known as the Light Combat Team. The vehicles in this team were to be built from three basic assemblies on a system known as the Common Chassis Concept. The first basic

assembly comprised the power plant, transmission, cooling and fuel systems, the second was made up of the steering system and final drives, while the third consisted of the tracks, road wheels and suspension system and the return rollers.

The first member of the Light Combat Team of weapons based upon the M24 to appear was the Gun Motor Carriage M19, which carried the twin 40-mm (1.57-in) M2 AA mount. In this version, the engine was mounted amidships and the steering system forward, with the twin gun mount in an open-topped turret at the rear; it was manned by a crew of six men. Only some 285 were completed before the end of the war, but the M19 remained standard US army equipment for many years thereafter.

The next self-propelled member of the Light Combat Team to appear was the Howitzer Motor Carriage M41, in which the layout was the same as for the M19. The armament was the 155-mm (6.1-in) M1 Howitzer, with a manually-operated recoil spade and folding crew platform. It was operated by a crew of twelve, eight of whom were carried in an accompanying vehicle. The howitzer had a traverse range from 17° left to 20° right, and an elevation range from -5° to +45°. Although 250 of these vehicles were ordered, only 60 had been completed by the war's end; like the M19, the HMC M41 remained in US army service for several years after the end of the war.

The last vehicle in the Light Combat Team was the Howitzer Motor Carriage M37. This entered service in November 1944 and mounted the 105-mm (4.13-in) M4 howitzer on a chassis in which the assemblies were arranged similarly to those on the M24 tank. The vehicle was manned by a crew of seven. The howitzer had a traverse range of 22.5° left and right and an elevation arc from -10° to +45°. Production had only just begun when the war ended so the vehicle never saw action in that war.

The final US light tank to appear in the Second World War was designed to be airportable. The requirement for such a tank had been expressed in February 1941 and an outline specification was issued in May of that year. It called for a tank of about half the weight of the M5A1, with dimensions suitable for it to be portable inside or beneath a transport aircraft. Proposals were requested from J. Walter Christie (whose fast tank had formed the basis for both British cruiser tanks and the Soviet BT and T-34 medium tanks), General Motors Corporation and the Marmon Herrington firm. The latter's designs were preferred, and a prototype ordered, featuring the 37-mm (1.46-in) M6 gun as main armament in a turret with 360° manual traverse, modified volute spring suspension, armour of 25-mm maximum thickness and a Lycoming engine. Powered turret traverse and the gun stabilization system were omitted to save weight. The prototype was delivered in the autumn of 1941, tested, modified as a result of the tests and the modified result put into production in March 1943: 830 were produced between then and February 1944, all by Marmon Herrington, and the production version designated Light Tank (Airborne) M22. It was never used in action by the US army, mainly because they lacked an aircraft or glider capable of carrying it. It was, however, supplied in quantity to the British army under Lend-Lease arrangements, as the British had designed the Hamilcar glider to carry their Tetrarch light tank and this was also capable of lifting the M22. In British service the M22 became known as the 'Locust', and it was used by 6 Airborne Division in the Rhine crossing in March 1945. The M22 carried a crew of three (commander, gunner and driver) and weighed 7.5 tons; the maximum armour thickness was 25 mm.

Below is a list of all US light tanks and the self-propelled weapons based upon them which saw service with the US or British armies in the Second World War, together with their armament:

NOMENCLATURE	ARMAMENT
M2A4	One 37-mm (1.46-in) L/50 gun in turret. Four .30 cal Browning MGs, one coaxial with 37-mm, two fixed in hull sponsons and one in AA mounting on turret roof.
M3A1, A2, A3 & A3A1 (Stuart)	One 37-mm (1.46-in) L/50 gun in turret. Three .30 cal Browning MGs, one coaxial with 37-mm, one in hull front and one in AA mounting on turret roof.
M5, M5A1 (Stuart)	As for M3A1 series above.
M22 (Locust)	One 37-mm (1.46in) L/50 gun in turret with coaxial .30 cal MG.
M24 (Chaffee)	One 75-mm (2.95-in) M6 (L/39) gun in turret. One .50 cal (12.7-mm) AA MG. Two .30 cal MGs, one coaxial with 75-mm and one in hull front plate.
GMC M19	Twin 40-mm (1.57-in) M2 AA guns in turret.
HMC M37	One 105-mm (4.13-in) M4 howitzer in open-topped fixed superstructure.
HMC M41	One 155-mm (6.1-in) M1 howitzer in open-topped fixed superstructure.

MEDIUM TANKS

The National Defense Act of 1920 had put tanks and tank development in the hands of the Infantry, and it was therefore as infantry support weapons that the few medium tanks developed in the 1920s and 1930s were designed. These were limited, by the terms of the War Department policy statement on tank development issued in 1922, to a maximum weight of 15 short tons. Only three prototypes were produced between 1921 and 1925 and a fourth, the T2, which closely resembled the Vickers Medium, in 1930. This tank mounted a 47-mm (1.85-in) gun together with a .50 and a .30 calibre machine-gun. The T2 was followed by a series of prototype medium tanks based on J. Walter Christie's designs and incorporating his suspension system of which the T4, in 1935–6, was the only one to reach a limited production. Fast and reliable, they were nevertheless thinly-armoured and the design was abandoned in favour of the T5, designed in 1938 by Rock Island Arsenal on the lines of the Light Tank M2 and incorporating as many of the latter's components as possible, in the interests of standardization. Its infantry support role was obvious from its armament, consisting of six .30 calibre Browning machine-guns and one 37-mm (1.46-in) high velocity gun; four of the machine-guns were mounted at the four corners of a lateral barbette across the full width of the tank, which was surmounted by a turret with 360° traverse carrying the 37-mm gun. The other two MGs were fixed and forward-firing in the hull front. It carried a crew of six men – commander, driver and four gunners. Trials of the T5 were completed in June 1939 and it was approved for service introduction as the Medium Tank M2; production of fifteen vehicles started in August 1939 at Rock Island Arsenal. An improved version standardized as the M2A1 was introduced in

1940, with thicker armour, a wider, vertical-sided turret and various other detail changes. As a result of the developing war in Europe, a National Munitions Program was introduced in June 1940 under which a contract for 1,000 M2A1 Medium Tanks was placed with the Chrysler Corporation in August 1940. Chrysler had agreed to build and operate a special plant, the Detroit Tank Arsenal, to be devoted to medium tank production, and production of the M2A1 was scheduled to start, at the rate of 100 per month, within a year.

The German PzKpfw IV with its 7.5-cm (2.95-in) L/24 gun used in the invasion of France and the Low Countries in 1940 had, however, rendered the M2A1 technically obsolete even before production had started. In June, therefore, the Chief of Infantry suggested to the Ordnance Department that US medium tanks should also mount 75-mm guns. It was agreed at a meeting in August that, as the turret of the M2A1 could not accept a 75-mm gun and in view of the urgency of the problem, a compromise solution should be adopted whereby the 75-mm gun should be mounted in a limited traverse mounting in a barbette on the right side of the M2A1 hull sponson, pending the design of a fully-traversing turret suitable to mount a 75-mm gun, and a tank capable of mounting this turret. Production of M2A1s was therefore halted after 94 had been produced by Rock Island Arsenal, these vehicles being used only for training in the US.

Meanwhile, design of the compromise version of the medium tank was carried out with commendable speed and the testing and acceptance for production of what became in service the Medium Tank M3 was completed in record time. Prototypes were produced in April 1941 and full-scale production had started in Detroit Arsenal, American Locomotive and Baldwin Locomotive by

Medium tank M3 (Lee/Grant), with M3 75-mm gun. (Author's Collection)

August of that year. Discussions had taken place with members of the British Tank Commission who had arrived in the USA in June 1940 to place contracts for US-built tanks for the British army, and who had been able to suggest improvements in the light of British battle experience. The M3 retained the overall dimensions, layout, suspension and engine of the M2A1, and a cast turret with hydraulic power traverse carried the 37-mm L/50 gun and a coaxial .30 calibre (7.62-mm) MG; a new 75-mm M2 (L/28.5) gun was mounted with limited traverse in a barbette in the right hull sponson. Both this and the 37-mm were gyro-stabilized in elevation to facilitate accurate fire on the move, an important innovation. The 75-mm gun's

performance compared favourably with that of the German 7.5-cm KwK (L/24), having a higher muzzle velocity. It also had an armour penetration performance similar to that of the German long 5-cm tank gun. A cupola mounting another .30 calibre MG was mounted on top of the turret, while one or two other .30 calibre MGs were mounted in the left hull front. Carrying a crew of six (commander, two gunners, two loaders and driver), the M3 weighed some 27 long tons in action. It was widely used by the US, British and allied armies, and as an interim tank it enjoyed a good reputation among its users. British units in the Western Desert particularly liked the anti-personnel capability of the 75-mm gun, British tanks hitherto lacking a high explosive round for their main armament. Later production mounted the longer M3 75-mm (L/37.5) gun in place of the M2, giving an improved armour-piercing performance. Various Marks of the M3 were produced, from M3A1 to M3A4. These differed only in minor details such as power plant and cast/welded armour instead of riveted plate, as all models were eventually up-gunned to take the M3 75-mm gun. The basic M3 was known as the 'Lee' in British service; modified M3s, with lower turrets and turret-mounted radios, were known by them as the 'Grant'. Some 600 M3 series tanks were shipped to the UK and British forces in the Middle East under Lend-Lease (from March 1941) or Cash-and-Carry arrangements. Production of the M3 ceased in August 1942, after a total of 4,924 had been built, and it was finally declared obsolete in April 1944. It had been only a stop-gap weapon and had severe tactical disadvantages, but it was the first tank available to the Allies with adequate dual-purpose armament and had provided a vital boost to flagging Allied morale at a time when it was felt that their tanks were no match for those of the Germans.

The M3 chassis was used as the basis for several variants such as the M31 ARV, M33 and M44 Full-Tracked Prime Movers for heavy artillery and self-propelled artillery Motor Carriages. The first SP variant was the Howitzer Motor Carriage M7, mounting a standard M1A2 105-mm (4.13-in) howitzer in a limited traverse mounting on an M3 medium tank chassis with an open-topped superstructure, plans for which were first made in June 1941. Two prototypes (T32) were built, tested and the design standardized as the HMC M7 in February 1942. Carrying a crew of seven, consisting of the commander, driver and the gun crew of five, the M7 weighed 22.6 tons and was armed with one .50 calibre (12.7-mm) AA MG on a ring

mounting at the commander's station. Production started in April 1942 and ended in September 1943. The British army ordered several hundred M7s, named 'Priest' in British Army service, which were used in the Battle of Alamein and the Italian and north-west Europe campaigns.

The second Motor Carriage to be based upon the M3 Medium Tank was the Gun Motor Carriage M12; this mounted the 155-mm (6.1-in) M1918M gun with limited traverse in an open-topped M3 super-structure, and was standardized in August 1942. Only 100 were built, being used mainly for training in the USA, production ceasing in March 1943. In December of that year, with the invasion of north-west Europe being planned, it was decided to refurbish 74 of them for possible use overseas. They were sent to Europe in June 1944 and were in fact used in several major actions for heavy bombardment. The M12 carried a crew of six (commander, driver and gun crew of four) and weighed 25.9 tons in action. The limber vehicle for this GMC was also based upon the M3 medium tank chassis; known as the Cargo Carrier M30, it carried the remainder of the 155-mm gun crew in addition to the commander and driver. It was armed with one .50 calibre (12.7-mm) Browning AA MG, and was identical to the M12 except for the omission of the latter's gun and recoil spade.

The M3 series of medium tanks had been produced as an interim measure, in order to get a tank armed with a 75-mm gun into service as soon as possible but, even while design of the M3 was in hand, several schemes for a medium tank mounting a 75-mm gun in a turret with 360° traverse were being prepared. These were considered at a meeting in April 1941, and the scheme selected for development proposed the use of the M3 lower hull, power plant, transmission and running gear, with a redesigned upper

Medium tank M4 (Sherman). (Author's Collection)

hull mounting a central turret with the 75-mm gun. This scheme was mocked-up in wood in the following month and designated Medium Tank T6. A prototype was completed in September 1941 and standardized the following month as the Medium Tank M4. Production was scheduled to take over from M3 medium tank production in early 1942 in a total of eleven plants; initial production was scheduled at a rate of 2,000 M4s a month on the personal orders of the President. The M4 pilot appeared in February 1942, by autumn of that year the tank was in full production and, in October, it went into action at the battle of Alamein with British troops, with whom it became known as the 'Sherman'. It was a popular tank with its users, proving to be reliable, simple to maintain, rugged and highly mobile, although it was certainly inferior to German and Soviet tanks in both firepower and protection. Produced in quantities not equalled in any other country during the Second World War, the M4 was the most widely used and the most important of all tanks in service with the US, British and Allied Armies. Between 1942 and 1946, some 40,000 M4 tanks, and variants based on its chassis, were built and used by every Allied nation in every theatre of war and in every armour role.

The M4 series ran to many models and several up-gunnings and up-armourings. The basic Medium Tank M4 carried a crew of five (commander, gunner, loader, driver and front gunner) and mounted the 75-mm (2.95-in) M3 (L/38.5) gun in a cast, centrally-mounted turret together with a coaxial .30 cal (7.62-mm) Browning MG. The turret was provided with hydraulic power traverse and the main armament was stabilized in elevation by a gyro-stabilizer. In addition to the coaxial MG another was mounted in a ball mounting in the hull front glacis plate, while a .50 cal Browning MG was provided as an AA MG

on the commander's cupola. The tank weighed between 30 and 31 tons, depending upon the model, model differences relating mainly to type of armour (cast or welded plate) and engine. These embraced the M4A1, M4A2, M4A3, M4A4 and M4A6. Only those models in which the armament was changed are separately described here; these retained their original model numbers with the calibre of the new gun in parenthesis after it. Thus the first up-gunning involved the substitution of the 76-mm (3-in) M1 (L/52) high velocity gun for the 75-mm, and tanks so modified mounted this gun in an enlarged turret. Tank models with the 76-mm gun were the M4A1 (76-mm), M4A2 (76-mm) and M4A3 (76-mm). Another version substituted the 105-mm (4.13-in) for the main armament; models so up-gunned were designated the M4 (105-mm) and M4A3 (105-mm) and were standardized for production in 1943. A final variation in M4 armament was provided by the British. This involved the substitution of the British 17-pdr (76.2-mm, or 3-in) high velocity gun for the 75-mm of the M4A4, and this vehicle was known as the 'Sherman VC' or 'Firefly'. The hull machine-gun (and gunner) were deleted from this modification.

Many special purpose variants of the M4 Medium Tank were built during its service life, including mine-clearing devices, ARVs, tank dozers, full-track prime movers, assault bridges, flame-throwers and self-propelled artillery weapons. Only the latter are dealt with here, where firepower is the subject, and they comprised the Gun Motor Carriages M10, M36 and M40 and the Howitzer Motor Carriage M43.

The Gun Motor Carriage M10 was based on the M4A3 chassis and mounted the 76-mm (3-in) M7 (L/52) gun in a low, open-topped turret with 360° traverse. The vehicle carried a crew of five, consisting of the commander, driver and the gun crew of three

Gun motor carriage M10. (Tank Museum 3564/D2)

men and weighed approximately 30 tons in action. A number of M10s were supplied to the British Army in 1944, by whom it was designated '3-inch SP Wolverine'; some 7,000 were produced between September 1942 and November 1943. The Gun Motor Carriage M36 was similarly based, but mounted the 90-mm (3.5-in) M3 (L/53) gun in place of the 76-mm in a new, larger turret. A successful tank destroyer capable of taking on the German Tigers and Panthers at long range, the GMC M36 was manned by a crew of five (commander, driver and gun crew of three), weighed some 29 tons and some 1,300 were produced before the end of the war.

In late 1943, it had been decided to base a series of complementary AFVs on the Medium Tank M4A3 chassis to form a 'Medium Weight Combat Team' in parallel with the 'Light Weight Combat Team' based on the chassis of the Light Tank M24

(Chaffee) and mentioned earlier in this chapter. The first of these was a self-propelled version of the 155-mm (6.1-in) M1 gun and the second mounted the 8-in (203-mm) M1 howitzer. Both weapons were interchangeable on a modified M4A3E8 chassis, mounted with limited traverse in open-topped superstructures. The 155-mm weapon was standardized as the Gun Motor Carriage M40 in March 1945, production having commenced in January of that year; 311 were produced by the end of the war. The complete vehicle weighed some 35 tons and carried a crew of eight, comprising the commander, driver and the gun crew of six men. It saw action in the north-west Europe campaign in the bombardment of Cologne. The 8-in howitzer version was standardized in August 1945 as the Howitzer Motor Carriage 8-in M43. Only 45 had been produced when production was halted by the cessation of

Gun motor carriage M18 (Hellcat). (Tank Museum 3002/C1)

hostilities. Its weight and crew were similar to those of the GMC M40.

There is one other GMC in the medium weight class to be mentioned before going on to the M4 medium tank's successors, and that is the Gun Motor Carriage M18, known colloquially as 'Hellcat'. The M18 was developed in response to a requirement for a fast tank destroyer first stated by the Tank Destroyer Command in December 1941. First proposals for such a vehicle by the Ordnance Department involved mounting the 37-mm (1.46-in) high velocity gun on a chassis employing the Christie suspension but, after the first prototype (T49) appeared in 1942, the requirement was changed as a result of British experience in the Western Desert, substituting the 57-mm (2.24-in) M1 gun for the 37-mm and torsion bar suspension for the Christie type. A modified prototype was tested in July 1942, but Tank Destroyer Command demanded an even more powerful gun and asked the Ordnance Department to

complete the second prototype with the 75-mm (2.95-in) M3 gun as mounted on the Sherman tank. This up-gunned version was designated as GMC T67 and the T49 project was cancelled. The T67 successfully passed its tests and was recommended for standardization, but in February 1943 the Tank Destroyer Command again requested a further up-gunning, suggesting the 76-mm (3-in) M1 gun in place of the 75-mm. Six more T67 prototypes were therefore built, mounting the 76-mm gun and redesignated T70. Trials of these were successfully completed and, apart from minor modifications, the T70 was approved for production. It was standardized for service as the Gun Motor Carriage M18 in February 1944. The M18 was a fast, highly mobile tank destroyer, weighing some 18 tons, manned by a crew of five (commander, driver and three gunner/loaders) and mounting the 76-mm (L/52) gun in an open-topped turret with 360° traverse. With a high power-to-weight ratio it had a maximum speed approaching 50 m.p.h. on roads and it was the fastest tracked AFV of any nation to appear in the Second World War. It was reliable, with well-shaped armour and a low silhouette, and was well liked by its crews. Some 2,500 Hellcats were produced between February and October 1944 and it was used in both the Italian and north-west Europe theatres in the Second World War by US tank destroyer battalions.

The question of a successor to the Medium Tank M4 is complicated by the changes in tank nomenclature and classification introduced by the US Army after the Second World War. Tanks which had been built during the war and classified as heavy tanks were downgraded to the medium tank category at this time, and are still so categorized. Nevertheless, once the M4 medium tank had reached the production stage in 1942, authorization was given to the Ordnance Department to proceed with the design and building of a prototype of a successor, provisionally called the M4X. Requirements called for a 30-ton vehicle mounting an automatic 75-mm (2.95-in) gun, carrying 4 inches of frontal armour and having a maximum speed of 25 m.p.h. After inspecting a wooden mock-up of the proposed tank, it was agreed that three prototypes should be built, each with different main armament. The first, designated T20, was to be armed with a 76-mm (3-in) gun and to have the horizontal volute spring suspension (HVSS) of the M4A3E8. The second, T20E1, on similar running gear, was to have the automatic 75-mm gun as main armament, while the third (T20E2) was to have torsion bar suspension and to mount a 3-in gun. All were to be powered by a new Ford tank engine, combined with a torque converter and Hydra-Matic transmission. The T20 was completed in June 1943, the T20E1 was cancelled and the T20E2 was armed with the

76-mm instead of the 3-in gun and then redesignated T20E3. All the prototypes suffered from transmission problems during trials. Development ceased at the end of 1944, by which time other developments were in the pipeline.

One of these was the T22 medium tank, a development of the T20 and identical to it except for the replacement of the T20 transmission by the standard M4 five-speed gearbox. This project had been initiated in October 1942 and prototypes completed in June 1943 but it too was abandoned in December 1944, by which time there was a requirement for a larger calibre gun. The T23 project had been authorized at the same time as the T22 and was based upon the T22, with the exception that the standard M4 vertical volute spring suspension and tracks were combined with an electric transmission. The T23 was armed with the 76-mm (3-in) M1A1 gun and was granted 'limited standard' status in November 1943; 250 were built between that date and December 1944. They were never generally issued and never saw action, being used in the USA only.

At the same time as the T20 requirements were drawn up in September 1942, the Ordnance Department suggested that a 90-mm (3.54-in) gun should be developed for future mounting in tanks of this series. A prototype was manufactured by March 1943 and was mounted for trials in a T23 prototype. The building of fifty trial vehicles was authorized in the following month, of which forty (designated T25) were to have the same characteristics as the T23 and ten were to carry heavier armour comparable to that of the German Tiger, just encountered in Tunisia. The ten heavier vehicles were designated T26. Two prototypes of the T25 were completed in March and April of 1944 and of the T26 by June of that year. In the same month, the T25 was abandoned in favour of the T26 which, by virtue of its

Medium tank M4 (Sherman VC – Firefly) with 17-pdr gun. (Tank Museum 380/E2)

heavier armour, was reclassified as a heavy tank in June 1944.

As this book deals with developments in tank armament only from 1939 to 1945, it is felt preferable to deal with tanks in the category which was applicable to them at that time. As there was no standardized medium tank after the M4 Sherman during the war, this section will therefore end here with a summary of US medium tanks and their armament, heavy tanks being discussed in the section which follows the summary.

Below is a list of all US medium tanks, and the self-propelled weapons based upon them, which were standardized for service in the US Army between 1939 and 1945, together with their armament:

NOMENCLATURE	ARMAMENT
M2 & M2A1	One 37-mm (1.46-in) high velocity gun in

NOMENCLATURE	ARMAMENT
	turret. Six .30 cal (7.62-mm) Browning MGs, four in corners of barbette and two fixed in hull front.
M3, M3A1, M3A2, M3A3 & M3A4 (Lee/Grant)	One 37-mm (1.46-in) L/50 gun in turret with coaxial .30 cal MG. One 75-mm (2.95-in) M2 (L/28.5) or M3 (L/37.5) gun in front RH sponson. One or two .30 cal MGs in left hull front and one in cupola atop turret.
HMC M7	One 105-mm (4.13-in) M1A2 howitzer in

NOMENCLATURE	ARMAMENT	NOMENCLATURE	ARMAMENT
	open-topped superstructure with limited traverse. One .50 cal Browning MG on AA ring mounting at commander's position.		One .50 cal (12.7-mm) AA MG on turret rear.
GMC M12	One 155-mm (6.1-in) M1918M howitzer in open-topped superstructure, with limited traverse. One .50 cal (12.7-mm) AA MG at commander's position.	GMC M10 (17-pdr SP Achilles)	One British 17-pdr (3-in/76-mm) gun (L/55). Otherwise as for GMC M10.
M4, M4A1, M4A2, M4A3, M4A4 & M4A6 (Sherman)	One 75-mm (2.95-in) M3 (L/37.5) gun and coaxial .30 cal (7.62-mm) MG in turret. One .50 cal (12.7-mm) AA MG on commander's cupola. One .30 cal (7.62-mm) MG in ball mounting in hull front plate.	GMC M36	One 90-mm (3.5-in) M3 (L/53) gun in turret with 360° traverse. One .50 cal (12.7-mm) AA MG on turret rear.
		GMC M40	One 155-mm (6.1-in) M1 gun in open-topped superstructure, with limited traverse.
M4A1(76), M4A2(76) & M4A3 (76) (Sherman)	One 76-mm (3-in) M1 (L/52) gun in place of 75-mm M3. Otherwise as for M4.	HMC 8-inch M43	One 8-in (203-mm) M1 howitzer in open-topped superstructure with limited traverse.
M4(105) & M4A3 (105) (Sherman)	One 105-mm (4.13-in) howitzer M4 in place of 75-mm M3. Otherwise as for M4.	GMC M18 (Hellcat)	One 76-mm (3-in) M1A1 (L/52) gun in open-topped turret with 360° traverse. One .50 cal (12.7-mm) AA MG on turret rear.
M4 Sherman IIC, IVC & VC (Firefly)	One British 17-pdr (3-in/76-mm) gun (L/55) Mk IV or VII in place of 75-mm M3. Otherwise as for M4.		
GMC M10	One 76-mm (3-in) M7 (L/52) gun on low open-topped turret with 360° traverse.		

HEAVY TANKS

Military thought in the United States was never enthusiastic for heavy tanks; their weight posed formidable transport problems, particularly overseas, and little requirement for tanks in this weight class could be seen. This lack of vision stemmed partly from the War Department policy statement of 1922, which stated a requirement for only light and medium tanks and partly from the years during which the Infantry branch had had responsibility for tanks. One of the unfortunate results of this wrong-headed decision was a failure on the part of the US army to realize that an important function of tanks was to engage enemy tanks, thus protecting and supporting the infantry in a more practical way. The engagement of enemy tanks was given to a separate command, the Tank Destroyer Command, which was equipped with a series of tracked SP anti-tank guns in which the gun was mounted in an open-topped turret. The lack of overhead cover for the turret crew meant that it was almost as vulnerable to airburst HE shell as the crew of a field-mounting gun, while the mixing of tank destroyers and tanks made for unnecessary complication of tactical and logistic planning and movement.

Nevertheless, the Chief of Infantry in May 1940 had suggested the development of a heavy tank in the 80 (short) ton weight class, armed with two 75-mm guns in turrets with partial traverse, two smaller turrets mounting 37-mm guns and a 20-mm and .30 cal machine-gun. This project was designated Heavy Tank T1, but the specification was revised in October of that year to comprise a 50 (short) ton tank armed with 75-mm and 37-mm guns mounted coaxially in a fully-traversing turret, as well as four .30 cal MGs. Two prototypes to this revised specification were produced in December 1941, and the vehicle was standardized as the Heavy Tank M6 in April of the following year. A production target of 250 vehicles a month was envisaged, but a projected total order for 5,000 was cut back to 115 in September 1942 and reduced still further to only 40 after the Armored Force Board reported adversely on trials of the vehicle in December of that year. In all, eight M6, twelve M6A1 and twenty M6A2 were built by Baldwin Locomotive between November 1942 and February 1944; they were never issued to operational units but were used for trials within the United States.

The US army was thus late to realize the requirement in the Second World War for heavy tanks, armed with high velocity guns of larger calibre than 75-mm (2.95-in), to counter the enemy's Panthers and Tigers. As stated above in the section on medium tanks, it was not until 1943 that approval was given for the procurement of ten T26 'heavy' medium tanks, and these were not available until March/June 1944. An order for production of some 500 vehicles would have been given in September 1943 had the Armored Force Board not preferred that the 90-mm (3.54-in) M3 gun be mounted instead on the M4 medium tank, and the commander of Army Ground Forces not considered that a 90-mm gun was 'undesirable in a tank, since it would encourage tank units to stalk enemy tanks', a role assigned to tank destroyers in the US Army's doctrine of the time. It was not until June 1944 that the Medium Tank T26 was redesignated as the Heavy Tank T26 and it was recommended by the Ordnance Department for standardization and production in December of that year. Army Ground Forces had tried another delaying tactic in July by requesting that it be redesigned with a 76-mm (3-in) gun, and it was thus not until December of that year that the T26 was approved for limited procurement. Production of twenty prototypes had begun in November 1944 and Ordnance Department recommended that these should be shipped immediately to Europe for battle testing. Again prejudice against heavy tanks surfaced in Army Ground Forces, who asked that they first go to the Armored Force for testing of their combat effectiveness. This would have wasted another month but luckily the German attack in the Ardennes on 16 December 1944 spotlighted the inadequacies of the M4 medium tank with its weak armour and 76-mm (3-in) gun and the US General Staff intervened on the 22nd to order the immediate despatch to Europe of all available T26 tanks. The first twenty arrived

Medium/heavy tank M26 (Pershing). (Tank Museum 3032/A2)

in the European Theatre of Operations (ETO) in January 1945 and were issued to combat units in February. Tank crews were favourably impressed with a tank which was almost a match for the Tiger in firepower and protection but very much more mobile and reliable, and full production was ordered. Some 2,400 had been produced by the end of the war, the tank having been standardized as the Heavy Tank M26 and named 'General Pershing' in March 1945. A few were shipped to the United Kingdom that year for test and evaluation, but the cessation of hostilities limited the number sent. The M26 was armed with the 90-mm (3.54-in) M3 (L/53) gun in a turret with 360° traverse, together with a coaxial .30 cal (7.62-mm) Browning MG. Auxiliary armament also comprised another .30 cal MG in the front hull plate and a .50 cal (12.70-mm) AA MG on the turret. Carrying a crew of five (commander, driver, co-driver, gunner and loader), the tank weighed 41 tons, had a maximum frontal armour thickness of 102 mm (4 in) and had a maximum road speed of 20 m.p.h. The M26 was reclassified as a medium tank in May 1946.

In response to a requirement from ETO for tanks mounting the 105-mm (4.13-in) howitzer, a version of the T26 (the T26E2) was designed to mount this weapon. Classified as 'limited standard' and designated the M45 in July 1945, this vehicle was produced in only a small quantity.

The following list gives all the heavy tanks that were standardized for service in the US army between 1939 and 1945, together with their armament and all variants:

NOMENCLATURE	ARMAMENT
M6	One 75-mm (2.95-in) M2 (L/32) gun and coaxial 37-mm (1.46-in) M6 (L/57) gun in fully-traversing turret. Three .50 cal (12.7-mm) Browning MGs, two in bow, one on turret as AA MG. Two .30 cal (7.62-mm) Browning MGs.
M26 (Pershing)	One 90-mm (3.54-in) M3 (L/53) gun and co-axial .30 cal (7.62-mm) Browning MG in turret.

NOMENCLATURE	ARMAMENT
M45	One .50 cal (12.7-mm) Browning AA MG on turret roof. One .30 cal (7.62-mm) Browning MG in hull front plate. One 105-mm (4.13-in) howitzer and coaxial .30 cal (7.62-mm) Browning MG in turret. One .50 cal (12.7-mm) Browning AA MG on turret roof. One .30 cal (7.62-mm) Browning MG in hull front.

American Tank Armament Development Summarized

Unlike the German and Soviet tank policy-makers, those in the United States had no very clear idea either of a tank's main function or of the importance of firepower among a tank's characteristics. They were further hamstrung by the subordination of tank development and tactics to the Infantry branch, by the separation of the tank destroyer function from the tank arm, by the prevailing isolationism before the Second World War and by the resulting shortage of Research and Development funds for the Army. The result was that, on the outbreak of war in 1939, the US army had fewer than 500 tanks in the whole of the United States.

Despite an amazing build-up of tank production in a very short time after the outbreak of war, the tanks to be produced, although reliable and easy to maintain, would be under-armoured and under-gunned for much of the war, relative to those of both the Soviet Union and Germany. It was thus the quantity of US tanks rather than the quality

that defeated Germany. It was the failure of those in command to realize, until late in the war, that an important function of the tank is to take on enemy tanks, and the most important characteristic of a tank to enable it to do this is firepower. This was responsible for the failure to up-gun the M4 medium tank. The issue was further clouded by the allocation of the tank-destroying function to a separate Tank Destroyer Command. Thus the 75-mm main armament of the Sherman remained in service long after it should have been declared obsolescent, its shortcomings being hidden by its success in the pursuit after Alamein. It was not until the campaigns in Italy and north-west Europe that its inadequacy was realized and the 76-mm (3-in) (L/52) rushed over to counter the German Panthers and Tigers. To the makers of US tank policy, firepower and protection were of less importance than mobility and reliability, and their tanks suffered in consequence throughout the war from being under-gunned and under-armoured, while the emphasis on mobility with its powerful radial engines, front sprocket drive and clumsy suspension gave the majority of US tanks an undesirably high silhouette.

At the outbreak of the war, the standard armament of US tanks was a 37-mm (1.45-in) high velocity gun. This compared well with the contemporary German and Soviet guns of the same calibre and with the British 2-pdr (40-mm). As the need for a dual-purpose gun of larger calibre was perceived, the 37-mm gun was either complemented (in the Medium Tank M3 series) or replaced (in the Medium Tank M4 series) by a 75-mm (2.95-in) medium velocity gun with reasonable armour-piercing and excellent anti-personnel performance. This gun remained the mainstay of US tank armament for most of the war, the only improvement being an increase in barrel length from 28.5 to 37.5 calibres, with its consequent increase in muzzle velocity and armour penetration. It was not until 1944 that the 76-mm (L/52) gun, with its greatly improved armour penetration performance, started to replace the 75-mm gun in the Sherman, while the light tank's 37-mm gun of the M5 (Stuart) was replaced by a 75-mm (L/39) gun mounted in the new M24 Light Tank (Chaffee). Apart from the substitution of a 105-mm howitzer for the Sherman's 75-mm gun in the close support version of the Sherman, again in 1944, and the introduction of a 90-mm (3.95-in) L/53 gun in the Heavy Tank M26 (Pershing) in early 1945, this was the sum total of main armament development for US tanks between 1939 and 1945.

Similarly, the tank destroyers M10 and M18 (Hellcat), with which the units of Tank Destroyer Command were equipped, both mounted the same 76-mm (3-in) L/52 gun from the time of their introduction (in September 1942 and February 1944, respectively) up to the end of the war, despite the need for more powerful weapons from 1943 onwards to deal with the German Tigers, Panthers and King Tigers. It was again not until 1944 that the 90-mm (3.95-in) L/53 gun as mounted on the Pershing heavy tank was taken into service with Tank Destroyer units on the M36 tank destroyer. Although mounted on variants of standard medium tank chassis in fully-traversing turrets, these guns would have been better employed in tanks with fully-armoured turrets. Although timely schemes for doing this were put forward by the Ordnance Department, they were rejected by the Armor Force and Infantry as unnecessary, thus leading to separate time- and production-wasting development for the redundant Tank Destroyer Command.

American developments in tank main armament during the Second World War can therefore be seen to have been barely adequate and rather less than impressive. In one or two other aspects of tank firepower, however, the Americans led the field. The introduction of gyroscopic gun stabilization in elevation was a far-sighted development leading to the ability to put down accurate fire from a moving tank. Although the early systems were not entirely satisfactory they have since been developed, with the introduction of sophisticated electronics, to give a high degree of accuracy in both azimuth and elevation, and stabilization systems have become standard equipment on tanks worldwide since the end of the Second World War. The Americans also favoured the use of periscopic sights mounted in the turret roof rather than telescopes requiring holes in the gun mantlet. Periscopes are less vulnerable, require the gunner to move his head less when elevating or depressing the gun and give the gunner greater protection from frontal attack.

Powered turret traverse, with alternative manual handwheel operation, was standard on American tanks, the power being provided hydraulically. The British had rejected hydraulics in the turret in favour of electrical traverse systems from early in the war, hydraulic fluid having been found to give an unacceptably high fire risk. The Soviets also preferred electrical to hydraulic power traverse systems, as did the Germans in the PzKpfw IV. In the Tiger and Panther they changed to hydraulic control.

Auxiliary armament throughout the war consisted of machine-guns of either .30 cal (7.62-mm) or .50 cal (12.7-mm). In common with the other combatants, US tanks mounted a machine-gun coaxially with the main armament and at least one other in the front hull plate. The .50 cal MG was usually employed in the anti-aircraft role, mounted on the roof of the turret in tanks or tank destroyers or the superstructure on SP guns.

Main armament ammunition included APCBC, AP and HE for all calibres. In addition, smoke rounds were provided for the 75-mm, 76-mm and 105-mm weapons, AP/CR for the 76-mm and 90-mm guns and HEAT for the 105-mm howitzer. Canister ammunition was provided for the 37-mm gun to increase its anti-personnel capability.

CHAPTER SEVEN

AMMUNITION

MAIN ARMAMENT

The ammunition fired by its guns obviously forms a very important part of a tank's firepower. After all, it is the effect of the ammunition at the target that counts, more than the size of the gun which fires it. Ideally for main armament the projectile needs to be as big as possible, so as to contain the maximum amount of explosive (in the case of a projectile relying upon chemical energy for its effect at the target) or to have the greatest possible mass (weight) if relying upon kinetic energy to achieve its target effect. The limitation on size/calibre of projectile is imposed by the capability of the turret to mount the gun required to fire it and the ability of the loader to handle it. A tank has to be able to engage successfully and knock out enemy tanks, but it also has a very important anti-personnel role. Its gun therefore has to be provided with ammunition capable of enabling it to fill both these tasks satisfactorily. The whole history of tank armament development has been influenced by the conflicting requirements for firing anti-personnel and anti-tank ammunition. The anti-personnel requirement is the more important but the anti-tank is the more exacting. A high explosive shell may produce some effect even if it does not score a direct hit on the target; even the smallest HE shell will do some damage to personnel. On the other hand, an armour-piercing projectile is only effective if it scores a direct hit and even then its remaining energy may be insufficient to do serious damage after

penetration. If a projectile could be devised that was equally effective against both armour and personnel, the gun could be designed around it and the need for compromise in designing a dual-purpose weapon would disappear.

In the Second World War, the anti-tank task was filled very largely by projectiles relying upon their kinetic energy for their penetrative effect, although both Germany and America also provided high explosive anti-tank ammunition which relied for its penetrative effect upon chemical energy. The anti-personnel task was carried out by high explosive fragmentation or case shot projectiles using chemical energy to achieve their effect. High explosive ammunition could also be used to good effect against buildings and certain types of defensive position.

This sounds an ideal mix, enabling the tank to cope with most types of target likely to be met on the battlefield, but there are snags. Projectiles relying upon chemical energy need fuzes to initiate the explosion at the target, and fuzes need a relatively low striking velocity (and thus muzzle velocity) to enable them to function reliably at the target. If the muzzle velocity is too low, accuracy is adversely affected and gun recoil will be insufficient to operate the semi-automatic breech opening/cartridge ejection gear. Projectiles relying upon their kinetic energy for target penetration, on the other hand, require as high a striking and muzzle velocity as possible, as kinetic energy is a function more of velocity than of mass. A gun firing both types of ammunition is therefore called

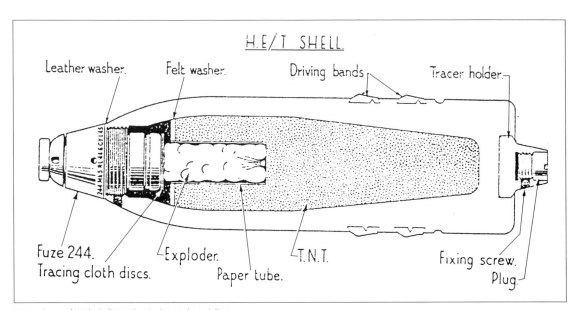

Sectional view of HE/T shell (British 17-pdr). (Author's Collection)

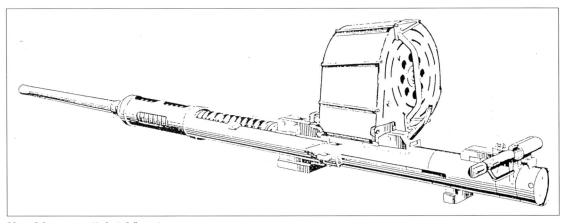

20-mm Polsten cannon. (Author's Collection)

a dual-purpose weapon. It should more accurately be described as a compromise weapon, as it can fulfil neither function with maximum efficiency. As these two categories of projectile are the basis of the compromise which the tank gun represents, ammunition developments between 1939 and 1945 will be dealt with in the following paragraphs under the main headings of 'Chemical Energy' and 'Kinetic Energy'. These will be subdivided according to the type and function of the ammunition concerned. All projectiles were provided with one or more circumferential driving bands of malleable metal, usually copper. These engaged with the lands and grooves of the rifling in the barrel of the weapon on firing, both to obturate and prevent leakage forward of the propellant gases and to impart spin to the projectile for greater accuracy.

Whatever its function, gun ammunition comprises two main parts, the propellant charge and the projectile. They may be loaded together (fixed or QF ammunition) or separately (semi-fixed, separate or bag-loaded (BL)). In fixed ammunition, as the name implies, the cartridge case and projectile are fixed together and loaded as one item. The propellant charge is fixed and cannot be varied. The majority of tank guns in the Second World War employed fixed ammunition, which has the advantage of enabling a higher rate of fire to be maintained (hence the Quick Firing (or QF) nomenclature) but has the disadvantage of cluttering the turret with empty cartridge cases for disposal. Semi-fixed and separate ammunition has the same disadvantage, as the propellant charge is again contained in a cartridge case, but in this case the projectile and cartridge case are loaded into the gun separately. This leads to a slower rate of fire, but this type of ammunition is used where a fixed round would be too heavy for the loader to handle

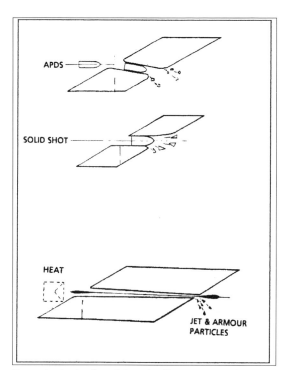

Diagram showing the effects of chemical and kinetic energy attack on armour. (Author's Collection)

7.62-mm DT MG. (Tank Museum 3235/B2)

Two 6-pdr Crusaders of British 6th Armoured Division knocked out (one still burning) in the initial British thrust for Tunis in November 1942. (Wilhelm Hartmann)

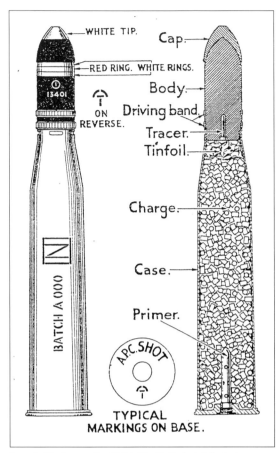

A round of fixed ammunition (British 17-pdr). (Author's Collection)

rearwards of the propellant gases, and consequently gives an even slower rate of fire. It has the advantage of not requiring the disposal of empty cartridge cases and is again used in the case of weapons of large calibre, where fixed ammunition would be either too heavy or too large to be handled within a turret.

PROPELLANT CHARGE

As stated above, in the case of all except BL ammunition the propellant charge is contained in a cartridge case. This is normally made from brass, a malleable metal that expands into the chamber of the gun on firing, thus sealing the breech against the rearward escape of propellant gases. This sealing is known as 'obturation', and the system of sealing which relies upon the cartridge case to achieve it is known as 'ammunition obturation'. After firing, it rapidly contracts to its former size, thus enabling it to be extracted from the chamber by the extractor levers in the gun's breech mechanism. All combatants in the Second World War employed brass as their cartridge case material. In Germany, however, towards the end of the war when material shortages were beginning to be felt and brass was in short supply, cartridge cases for the German forces were fabricated from steel with success, despite its greater tendency to corrode. Corrosion was inhibited in this case by the application of enamel and lacquer. Steel has continued to be used for many cartridge cases since the end of the Second World War, another development arising from wartime research. Bases of cartridge cases were rimmed, the rim providing a purchase for the extractor levers in the breech mechanism when extracting the empty case after firing.

The propellant charge consisted of sticks or grains of propellant, normally nitro-cellulose based, packed to a carefully

or too long for loading in a turret. In the case of separate ammunition, the propellant charge is contained in bags within the cartridge case, and may be varied by extracting one or more of the bags according to the range to the target and the muzzle velocity required. BL ammunition again has separate charge and projectile but the charge is contained in bags only, with no cartridge case. Again the charge may be varied according to the range over which it is to be fired. BL ammunition requires a different breech mechanism and method of obturation (breech obturation) from that used with cased ammunition which relies upon the expansion of the cartridge case to prevent the escape

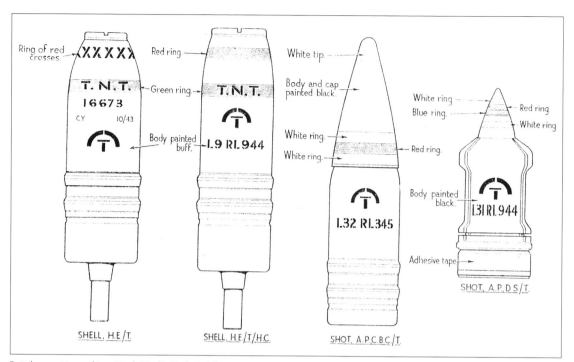

Typical ammunition markings (British 17-pdr). (Author's Collection)

measured weight to give the optimum projectile muzzle velocity. The charge was initiated by a primer which was screwed into the base of the cartridge case and was itself detonated by either a percussion cap, operated by the gun firing pin, or an electric initiator operated by a firing contact in the breech block. British, US and Soviet tank guns all employed percussion operation. The Germans used electric primers which were more reliable as they eliminated the firing interval which elapsed in percussion systems between the gunner pressing the trigger and the primer firing, due to the mechanical linkage involved. Electric primers had, however, to be screened against induced currents such as those from radio or radar, and the system protected against damp. The percussion or electric cap initiated the main primer composition which in turn ignited the main propellant.

CHEMICAL ENERGY PROJECTILES

ANTI-PERSONNEL
High Explosive (HE) Fragmentation
This was the most common type of anti-personnel ammunition used by tank guns in the Second World War and was used by tanks of all combatants. The principal cause of personnel casualties in that war was fragmentation from HE ammunition. To be effective it needs to have a minimum calibre of about 3 inches and for this reason it was not issued to British tanks armed with the 2-pdr (40-mm); neither was it available for the British 6-pdr (57-mm) until 1943, by which time the 6-pdr was being replaced by the British and US 75-mm guns. A high explosive projectile consists of a thin-walled steel casing, aerodynamically shaped, containing an

.30 cal Browning MG. (Tank Museum 3259/E4)

7.92-mm MG34. (Tank Museum 2973/C5)

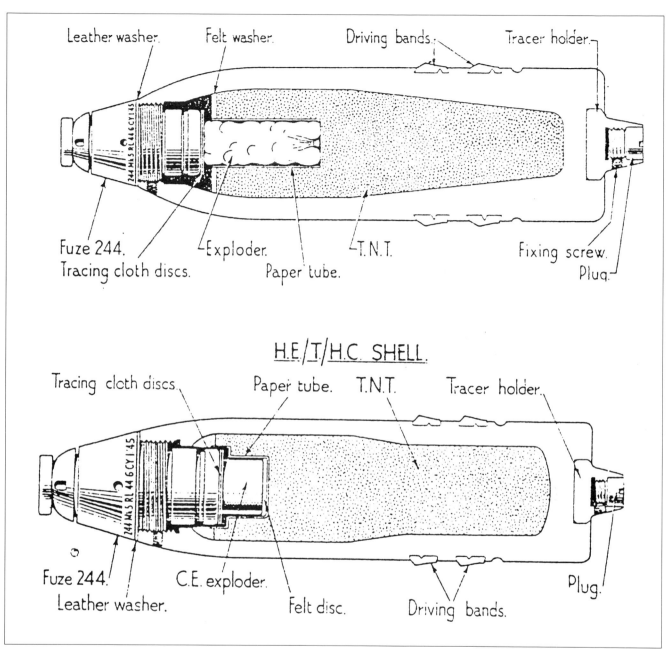

Leather washer.   Felt washer.   Driving bands.   Tracer holder.

Fuze 244.   Exploder.   T.N.T.   Fixing screw.
Tracing cloth discs.   Paper tube.   Plug.

H.E./T/H.C. SHELL.

Tracing cloth discs.   Paper tube.   T.N.T.   Tracer holder.

Fuze 244.   C.E. exploder.   Plug.
Leather washer.   Felt disc.   Driving bands.

17-pdr HE/T and high capacity HE/T/HC shells. (Author's Collection)

explosive filling and carrying a nose-mounted fuze to detonate the explosive charge at the target or at an appropriate point in its flight. The casing is designed to produce the maximum number of lethal-sized fragments on detonation of the explosive filling. Fuzes were of either direct or delayed action and explosive fillings were generally of TNT.

Case Shot or Canister

This was a projectile designed for use at short range against personnel in the open, and worked on the shot-gun principle. A thin-walled, flat-nosed casing was filled with balls of lead, steel or cast iron embedded in resin. Used to great effect in the First World War, it found little use in the Second. Its issue was limited to the US 37-mm tank gun, although rounds for the 75-mm (2.95-in), 76-mm (3-in) and 90-mm (3.54-in) US tank guns were developed, the German 7.5-cm (2.95-in) KwK (L/24) and Soviet 76.2-mm (3-in) and 85-mm (3.35-in) tank guns. It was not an effective round for weapons of a calibre less than about 75-mm as not enough balls of sufficiently large diameter could be contained in the projectile.

Carrier Shell

Filled with anti-personnel chemical agents, these were prepared, but not issued, by both sides in the Second World War. Again a calibre of 75-mm or above is desirable for such shell, which functions by emitting the chemical content from the base of the projectile on striking the target.

ANTI-TANK

High Explosive Anti-Tank (HEAT)

Also known as Hollow Charge (HC) or, by the Germans, as Hohlladung (Hl), the HEAT projectile is fired at a relatively low velocity and is therefore most accurate at shorter ranges. It relies for its penetration of armour on the chemical energy generated by a high velocity, high temperature jet of high explosive. The projectile consists of a thin-walled shell containing a high explosive charge packed around a conical metal liner, with the apex of the cone pointing towards the base of the projectile. The charge is initiated at the base, at the time under examination by a base fuze. On initiation, the detonating wave moves through the explosive towards the apex of the cone, which collapses and forms the high speed jet moving at 90° from the cone apex. The jet, with its tip moving at a velocity in the region of 8,000 metres per second, is followed by a slower-moving slug of metal from the cone. On impacting with an armoured target, it causes the metal of the target to flow away from the point of impact leaving a hole in the armour. Not as accurate as kinetic energy anti-tank ammunition because of its lower velocity, HEAT projectiles nevertheless have great armour penetration provided that the target is hit, and penetration is independent of striking velocity. In the Second World War penetrations of armour up to 3.5 times the calibre of the shell were common. However, accurate fuzing to ensure that the initiation of the shaped charge takes place at the optimum distance from the target is essential. The stand-off distance of the cone from the target at initiation is critical for good performance. Because of their low velocity, equivalent to a conventional HE round, HEAT ammunition was able to give an enhanced anti-armour performance to low velocity weapons such as howitzers. HEAT rounds were provided for all German 7.5-cm and 8.8-cm tank guns, for the US 105-mm howitzer and for the British 95-mm CS howitzer.

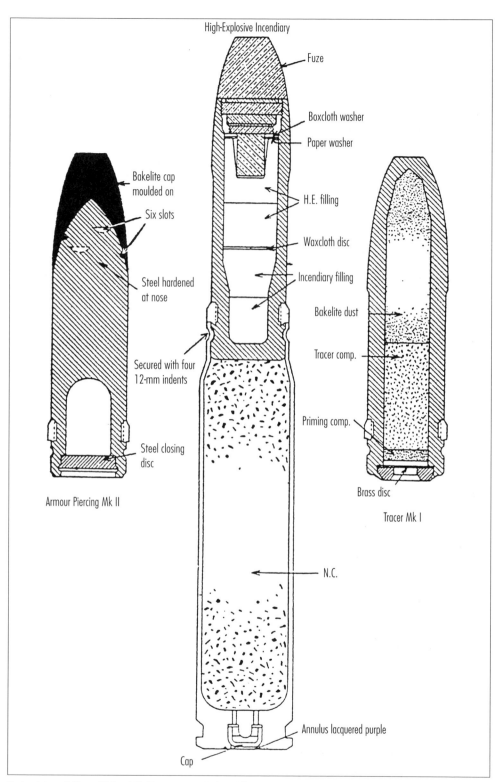

High-Explosive Incendiary

Fuze

Boxcloth washer

Paper washer

Bakelite cap moulded on

Six slots

H.E. filling

Waxcloth disc

Steel hardened at nose

Incendiary filling

Bakelite dust

Tracer comp.

Secured with four 12-mm indents

Priming comp.

Steel closing disc

Brass disc

Armour Piercing Mk II

Tracer Mk I

N.C.

Annulus lacquered purple

Cap

Sectional views of 20-mm HE/I and AP/T ammunition. (Author's Collection)

7.92-mm BESA MG. (Tank Museum 3859/D3)

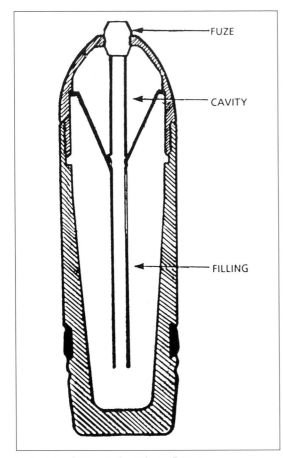

FUZE

CAVITY

FILLING

Sectional view of HEAT projectile. (Author's Collection)

KINETIC ENERGY PROJECTILES
Armour-Piercing (AP)

Anti-tank ammunition with AP projectiles was provided for all medium- and high-velocity tank guns of both sides in the early years of the Second World War, when it was adequate for penetrating the relatively thin armour of the tanks of the period. The simplest of all anti-tank projectiles, the AP projectile was a solid hardened steel shot with an ogival nose which depended upon the combination of its weight and striking velocity to achieve penetration of the target. The kinetic energy available with all KE projectiles is calculated from the formula $\frac{1}{2}MV^2$, where M is the mass (weight) of the

projectile and V is its striking velocity, from which it can be seen that an increase in velocity has a greater influence on kinetic energy than an increase in mass. The simple AP shot was soon superseded by the APC as it was found to be too easily deflected by sloped armour, off which it tended to ricochet after making a mere scoop in the armour. It also tended to shatter, particularly at close ranges and higher velocities, against face-hardened armour. It was fitted with a pyrotechnic composition tracer in the base to ease the problem of following its flight.

Armour-Piercing, High Explosive (APHE)

Like the AP shot, this was a thick-walled shell with a hardened steel casing and a small HE filling. A base-mounted fuze was intended to detonate the shell inside the target but, in small calibres, the HE content did little if any more damage than the equivalent solid shot. It was originally issued for the British 2-pdr (40-mm) tank gun but was withdrawn by the end of 1940.

Armour-Piercing, Capped (APC)

This type of projectile replaced the simple AP shot, which it resembled except for the provision of a penetrative cap over the nose, the function of which was to turn the projectile into a sloping target on striking it, thus allowing it to penetrate the armour at or near normal (i.e. at 90°). The cap also reduced the tendency of the AP shot to shatter when striking face-hardened armour. APC projectiles were also fitted with a base tracer. The poor ballistic shape of the APC shot caused it to be replaced by the APCBC shot.

Armour-Piercing, Capped, Ballistic Cap (APCBC)

This projectile consisted of an APC shot fitted with a lightweight ballistically-shaped cap to

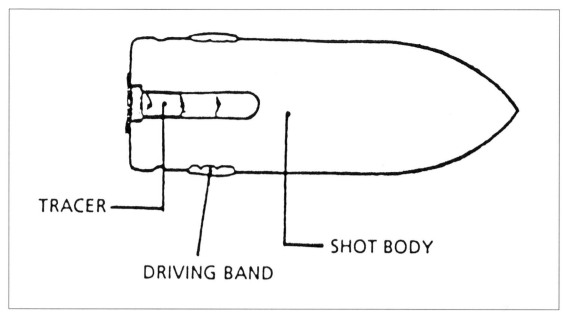

AP projectile. (Author's Collection)

An M4 Sherman of 1st US Armoured Division knocked out by AP shot in Tunisia in February 1943. The penetration can just be seen below the commander's cupola. (Wilhelm Hartmann)

Remains of a German PzKpfw III knocked out by AP fire in Tunisia in 1943. Set on fire by the initial AP penetration, the tank has been blown to pieces by the resultant ammunition and petrol explosion. (Wilhelm Hartmann)

A US M3 medium tank knocked out by 88-mm AP fire in Tunisia, 1943. (Wilhelm Hartmann)

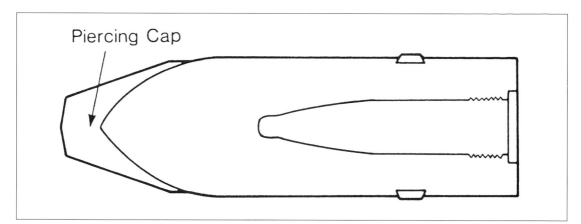

APC projectile. (Author's Collection)

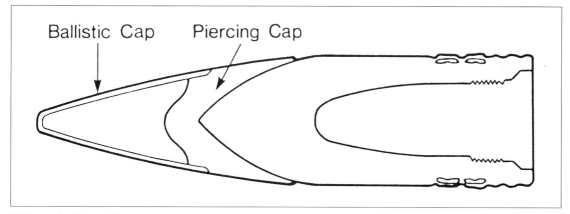

APCBC projectile. (Author's Collection)

improve accuracy and range. It was in use by all combatant tank troops in the Second World War and was the most universally used of all kinetic energy anti-tank rounds. It too was provided with a base tracer. The Germans and Soviets employed a version which contained a small explosive charge, but the explosive charge was not reliable, neither was it large enough to cause much damage. This type of projectile was known as APCBC/HE.

Armour-Piercing, Composite, Non-Rigid (AP/CNR)

The AP/CNR projectile was the first of a new generation of anti-tank projectiles in which various methods of greatly increasing muzzle velocity, and thus penetration of armour, of existing guns was tried. All the projectiles which follow belonged to this generation, which in fact achieved a startling increase in both velocity and penetration at the cost of a reduction in long range accuracy. The principles governing the design of postwar kinetic energy projectiles were developed during the Second World War, both in the use of materials and in the imaginative application of the laws of ballistics. Full calibre steel shot had limited applications, particularly with the

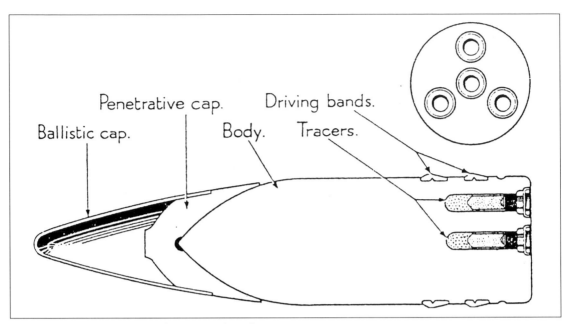

17-pdr APCBC/T shot, showing layout of the four tracers. (Author's Collection)

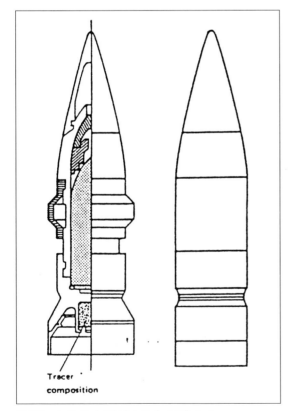

AP/CNR projectile (2-pdr Littlejohn). (Author's Collection)

development of larger calibre anti-tank guns. Steel projectiles could not withstand the stresses of very high velocity impact on armour plate, so it became necessary to find better materials. At the same time, it was necessary to produce a projectile that would have different ballistic characteristics in the gun, in flight and at the target. The first attempt to find an answer came with the AP/CNR projectile, a British solution for the 2-pdr (40-mm) tank gun, which was the first to reconcile internal, external and terminal ballistics. It consisted essentially of a dense (tungsten carbide) sub-calibre projectile contained in a full-calibre flanged carrier. A conical adaptor at the muzzle (the Littlejohn adaptor) swaged down the flanges of the carrier as it passed through the muzzle from 40 mm down to 30 mm, thus concentrating the kinetic energy of the shot over a smaller cross-sectional area and giving a very high muzzle velocity and good anti-tank performance at close range. At the target, the steel outer carrier shattered after making the initial indentation in the armour, leaving the dense sub-calibre core to penetrate the armour. This type of ammunition was successfully used by British units in the battles of the Western Desert, but the 'squeeze' at the muzzle wasted energy, and research by both sides was devoted to finding a less wasteful method of achieving the same result. The Germans tried a taper-bore gun based on the Gehrlich principle in 1943. It was a 7.5-cm (2.95-in) weapon known as the Project 0725, due to have been mounted on the Henschel prototype for the PzKpfw Tiger, but was dropped due to the availability of the 8.8-cm (3.46-in) KwK36 (L/56) gun.

Armour-Piercing, Composite Rigid (AP/CR)

The Germans introduced a range of AP/CR ammunition for their 5-cm (1.96-in), 7.5-cm (2.95-in) and 8.8-cm (3.46-in) tank guns in 1943, known as Panzergranate 40 (AP40). Similar in outline and principle to the British squeeze-bore Littlejohn projectile, the AP40 projectile could be fired from a normal gun barrel. The British introduced a similar

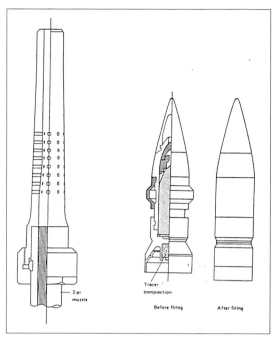

Littlejohn 2-pdr adaptor and projectile. (Author's Collection)

projectile on a limited scale for the 6-pdr (57-mm) anti-tank gun in the same year. In this type of projectile, the sub-calibre tungsten carbide core was carried in a

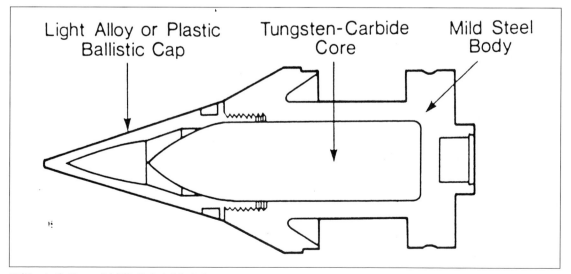

AP/CR projectile (German Gehrlich). (Author's Collection)

lightweight full-calibre outer projectile which disintegrated on striking the target, leaving the sub-calibre core to penetrate the target. Shortage of tungsten towards the end of the war curtailed German production of a successful type of projectile that was intermediate between the Littlejohn and the later APDS of the Western Allies. AP/CR shot was provided with a base tracer.

Armour-Piercing, Discarding Sabot (APDS)

This was a Second World War US development of the AP/CR principle which was highly successful and which continues in use in both NATO and the former Eastern Bloc countries in a further developed form. First mooted in the USA in 1942, it was developed in 1943 and issued to British troops for the 17-pdr (3-in) gun in 1944. It represented a logical progression from the

variable geometry of the AP/CR projectile to a two-part projectile, the hard, dense tungsten carbide sub-calibre projectile was carried in a full-calibre light alloy 'sabot', which provided the large base area required in the gun but which disintegrated after leaving the muzzle, allowing the sub-projectile to fly at enhanced velocity to the target. The discarded segments of the sabot caused some danger to exposed troops in the vicinity of the muzzle and were liable to damage any muzzle attachments, such as a muzzle brake. Nevertheless, the APDS projectile was a great success. It was used only by British and US forces in the Second World War.

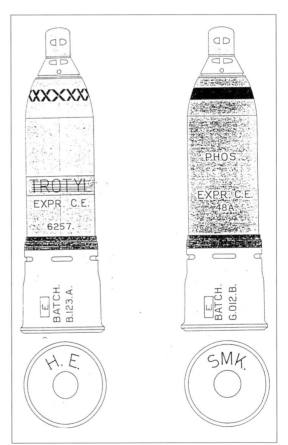

British 3.7-in close support howitzer HE and smoke rounds. (Author's Collection)

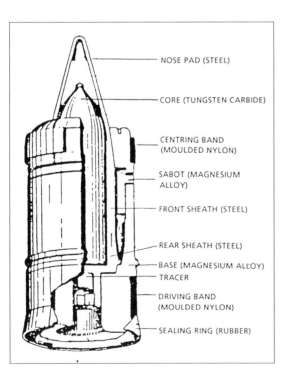

APDS projectile. (Author's Collection)

MISCELLANEOUS PROJECTILES
Smoke

Smoke was used extensively by both sides in the Second World War as a tactical aid for concealing troop movements and as a local protection device for concealing the withdrawal or changing of position of individual tanks in action. The former was normally provided by carrier smoke shells fired from a tank's main armament and the latter by smoke grenades fired from dischargers or small mortars on the tank turret, in the case of British, US and German tanks. As mentioned earlier, the Red Army preferred to generate smoke screens by injecting oil into tanks' exhaust systems.

Smoke shells were thin-walled projectiles filled with a pyrotechnic composition which, when ignited, produced vaporized products which reacted with atmospheric moisture to produce aqueous droplets. Screening smoke could be produced by compositions which either burned steadily to evolve smoke that built up into an effective screen, which lasted as long as the composition burnt, or produce an instant screen by the bursting of a container filled with phosphorus. The former type were normally used for tactical screening and were filled in shells in which the smoke composition was emitted or ejected from the base of the shell after it had struck the ground. The smoke composition was normally Hexachlorethene (HCE) which produced an effective and long-lasting screen, provided that there was some moisture in the air. In dry desert conditions of low relative humidity it was not effective, producing a thin screen. The latter were used in local smoke projecting devices and normally consisted, in British service, of white phosphorus and in German service of an oleum/pumice mix

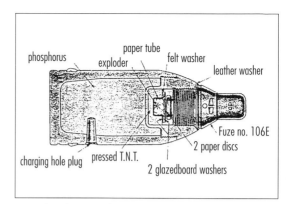

Section through 3.7-in CS howitzer smoke projectile. (Author's Collection)

filled in bursting canisters, initiated by high explosive bursting charges. They were propelled from external grenade launchers mounted on the outside of the tank turret or from small calibre (2-in) mortars fired and loaded from inside the turret. White phosphorus is an unpleasant and difficult chemical as it burns spontaneously on exposure to air. Great care has to be taken in the filling and storing of ammunition containing it. Because of the high temperature at which it burns it tends to 'pillar' instead of clinging to the ground.

Illuminating

Provided only on a small scale, for low velocity high trajectory weapons, and used by both sides in the Second World War for battlefield illumination. Thin-walled, ballistically-shaped projectiles were used, containing a thin-walled canister filled usually with a magnesium composition as the light-producing medium, mixed with some oxygen-rich substance to support combustion. The canister was provided with a parachute to slow down the canister's descent. The shell was provided with a nose time fuze, to eject the canister from the projectile base at the correct point of its trajectory.

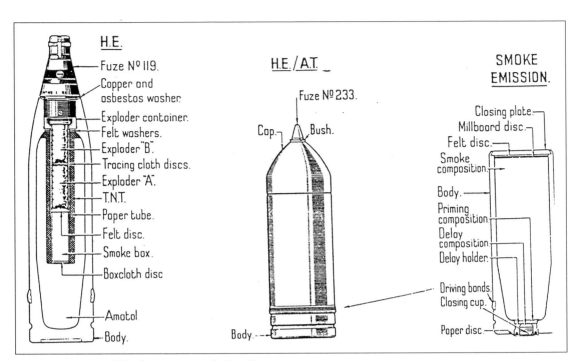

British 95-mm howitzer HE, HEAT and smoke projectiles. (Author's Collection)

Chemical

Although produced and stockpiled by both sides, shells filled with chemical warfare agents were not used in the Second World War.

AUXILIARY ARMAMENT

MACHINE-GUNS

Machine-guns are the main weapons available to tank crews for the attack of personnel, unarmoured or thinly-armoured vehicles and aircraft. In the Second World War, most tanks of both sides carried one mounted coaxially with the main armament and fired by the tank's gunner and one mounted, either fixed or flexibly, in the front of the hull, operated by the co-driver or driver. Occasionally, and particularly in tanks produced early in the war, other machine-

guns were located in sub-turrets or flexibly mounted in the rear of the main turret. These guns were all of standard rifle calibre of the country concerned. Finally, a machine-gun for anti-aircraft use was often mounted on the turret roof (or superstructure roof, in SP guns). This was usually of the same calibre in British and German tanks, or of larger (.50 calibre or 12.7-mm) calibre in the case of the United States and the USSR, respectively.

Tank MGs, with the exception of the British BESA guns, could be dismounted and used on bipods or tripods in the ground role if required, being virtually unmodified infantry light or medium machine-guns. The BESA, however, was designed primarily as a tank machine-gun and was too bulky and heavy to be used dismounted. Tank machine-guns could be either belt or magazine fed, and both types were used by both sides in the war. As the machine-gun is by nature an area

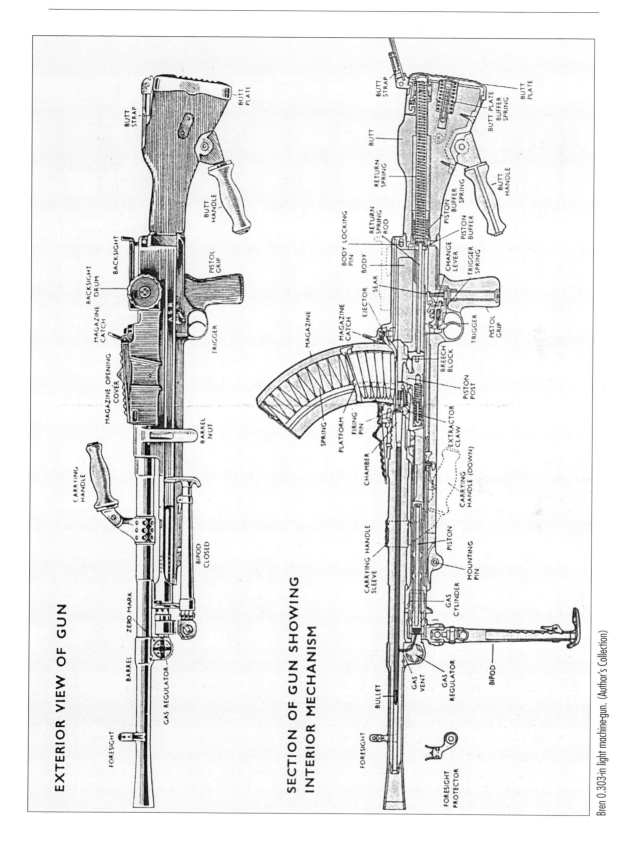

EXTERIOR VIEW OF GUN

SECTION OF GUN SHOWING
INTERIOR MECHANISM

Bren 0.303-in light machine-gun. (Author's Collection)

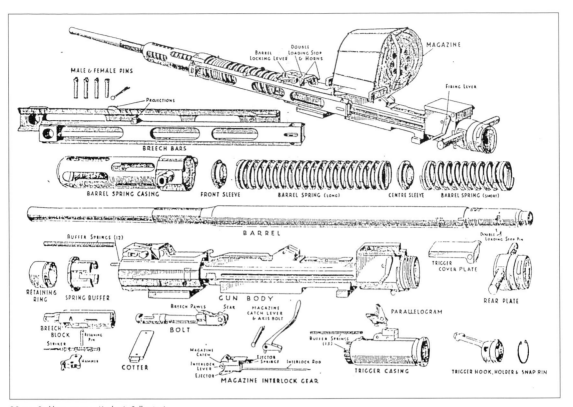

20-mm Oerlikon cannon. (Author's Collection)

weapon, with fall of shot difficult to spot, particularly in the fog of battle, all countries provided their tank MGs with tracer rounds. Other varieties were ball and armour-piercing ammunition, with incendiary rounds in some cases for anti-aircraft use.

Types of tank machine-gun used by the combatant countries in the Second World War are listed below, together with their calibres and methods of feed:

COUNTRY	MG	CALIBRE	METHOD OF FEED
Britain	Vickers	0.303 in	Belt
		0.5 in	do.
	BESA	7.92 mm	do.
		15 mm	do.
	Browning	.30 cal	do.
		.50 cal	do.
USA	Browning	.30 cal	do.
		.50 cal	do.
USSR	Degtyarev	7.62 mm	Drum
	DShK	12.7 mm	do.
Germany	Dreyse MG13	7.92 mm	Box Mag
	MG34	do.	Belt or Belt Drum
	MG42	do.	Belt

All except the Vickers guns were air-cooled. Small arms ammunition (SAA), like that of main armament, consists of a cartridge case and a projectile. It is fixed, in that the cartridge case and bullet are joined and loaded as one item. Bullets are of one of two types, solid and filled.

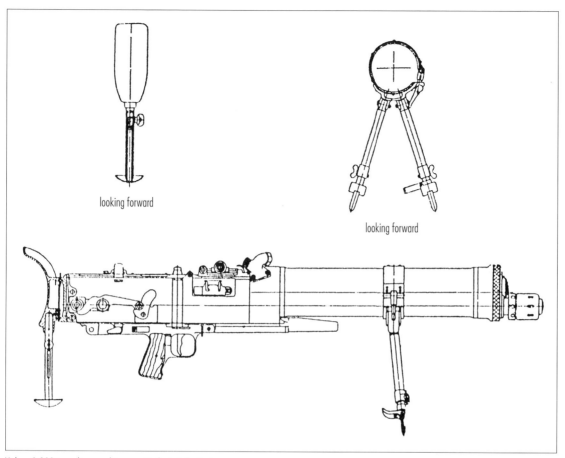

looking forward

looking forward

Vickers 0.303-in medium machine-gun. (Author's Collection)

CARTRIDGE

The small arms cartridge consists of a case of brass or steel containing a percussion cap in the base, the propellant and the bullet crimped to the neck of the case. The case is necked and may be rimmed or rimless at the base. The rim in a rimmed case is provided to enable the extractors in the MG's breech mechanism to extract the empty case after firing; the same function is performed in a rimless case by a groove or cannelure around the base of the cartridge. The percussion cap in the base is struck and fired by the gun's firing pin, thus igniting the propellant charge contained in the case.

Propellant is usually granular and, on ignition, propels the bullet, which is slightly wider than the barrel, so that it engages in the barrel rifling and provides obturation forwards. Rearward obturation is provided by the expansion of the cartridge case. The bullet is held firmly in the neck of the cartridge case long enough for a high pressure to be built up before the bullet is propelled up the barrel.

The majority of MG cartridge cases during the Second World War were rimless, including the German 7.92-mm, British BESA 7.92-mm and 15-mm, Soviet DT 7.62-mm and DShK 12.7-mm and US .30

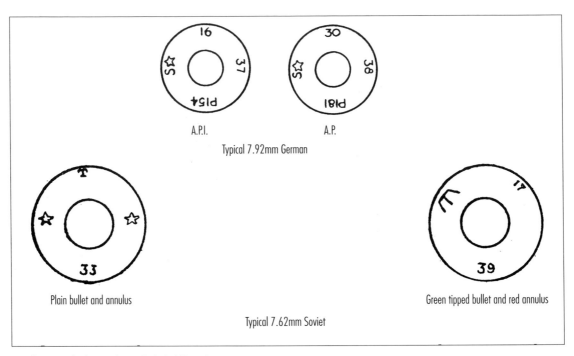

A.P.I.   A.P.

Typical 7.92mm German

Plain bullet and annulus   Green tipped bullet and red annulus

Typical 7.62mm Soviet

Typical SAA cartridge base markings. (Author's Collection)

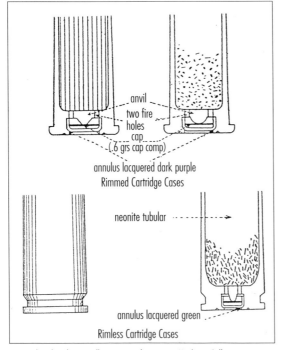

anvil
two fire
holes
cap
(.6 grs cap comp)
annulus lacquered dark purple
Rimmed Cartridge Cases

neonite tubular

annulus lacquered green
Rimless Cartridge Cases

Rimmed and rimless small arms cartridge cases. (Author's Collection)

cal and .50 cal rounds. The .303-in rounds for the British Vickers MG were rimmed. German and Soviet ammunition used steel case material; British and US rounds used brass.

BULLET
Solid Bullets

These were used for anti-personnel (ball) and anti-tank (armour-piercing) roles and consisted of an envelope and a core. The core in ball ammunition was usually a lead/tin/antimony alloy while a tungsten or steel alloy was used as the core in AP ammunition. The envelope was made from a ductile alloy such as nickel, cupro-nickel or gilding metal.

Filled Bullets
Tracer bullets are the main type in this category; others include incendiary and

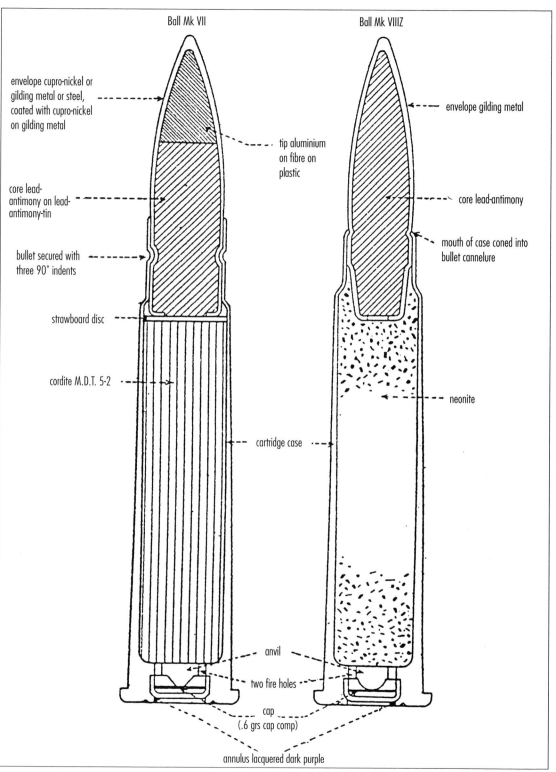

Ball Mk VII

Ball Mk VIIIZ

envelope cupro-nickel or gilding metal or steel, coated with cupro-nickel on gilding metal

envelope gilding metal

tip aluminium on fibre on plastic

core lead-antimony on lead-antimony-tin

core lead-antimony

bullet secured with three 90° indents

mouth of case coned into bullet cannelure

strawboard disc

cordite M.D.T. 5-2

neonite

cartridge case

anvil

two fire holes

cap (.6 grs cap comp)

annulus lacquered dark purple

Sectional views of 0.303-in cartridges. (Author's Collection)

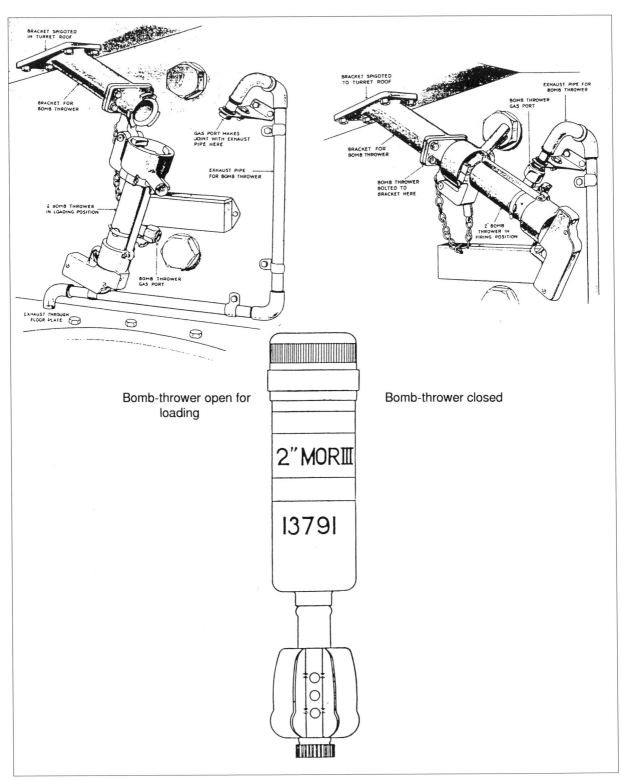

Bomb-thrower open for
loading

Bomb-thrower closed

2-inch bomb-thrower and mortar bomb. (Author's Collection)

tracer/incendiary, used primarily for spotting and observation. The tracer composition was ignited when the round was fired, the incendiary composition on impact of the bullet with the target. Tracer rounds were particularly necessary when firing from AFVs so as to assess where bullets were striking. Delayed ignition of the tracer composition was essential to prevent the firer's position being revealed. Tracer ammunition had to be evenly distributed throughout the belt/magazine, and its trajectory had to match that of the solid bullets at least up to the range at which the trace burnt out.

GRENADES

Apart from the hand grenades that formed part of the crew's close defence personal weapons, British and German tanks in the Second World War incorporated bomb-throwers, mounted externally or internally, for close-in defence of the vehicle. These projected grenades of two types, anti-personnel and smoke.

British tanks were the only ones to carry smoke bomb-throwers in the early stages of the war. Light tanks, Matilda infantry tanks and cruiser tanks mounted two 4-in single-shot throwers mounted on the outside of the turret for operation by the tank commander. These were replaced in 1941–2 by the 2-in breech-loading bomb-thrower mounted in the turret roof and loaded and fired from inside the turret. Both types of weapon were designed for close-in defensive screening, and had ranges out to 150 metres in the case of the 4-in weapon and range variable from 20 to 110 metres in the case of the 2-in bomb-thrower.

German tanks had two types of facilities for generating defensive smoke, a five-candle device mounted on the tail plate and operated from inside the vehicle on early tanks and, on later models of the PzKpfw III and the Tiger I, three projectors mounted on each side of the turret at the front, angled so as to produce a semi-circular screen. These projectors were single-shot, loaded externally but fired electrically from inside the turret, and fired the 90-mm smoke grenade. Early Tiger I tanks for use on the Eastern Front also mounted five S-Mine anti-personnel mine dischargers around the roof of the hull superstructure. These too were single-shot weapons, fired electrically from inside the turret, and were used against Soviet tank-hunting parties in close country.

Later German tanks such as the PzKpfw Panther and King Tiger had a bomb-thrower mounted in the turret roof with independent 360° traverse and fixed elevation, loaded and fired from within the turret, for close defence. This was provided with both smoke and anti-personnel grenades, as well as illuminating and coloured smoke bombs.

AMMUNITION STOWAGE

Correct stowage of ammunition in a tank helps towards a high rate of fire, both from the main armament and from auxiliary weapons, and is thus a factor in a tank's firepower. Obviously, it would not be possible to stow all the ammunition for a weapon beside it; there would not be enough room in the turret for the 50 to 90 rounds of main armament ammunition stowed in the average tank of Second World War vintage, to say nothing of the boxes, drums or bags of machine-gun ammunition and the smoke and other auxiliary armament ammunition. Ammunition stowage within a tank is therefore divided into two categories:

1. Ready rounds: those required immediately when a target is engaged.

A Tiger Model E of No. 1 Company of 501 Heavy Tank Battalion with tracks broken by mines and two ineffective strikes by 6-pdr anti-tank guns on the front vertical plate, in Operation Eilbote I Tunisia, January 1943. (Wilhelm Hartmann)

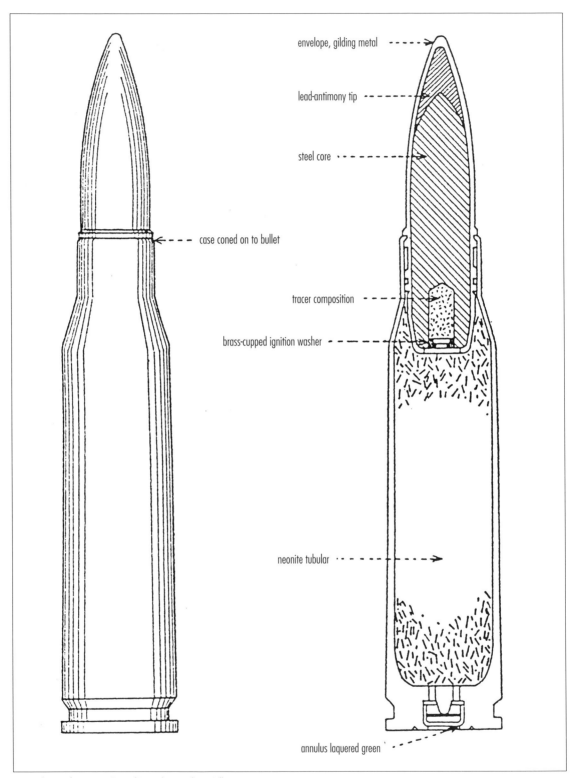

envelope, gilding metal

lead-antimony tip

steel core

case coned on to bullet

tracer composition

brass-cupped ignition washer

neonite tubular

annulus laquered green

Sectional view of 15-mm BESA AP/T cartridge. (Author's Collection)

2. Replenishment rounds: used to replenish the ready rounds as they are fired.

Ready rounds are stowed as near to the loader as possible, preferably in a position where he has to manoeuvre them as little as possible between the stowage position and the gun breech. Other rounds can be stowed wherever space is available, as long as they are accessible from within the turret.

To reduce handling and manoeuvring by the loader to a minimum, ready rounds of fixed ammunition should therefore ideally be stowed horizontally, in the turret or the turret basket, with the projectile pointing towards the front of the turret, in the attitude in which they will be loaded into the gun. Ammunition is the most common cause of fire in tanks when hit and, as the turret is the most vulnerable part of a tank, it is obviously desirable to keep the number of rounds stowed there to a minimum, the remainder being stowed below the turret ring in the hull.

With the small calibre fixed ammunition of the early years of the war, rounds tended to be stowed vertically in bins on the floor of the turret basket. As the calibre of main armament increased, however, the length of round dictated horizontal stowage. Horizontal stowage of main armament rounds was generally in open racks, the rounds retained by quick-release clips, or in boxes or bins beneath the turret basket and along the hull side walls. In many tanks the turret basket had no floor, the turret crew sitting in seats attached to the turret ring thus allowing fairly free access to the stowage beneath. In Soviet medium and heavy tanks the poor turret crew in action had to step over opened ammunition boxes which formed the turret floor.

The ease with which ammunition was ignited within the tank by hot shot or armour fragments penetrating the cartridge case when a tank was hit by enemy fire was a cause of great worry to tank crews and

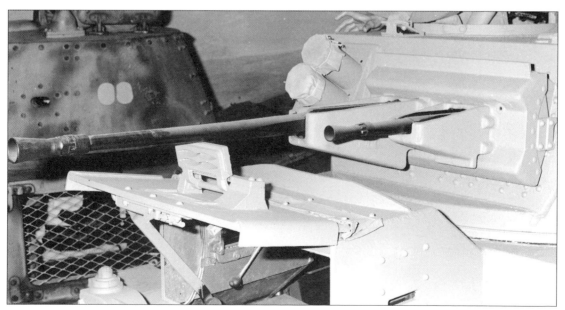

15-mm BESA MG, coaxially mounted with the 7.92-mm version. (Tank Museum 5386/D5)

Valentine III of British 6th Armoured Division knocked out in the initial British thrust towards Tunis in December 1942. (Wilhelm Hartmann)

designers during the Second World War and much research was devoted to seeking to reduce the fire risk. At first it was thought that the provision of armoured bins for ammunition would prevent or reduce the incidence of ammunition fires, but it was found that hot fragments of a struck ammunition bin caused as many fires as the bin prevented, with rather more damage being caused by the enclosure of the ammunition within the confined space of the bin

The Americans experimented with water-jacketed bins, in the hope that water would be released into the penetrated cartridge case, thus quenching any fire before it could ignite the round, but results were inconclusive before the war's end. The British tried another tack, by keeping replenishment ammunition out of the tank altogether in an armoured trailer called a Rotatrailer. This was soon rejected by user units on account of the restriction the trailer placed upon the tank's manoeuvrability when travelling across rough country and when reversing, and the rail-head in North Africa was soon full of Rotatrailers in new condition, abandoned by their units at the first opportunity.

There is unlikely to be a solution to the problem of preventing the ignition of a highly explosive cargo such as ammunition by a projectile which, when penetrating the armour of an AFV, generates numerous extremely hot, high velocity fragments inside the vehicle and which can itself penetrate the stowed ammunition and its bins. The problem has exercised the best minds in the tank design business since the end of the Second World War, but no universally successful solution to the problem has yet been found.

CHAPTER EIGHT

FIRE CONTROL SYSTEMS

In the Second World War tank fire control systems were relatively simple, and comprised the following elements that enabled the crew to search for, locate and engage a target:

1. Vision devices for crew members.
2. Inter-communication between crew members.
3. Means of estimating range to target.
4. Sight(s) for gunner.
5. Turret traverse system.
6. Gun elevation system.
7. Gun firing system.

Although the combatant countries differed in the detail of their construction and use, the components of their fire control systems were remarkably similar in general principles, and achieved broadly similar results in action. The components will be considered in detail separately in the following pages and the performance of each country's system will be compared and evaluated in a summary at the end of this chapter.

1. VISION DEVICES

All members of a tank crew are responsible for observation, all playing their part where necessary in the process of target-seeking. All must have some means of seeing out of a closed-down vehicle. This is necessary in any case to prevent their being overcome by motion sickness in a closed-down tank moving across country without a stable horizon being visible. These devices gave an unmagnified ×1 view and consisted, in the tanks with which most countries started the

war, of narrow vision slits cut through the armour, backed by thick laminated toughened glass blocks which could be replaced from inside the vehicle if they became damaged by fragments or bullets. These were provided for all crew members except the gunner, who had his optical sight. In the case of the driver, who by virtue of his position, generally played only a negligible part in fire control but who needed a wide field of view when driving closed down, his vision block was larger and was given a much larger hole in the front armour, but it could be covered by an armoured visor operable from inside the vehicle in action. In addition, German tanks up to the PzKpfw Panther were provided with a pair of cranked telescopes, known as KFF-2, for the driver. These had two separate holes through the armour, and were for use when the armoured visor was closed. These were abandoned on the Panther and later tanks as slits and holes through the armour obviously weakened it, and the driver was instead provided with a two-position seat so that, when not closed down, he could drive with his head out of his hatch in the hull roof. As armour got thicker as the war progressed, it became increasingly difficult to provide adequate vision through slits in it. In any case, the light transmission of the laminated glass blocks was poor, reducing their efficiency in poor light conditions. The slit/glass block solution was therefore gradually abandoned in favour of episcopes or periscopes through the turret or hull roof, giving a greater field of view and being less vulnerable to attack (although more vulnerable to weather and accidental damage)

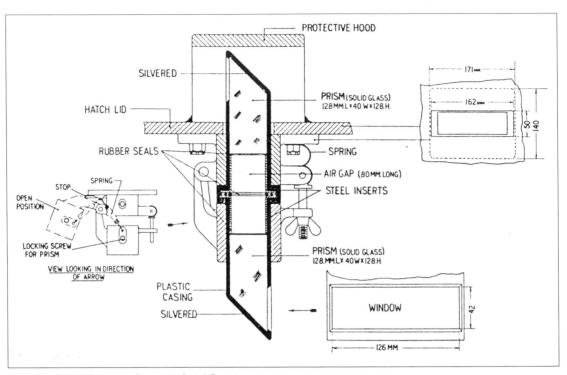

PROTECTIVE HOOD

SILVERED

HATCH LID

PRISM (SOLID GLASS)
128 MM L × 40 W × 128 H.

RUBBER SEALS

SPRING

STOP

SPRING

OPEN
POSITION

AIR GAP (80 MM LONG)

STEEL INSERTS

LOCKING SCREW
FOR PRISM

PRISM (SOLID GLASS)
128.MM L × 40 W × 128 H.

VIEW LOOKING IN DIRECTION
OF ARROW

PLASTIC
CASING

SILVERED

WINDOW

171 ᴍᴍ

162 ᴍᴍ

50

140

42

126 MM

Section through a typical episcope and mount. (Author's Collection)

than the earlier method. An episcope was defined, at least in the British service, as a periscope in a fixed mounting. A periscope, on the other hand, could be traversed and elevated independently in its mounting. Both types of instrument had removable top prisms which could be replaced from inside the vehicle. In addition to vision slits, glass blocks, episcopes and periscopes, many tanks up to 1943 incorporated one or more pistol ports in the turret armour, which could be closed by conical armour plugs from inside the tank and which could also be used for vision if required. The commander's position demanded special treatment in view of his key role in the fighting of his tank; he needed all-round vision to carry out his task properly, both when opened up and closed down. When opened up, he commanded with his head out of his hatch but in action this made him especially vulnerable to sniper and HE fire. He needed some means of all-round vision when closed down, and the universal solution adopted by all combatants before the end of the war was to give him a fixed or rotateable cupola, provided with either vision slits/glass blocks or episcopes, giving him 360° ×1 vision. The British rejected the fixed, dustbin-like cupola with vision slits/episcopes in favour of the rotateable, flat cupola with periscopes from the Churchill onwards – the Americans did likewise. The German and Red Armies retained the fixed type of cupola with vision slits and glass blocks or, in the German case of the PzKpfw IV, Panther and later tanks, with episcopes. Tank commanders were also provided with binoculars to give increased magnification, usually about ×6, for target identification. German tank commanders were provided with periscopic

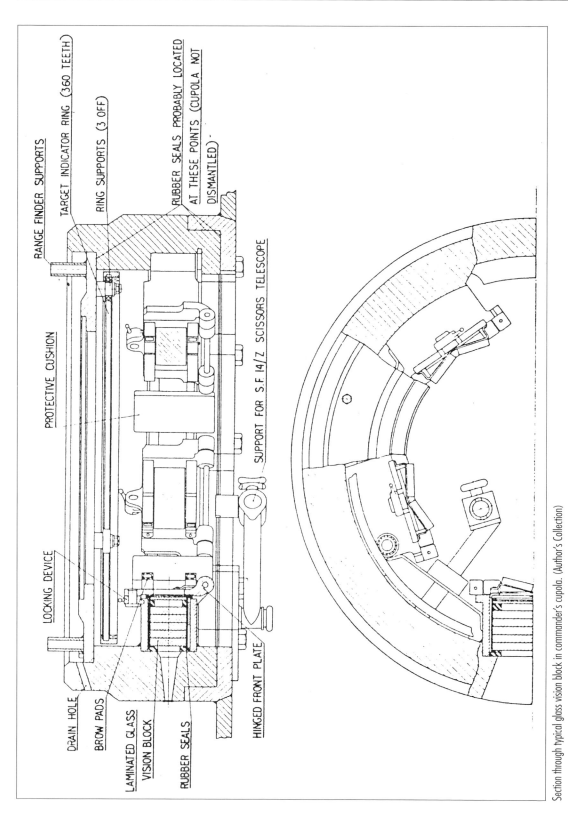

Section through typical glass vision block in commander's cupola. (Author's Collection)

binoculars, for which a mounting was provided on the cupola, enabling the commander to observe without exposing his head.

2. Crew Intercommunication

Clear communication between crew members is obviously essential to the correct and rapid application of a tank's firepower. In British tanks at the outbreak of the Second World War, communication between the tank commander and his crew was by means of the unassisted human voice, coupled with such hand and foot signals as they might devise. In the noise of a tank in the heat of battle, such a system was open to misunderstanding and repetition, thus slowing down the target engagement process. German tanks, by contrast, provided headsets for all crew members, connected to an intercommunication system in the tank radio. By 1941, the British had introduced a Tannoy set for crew intercommunication and, later still, a radio set (the No. 19 set) which incorporated an intercommunication facility. In the Red Army, few tanks were provided with radios until late in the war; by 1944, however, they had adopted a similar system to that used in the British, US and German tanks. These systems enabled the commander to communicate orders to and converse with his crew members above the noise within the tank and thus, by reducing the possibility of misunderstood orders, increased the speed of engagement.

3. Range Estimation

Accurate estimation of the range to a target is essential to the obtaining of a hit with low velocity ammunition and highly desirable with any type of ammunition. Until the invention of the laser and ground radar after the Second World War it was the most common and largest source of error in tank gunnery. The most common method was by the commander's guesswork, a method which, despite specialized training in the art, remained open to gross error of the order of 25%, particularly when estimating range over water or open country without features to give an idea of scale. This was the least accurate but the cheapest method of range estimation; there were four others available during the Second World War, each used at some time by all the combatants with varying degrees of success.

(i) **Observation of fall of shot**
     This method, usually combined with an initial estimation of range by the commander, depended upon observation of the fall of the first shot and correcting from this. It could be a lengthy procedure, revealing the tank's position in the process, but it was the method most commonly used by both sides in the Second World War.

(ii) **Stadiametric**
     This was an optical method that depended upon the angle subtended at the tank by a target of known dimensions at various key ranges. By comparison of the target with markings in the gunner's sight, a reasonable estimate of range could be obtained. The drawback to this system lay in the need for the target to be in a specific position relative to the tank (e.g. broadside on), which was rarely the case, and for the identity and dimensions of the target to be known when the range figures and tank outlines were incorporated in the sight. Despite these disadvantages, the stadiametric system was marginally

more accurate than unaided estimation of range by the tank commander and was used by Soviet tank crews in the Second World War.

(iii) **Stereoscopic**

The stereoscopic rangefinder is an optical instrument that works on the principle of stereoscopic vision, and had been in use for many years prior to the Second World War in the artillery units of some countries. Consisting of a long tube with a prism and lens system at each end and two eyepieces in the centre, the rangefinder depended for its efficiency on the possession by the operator of stereoscopic vision; the operator adjusted the two images of the target until he obtained a single stereo image, then read off the range. The Germans used this system in their field artillery units, and proposed the introduction of such a rangefinder in the redesigned Panther turret that was in prototype form at the war's end. The American Army also favoured this type of rangefinder and investigated its possible use in tanks. Surprisingly, they did not realize, until the investigation results were known, how few men possess stereoscopic vision good enough to enable them accurately to operate this type of rangefinder. Presumably the Germans either possessed better vision or they accepted poorer results.

(iv) **Coincidence**

Another optical method, the coincidence rangefinder is similar in appearance and general description to the stereoscopic type. In this system, however, the operator has to bring the two images in his eyepieces into coincidence. Accuracy of range measurement depends upon the base length of the instrument, the distance between the two object lenses. Many more men are able to operate this type of rangefinder accurately than can use the stereo rangefinder successfully. Its use reduced the average error in range estimation to 6%, and it was therefore the preferred choice of the British Army. None was adopted, however, largely on the grounds of lack of robustness and of adequate room for its installation at the commander's position in British tanks of the Second World War.

Optical systems of range estimation had the advantage of being passive, in that the enemy had no indication that he was being ranged upon. Observation of fall of shot and the postwar laser and radar rangefinders have the disadvantage of being active methods which can reveal to an alert enemy not only that he is being ranged upon but also whence the rangefinding is being carried out, thus giving the operator's position away.

4. SIGHTS

Sights need to be provided for the main armament gunner and the operators of any auxiliary weapons not coaxially mounted with the main armament. In addition to these sights, some simple form of open sight is required for the tank commander to enable him to line up, approximately, the main armament with the target so as to bring the target into the field of view of the gunner's sight. Gunners' sights in the Second World War were optical instruments of either straight-tube or periscopic

Tank commander's sighting vane (on Churchill VIII). (David Dring)

A) TELESCOPIC SIGHTS

These were optical instruments containing an eyepiece lens system, an object lens system and one or more adjustable range scales and aiming marks contained in a long tube. The eyepiece lens system, with its focusing adjustment, rubber browpad and rubber eyeguard or light excluder, was mounted conveniently for the gunner's eye while the object lens fitted into a hole in the armour. The instrument was mounted coaxially with the weapon. In the case of the main armament sight it contained graticules for both main armament and coaxial machine-gun. The aiming mark for the former carried adjusters for adjusting the aiming mark to coincide with the point of aim of the gun. In later instruments, provision for illumination of the graticule for use in poor light was made. In this case, graticules had to be engraved in the glass rather than printed on it in order for them to be seen. Sighting telescopes were normally monocular and of single magnification, but the Germans introduced a binocular version in the early PzKpfw Tiger and Panther. In later models they reverted to monocular telescopes, but having dual magnification of ×2.5 and ×5. The three chief drawbacks to the simple straight tube telescope were:

(i)   Coaxial mounting of the telescope meant that it elevated and depressed with the gun; this in turn meant that the gunner had to move his head up and down through quite a large and uncomfortable angle to keep his eye to the eyepiece.

(ii)   There was nothing to prevent a lucky shell fragment or bullet from entering through the hole in the armour and passing down the length of the telescope into the gunner's eye.

type, providing magnification of up to ×3 and with a comparatively narrow field of view, to enable the gunner accurately to identify and lay his sight on a target. Ideally, the gunner also needed a wide angle vision device in the same instrument as his weapon sight. If this could not be achieved, for example with a sighting telescope, he needed a ×1 periscope or episcope to give him the wide field of view necessary to enable him to pick out target positions indicated by the commander. Auxiliary weapon sights were either the open sights of the weapon, as used in its ground role, or simple telescopic instruments giving small magnification, while commanders' sights for alignment of turret with target were of the open type.

Stationary eyepiece sighting telescope. (Avimo Ltd)

(iii)   The requirement for a hole through the frontal turret armour, thus weakening it.

The British and Soviet armies nevertheless employed simple straight tube sighting telescopes in tanks of native design for most of the war. The Germans, on the other hand, used variations of this type of sight for both main and auxiliary armamant from the introduction of the PzKpfw II early in the war, while the American army used periscopic sights exclusively. The straight tube telescope had one great advantage over periscopic sights, this being the fact that it was mounted coaxially and rigidly with the gun and there was therefore no linkage to introduce error between gun and sight.

The German telescopic sights are worthy of special mention, both for their greater convenience to the gunner, their reduction of vulnerability, answering the drawbacks in (i) and (ii) above and the sheer quality of their design and manufacture, as befitted a country with what was then the most advanced optical industry in the world. These advantages were achieved by breaking the telescope tube near to the gun trunnions and inserting a combined optical and mechanical hinge between the two parts of the tube. Protection to the gunner was afforded by inserting an armour plate between the two components of the hinge. By this means the gunner did not have to move his head with the elevation and depression of the gun as the eyepiece remained stationary. This series of stationary eyepiece telescopes was known as Turmzielfernröhre (TZF: turret sighting telescope) and was copied by the Soviet Union towards the end of the war.

B) PERISCOPIC SIGHTS

The American version of this type of sight consisted of a large periscope giving a wide

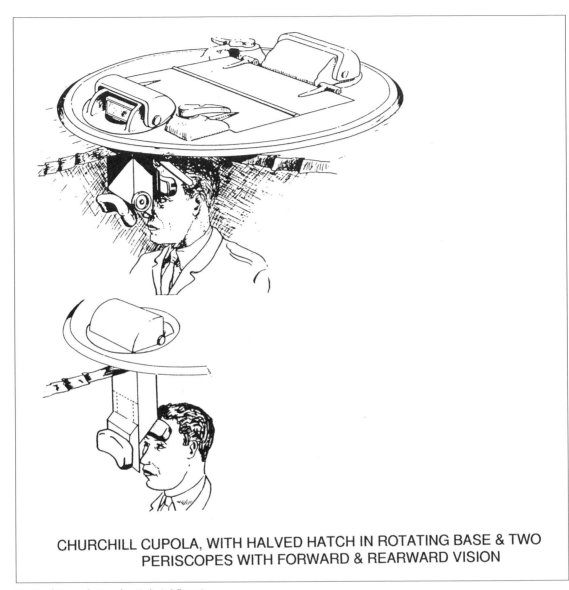

CHURCHILL CUPOLA, WITH HALVED HATCH IN ROTATING BASE & TWO PERISCOPES WITH FORWARD & REARWARD VISION

Two typical commanders' cupolas. (Author's Collection)

angle of view with ×1 magnification, containing a vertically-mounted telescope at one side with a focusing eyepiece and light excluder, graticule, graticule adjusters, range scale(s) and aiming mark(s) and giving a magnification over a narrow field of view in the region of ×3. The periscope was mounted in the turret roof in front of the gunner's position and connected to the gun cradle by means of an adjustable linkage. Its advantages over the straight tube telescope were:

(i)   Less vulnerable to attack.
(ii)   Gunner's head movement limited to small backward and forward

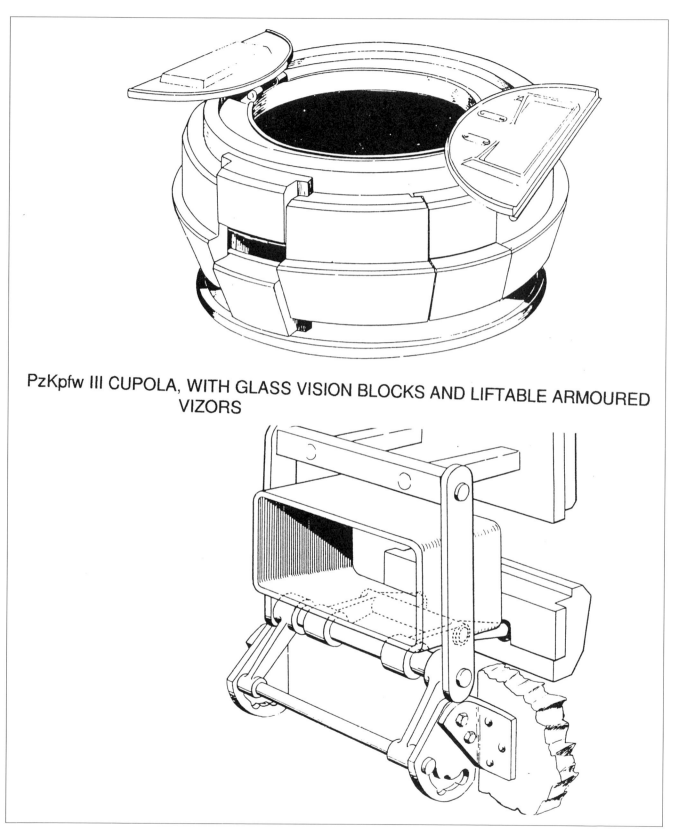

PzKpfw III CUPOLA, WITH GLASS VISION BLOCKS AND LIFTABLE ARMOURED VIZORS

movement when gun elevated or depressed.

(iii) Wide angle ×1 and narrow field ×3 vision available through same without gunner having to remove his eyes from the instrument.

The Soviet version differed from the American in resembling more a panoramic telescope with a rotatable head and thus lacking the wide field of view of the ×1 window of the US type of sight. Both types shared advantages (i) and (ii) above, as well as the disadvantage of all roof-mounted instruments, namely vulnerability to weather and accidental damage. This was minimized by the welding of an armoured cowl over the slot in the armour through which the periscope head protruded. The problem of sighting in heavy rain was not solved until after the war, when miniature screen wipers were developed for cleaning the sight head. German designers also converted to the idea of periscopic sights towards the end of the war, although none had been approved for service before the war's end.

C) OPEN SIGHTS

Open sights were restricted in tanks in the Second World War to use with auxiliary armament such as machine-guns in ball or AA mountings. In the latter role they consisted of a combination of rear sight and ring sight and they were used in conjunction with tracer ammunition to get into the area of an aircraft target. With ball-mounted weapons, the sight was the open sight used in the ground role as a light machine-gun, consisting of simple back and fore sight; for use in its ball mounting in the tank a larger than normal hole was required in the armoured ball so that the gun with its sight could be mounted and the sight used. Use of this type of sight was restricted to Soviet

tanks, where the Degtyarev LMG was employed.

A form of open sight was also provided for tank commanders so that the gunner could be brought quickly to the area in which a target had been located. In British tanks this consisted of a pair of folding vanes (the Blade Vane Sight) mounted on the turret roof, aligned with the gun, or of a frame sight mounted parallel to the front of the turret again on the turret roof in front of the commander's position. These could be seen through the commander's vision device and the turret quickly aligned with the target.

D) SIGHTS FOR INDIRECT FIRE

A special type of sight, known as a dial sight, was required for indirect fire with low velocity artillery type weapons with high angles of elevation. These were usually SP field guns and howitzers and the sight was usually that used with the weapon on its field mounting. It was used in conjunction with the range tables for the gun, and all combatant armies in the Second World War employed this type of sight for their self-propelled low velocity weapons. Adjustments included angle of sight (with a levelling bubble), tangent elevation and range (with scales for each nature of ammunition inscribed on a range drum) and cross-levelling (with bubble). Although not strictly speaking a sight, a clinometer was provided for measuring angles of sight for low velocity tank guns when firing HE in semi-indirect fire. An accurately machined level plane for seating the instrument was provided on the breech ring of the weapon. Most US, German and British tank guns of 75-mm calibre and above and of low to medium velocity were provided with clinometers and breech clinometer planes in the Second World War. Soviet tanks, however, lacked this facility.

A modern periscopic sight. (Barr & Stroud)

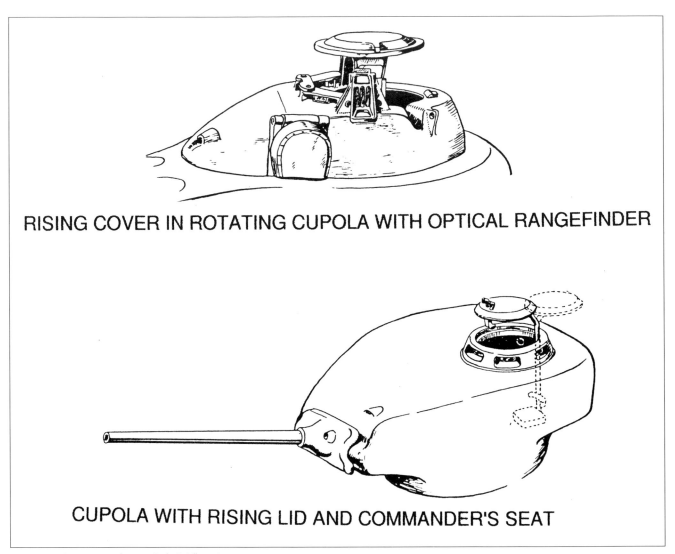

RISING COVER IN ROTATING CUPOLA WITH OPTICAL RANGEFINDER

CUPOLA WITH RISING LID AND COMMANDER'S SEAT

Some more cupola types. (Author's Collection)

5. TURRET TRAVERSE SYSTEMS

All tanks in service with both sides during the Second World War mounted their main armament in a turret capable of being traversed through 360°. Due to the weight and out-of-balance of the turret, some form of reduction gearbox was required to enable the gunner to achieve this on his own. Early in the war, tanks were provided with a traverse gearbox operated by hand, the gunner being provided with a horizontal handwheel which he turned in the direction in which he wished the turret to move. A locking device was provided for locking the turret when the tank was travelling out of action. This type of system was adequate for the light turrets in service at the time but, as turrets increased in weight with increases in armour thickness and calibre of armament, it was found to be both

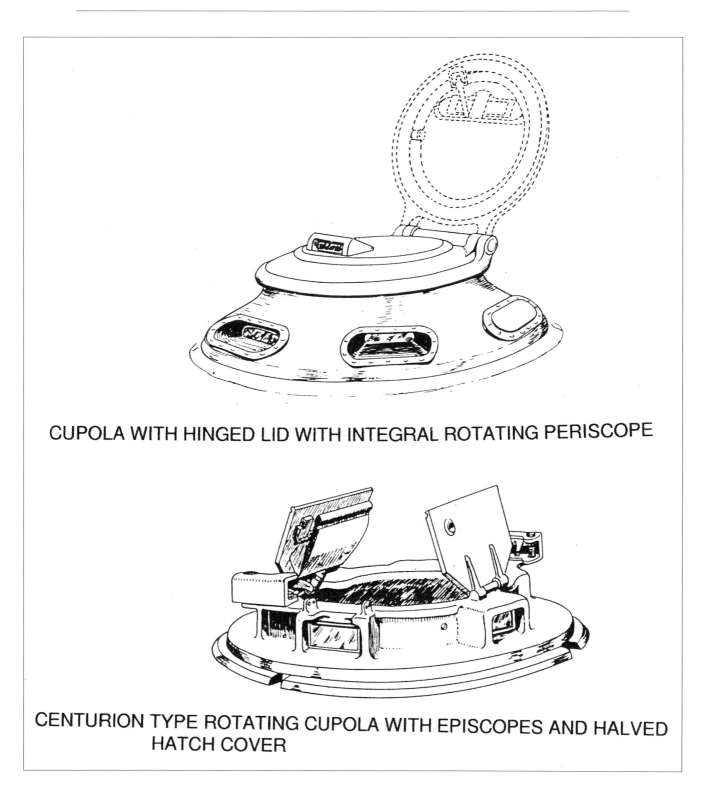

CUPOLA WITH HINGED LID WITH INTEGRAL ROTATING PERISCOPE

CENTURION TYPE ROTATING CUPOLA WITH EPISCOPES AND HALVED HATCH COVER

too slow and too heavy for the gunner to use unaided. The angular speed of a tank turret needs to be as fast as possible in the slew mode when switching through large angles, variable when tracking a moving target and very slow when fine-laying on a target. Manual traverse was adequate for making a fine lay on the target, but for tracking if the target speed was slow, it was soon found that some form of power assistance was needed. The British, in the Infantry Tank Mark II (Matilda) and Cruiser tanks, were the first to provide this, in the form of an hydraulic system. It gave excellent smooth operation but suffered from leaks, sand ingress in the Western Desert and posed an increased fire risk. It was also expensive to manufacture, as it involved much fine machining. The Germans opted for an electrical system in their contemporary PzKpfw IV medium tank, but early electrical systems suffered from lack of smoothness, particularly at low speeds. These early powered systems also incorporated manual operation, usually used for making the final lay on a target. The Soviet T-34 and KV tanks at this time also employed electrical power, both manual and power drives using the same epicyclic gearbox, requiring no switching from power mode to manual or vice versa. The Americans, on the other hand, used both electrical and hydraulic systems in different versions of the Sherman. British and German ideas changed over as the war progressed, the Germans moving to hydraulic traverse for the Panther and Tiger while the British turned to electrical systems for Churchill, Comet and Challenger. As far as maximum slewing speeds were concerned there was little to choose between the two systems, but otherwise the electrical was preferred by the British and Red Armies on the grounds of cheapness, lower fire risk, ease of installation, maintenance and repair, and ease of integration into a turret stabilization system if required. All systems offered alternative manual control.

6. GUN ELEVATION SYSTEMS

In view of the requirement for tanks to fire on the move, early British tanks in the Second World War employed shoulder control of the gun in elevation. This method was simple and reasonably accurate provided that the pitching of the tank was not too violent, but it required the gun to be in balance around its trunnions and this, as guns became progressively longer and heavier as the war continued, became increasingly difficult to achieve without the gun breech projecting too far into the turret. Mechanical systems were therefore adopted for tanks armed with the 6-pdr or bigger guns, such systems involving a gearbox, an elevating rack and pinion and handwheel control for the gunner. With such a system, firing on the move, unless from a smooth road surface, became virtually impossible. Despite this drawback, tanks of all the combatant countries adopted this system of controlling the gun in elevation, crews opting to halt to fire. Gun mountings were fitted with mechanical locks inside the turret for use when travelling out of action, while long-barrelled guns were also provided with external crutches for the same purpose, to avoid putting too much stress on the elevating gearing. There was little development in tank elevation gear after the introduction of manual geared systems until the introduction by the US tank designers of electrical gun stabilization systems, thus once again permitting firing on the move with reasonable accuracy. These systems were introduced on the Light Tank M3 (Stuart) and the Medium Tank M3 (Lee/Grant) and on all subsequent American tanks and they revolutionized tank gunnery. An improved system was introduced on the British Centurion just prior to the war's end, and all subsequent main battle tanks have incorporated stabilization systems for both gun and turret. Although the early American systems were treated initially with suspicion by British users of tanks fitted with them, they came to be regarded as essential as familiarity grew and system accuracy improved. If early systems did not enable gunners to achieve a first round hit on the move, at least the gunners were able to keep the guns laid on or near to the target so that, when their vehicle halted, they were able immediately to fine lay and to engage it with minimum delay and maximum chance of hitting it.

7. Gun Firing Systems

As was mentioned in the chapter on ammunition, a gun is fired by the detonation of a cap in the base of the cartridge case. In the majority of cases in the Second World War, this detonation was achieved mechanically by means of linkage from a firing trigger (located on or near to the turret traverse or the gun elevation control) to a firing pin located in the breech ring. Only in the case of the German tanks was initiation of the charge achieved electrically. One of the sources of error in a tank fire control system is the interval which elapses between the gunner squeezing the trigger and the gun firing, and it is essential to reduce this interval, known as the firing interval, to a minimum. One of the disadvantages of any mechanical linkage is the need, due to wear and vibration in the system, for constant lubrication and adjustment in order to maintain a consistent 'feel' to the trigger; another is the cumulative delay caused in each link and joint in the system, between the gunner pulling his trigger and the gun firing. It is a primitive and not very satisfactory system, and it is therefore all the more surprising that it took so long for Allied tank, gun and ammunition designers to adopt an electrical system. The advantages of an electrical over the mechanical firing system are many: with no mechanical links in the

chain the firing interval is reduced to a constant minimum, maintenance is reduced and 'feel' at the trigger is constant. The chief disadvantages of electrical systems are their vulnerability to damp and the need for insulation against induced electrical currents from, for example, high-power radio and radar sets. Mechanical firing systems were universally used for coaxial machine-guns. Despite these disadvantages the overall balance is in favour of electrical firing systems for tanks, as has been shown by their almost universal adoption in postwar tanks.

Fire Control System Development Summarized

Development in tank fire control systems during the Second World War was probably as great as in any other aspect of tank firepower in the same period. To take the various components individually:

Crew Vision: the trend was away from slits in the front and side armour, combined with laminated glass vision blocks, towards periscopes or episcopes for all crew members and all-round vision cupolas for the tank commander.

Crew Intercommunication: early in the war unaided voice communication was superseded by tank radios incorporating a crew intercommunication system, first by Germany, then by the US and Britain and lastly by the USSR. This has remained the norm up to the present.

Range Estimation: of all the components of a fire control system, range estimation showed the least development during the Second World War. Visual estimating techniques made little impression on the chief cause of gunnery error, and optical range measuring instruments proved too delicate for tank use,

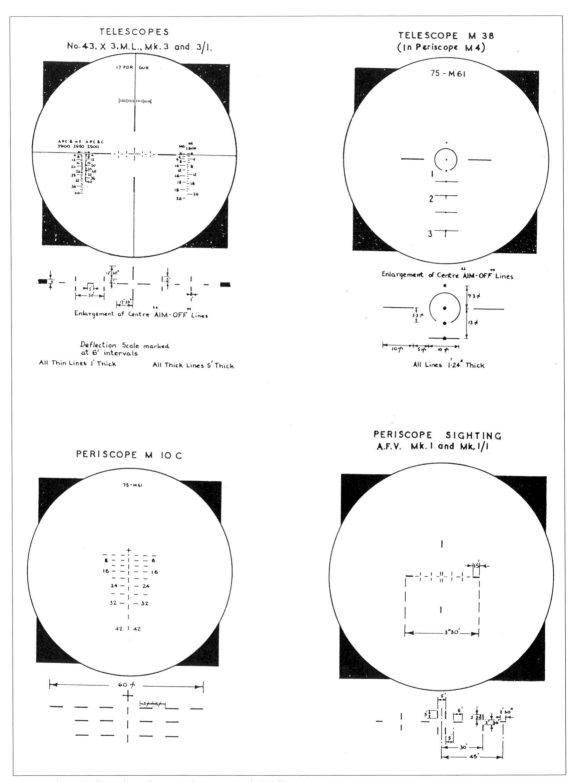

Some typical graticules from sighting telescopes and periscopes. (Author's Collection)

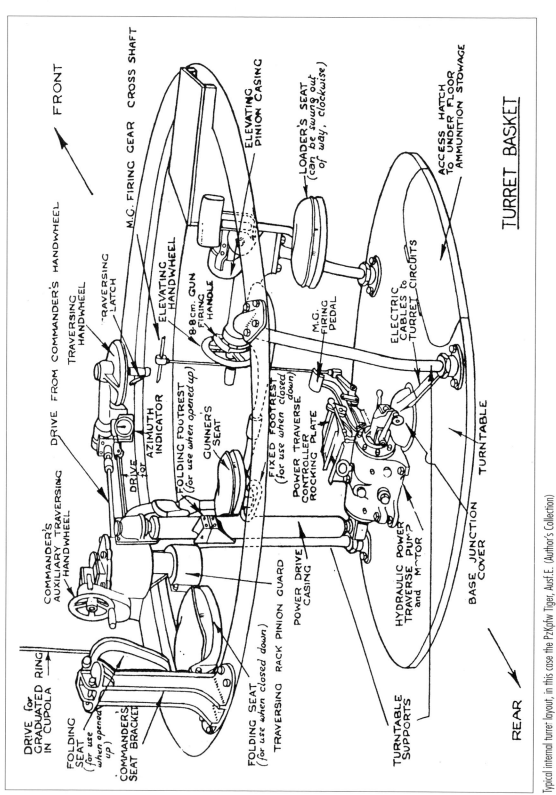

TURRET BASKET

Typical internal turret layout, in this case the PzKpfw Tiger, Ausf.E. (Author's Collection)

as well as demanding too much space. US and German preference for an optical system which few men were equipped to operate accurately did little to encourage its use. It was not until the invention of the laser range-finder after the war that range estimation errors could finally be eliminated from tank gunnery.

Sights: the early simple straight tube telescopes were replaced first by more sophisticated versions with adjustable range scales, illuminated graticules and, in the case of German tanks, by the stationary eyepiece type. This type was copied by the USSR in their later tanks, but was improved still further by the Germans before the end of the war by introducing binocular or dual-magnification models. The Americans preferred periscopic sights, with which all their wartime tanks were equipped, and this type was later adopted by the British. The majority of tanks produced postwar have confirmed this preference.

Turret Traverse Systems: early manual systems were soon replaced by powered systems with alternative manual control as turret weights and out-of-balances increased. Opinions differed between the combatant countries as to the best method of powering the systems and performance of electrical and hydraulic systems were comparable. The greater complication and fire risk of hydraulic systems persuaded the British to adopt electrical systems after their early flirtation with hydraulics. Germany used both types, as did the USA, but the USSR preferred electrical systems.

Gun Elevation Systems: The early replacement of shoulder-controlled elevation systems by manually-operated geared systems was necessitated by the increasing weight and out-of-balance of tank main armament. The biggest and most important development in gun elevation was the American powered gyroscopic stabilization system which reintroduced the ability to fire accurately on the move. All postwar main battle tanks have incorporated developments of this original system, possibly the most important development in fire control of the Second World War.

Gun Firing Systems: the most important development here was the German electrical primer firing system, which proved vastly superior to the mechanical systems of other countries in minimizing and standardizing the firing interval with a much-reduced requirement for maintenance. Again, this development has been almost universally adopted since the war for postwar tanks.

APPENDIX A

BRITISH TANK GUNS AND AMMUNITION

AUTOMATIC WEAPONS
1. Bren Light Machine-Gun

Calibre	0.303 in (7.7 mm)
Length overall	43.25 in (1,099 mm)
Weight	23 lb (10.5 kg)
Rate of fire	Single shot or 550 rds/min (cyclic)
Cooling	Air
Feed system	30-round box magazine or 100-round drum magazine for AA use
Muzzle velocity	2,400 ft/sec (727 m/sec)
Date into service	August 1938
Ammunition types	Ball
	Tracer (burn-out at 1,000 yds)
	AP(to penetrate 10 mm at 90° impact at 100 yds

The Bren LMG was copied from the Czech ZB 33 LMG and replaced the Lewis gun as the standard LMG of the British army. It was issued to virtually all British AFVs for local ground defence and, on the collapsible Lakeman mounting, in the AA role.

2. Vickers Medium Machine-Gun

Calibre	0.303 in (7.7 mm)
Length overall	45.5 in (1,156 mm)
Rate of fire	450 rds/min
Cooling	Water
Feed system	250-round belt
Muzzle velocity	2,440 ft/sec (743 m/sec)
Date into service	1912
Ammunition types	As for Bren LMG

Although a highly efficient gun, capable of prolonged sustained fire, the Vickers MMG was too bulky and its water jacket too vulnerable for AFV use. It was replaced by the 7.92-mm BESA MG (see below). It was fitted to the Vickers Medium, the Infantry tanks Marks I and II, the Cruisers A9, A10 and A13 and to the Light Tank Mark VIB early in the Second World War.

3. Vickers Heavy Machine-Gun

Calibre	0.5 in (12.7 mm)
Length overall	47.5 in (1,207 mm)
Rate of fire	650–700 rds/min
Cooling	Water
Feed system	100-round belt
Muzzle velocity	2,550 ft/sec (777 m/sec)
Date into service	1931
Ammunition types	Ball
	Semi-AP (to penetrate 15 mm of armour at 100 yds range)
	Semi-AP (Trace) (tracer burn-out at at 800 yds range)
	AP (to penetrate 18 mm of armour at 100 yds range)

Essentially an enlarged version of the Vickers MMG (above), it had the same faults as its smaller relative when used in a tank. It was fitted in the Light Tank Mark VIB (with a coaxial Vickers MMG) and in the Infantry tank Mark I at the outbreak of war.

4. BESA Medium Machine-Gun

Calibre	7.92 mm (0.31 in)
Length overall	43.5 in (1,105 mm)
Weight	47 lb (21.3 kg)
Rate of fire	Low: 450–550 rds/min. High: 750–850 rds/min
Cooling	Air
Feed system	225-round belt
Muzzle velocity	2,550 ft/sec (777 m/sec)
Date into service	1939
Ammunition types	AP/T Ball Incendiary

Produced under licence by BSA, the BESA MMG was developed from the Czech ZB37; it was a reliable and accurate weapon but, like the Vickers, it was a heavy and bulky gun, requiring a large opening in the tank's armour, and it could not be easily used dismounted in the ground role. It was the standard British AFV MG in the Second World War, and was used in virtually all British tanks, SP guns and armoured cars until replaced by the American .30 cal Browning M1919 gun.

5. BESA Heavy Machine-Gun

Calibre	15 mm (0.59 in)
Length overall	80.75 in (2,051 mm)
Weight	125.5 lb (57 kg)
Rate of fire	Single shot or 450 rds/min
Cooling	Air
Feed system	25-round belt

Muzzle velocity	3,000 ft/sec (915 m/sec)
Date into service	1939
Ammunition types	Tracer AP (to penetrate 31 mm at 200 yds)

Essentially a scaled-up version of the BESA MMG (above), intended to replace the 0.5 in Vickers HMG, it was used only in the Light Tank Mark VIC, the Guy and Humber armoured cars, with a 7.92-mm BESA MMG coaxially mounted, and in the Light AA tank Mark II (in a twin mounting).

6. Oerlikon and Polsten cannon

Calibre	20 mm (0.79 in)
Length overall	87 in (2,209 mm) (Oerlikon) 85.75 in (2,178 mm) (Polsten)
Weight	141 lbs (64 kg) (Oerlikon)
Rate of fire	450 rds/min (both)
Cooling	Air (both)
Feed system	60-round drum magazine (both)
Muzzle velocity	2,725 ft/sec (830 m/sec) (both)
Date into service	1939 (Oerlikon) 1944 (Polsten)
Ammunition types	SAP/HEI HE/incendiary HE/incendiary/tracer

The Oerlikon was produced in the UK under licence from the Swiss firm of Oerlikon in large numbers, primarily for the Royal Navy as an AA weapon but also for the army in the same role. It was fitted on a twin mounting on the Crusader AA tank Marks II and III. The Polsten was developed in Poland in the 1930s as a cheaper redesign of the Oerlikon, and the design team escaped to the UK after the German invasion of Poland. It was used on the Centaur AA tank Mark I in a twin mounting and also as a coaxial weapon in the first ten prototype A41 Centurion Mark I tanks at the end of the war.

7. Bofors Anti-aircraft Gun

Calibre	40 mm (1.57 in)
Length overall	117.7 in (2,990 mm)
Rate of fire	120 rounds/min (cyclic), 60–90 rounds/min in action
Cooling	Air
Feed system	4-round charger
Muzzle velocity	2,700 ft/sec (823 m/sec)
Date into tank service	1943
Ammunition types	HE/Tracer (weight: 2 lbs) AP/Tracer (weight: 2.75lbs)

The Swedish-designed Bofors gun was adopted for British service in 1937 and was produced throughout the Second World War in large numbers and a total of seventeen Marks; only the Mark VI was produced for tank use. It was used only on the Crusader AA tank Mark I, for which it was specifically designed. It incorporated joystick control of both powered traverse and powered elevation and had an effective AA range of 1,500 yards. It had a telescopic sight (No. 39 Mark I) for use against ground targets and an anti-tank performance equivalent to that of the 2-pdr tank gun.

TANK MAIN ARMAMENT
8. Ordnance, QF, 2-pdr

Calibre	40 mm (1.57 in)
Length of bore in calibres	L/50
Length of gun overall	82 in (2,083 mm)

Maximum rate of fire	22 rds/min
Maximum range	8,000 yds (7,317 m) at 25° elevation
Maximum range on sight	1,500 yds (1,371 m)
Ammunition types and MV	AP/T: 2,800 ft/sec (854 m/sec). Shot weight: 2 lb 6 oz APCBC/T: 2,600 ft/sec (793 m/sec). Shot weight: 2 lb 11 oz AP/CNR: Mark I 4,200 ft/sec (1,280 m/sec). Weight: 1 lb 4 oz Mark II: 3,900 ft/sec (1,189 m/sec). Weight: 1 lb
Date into tank service	1936, on prototype A9

The 2-pdr was the main armament of all Cruiser and Infantry tanks up to 1942, and of most armoured cars and the Tetrarch and Harry Hopkins light tanks until after the end of the war. To increase its armour penetration performance, it was fitted with the Littlejohn squeeze muzzle attachment for firing AP/CNR ammunition. At the time of its introduction, the 2-pdr was arguably the best tank gun in service worldwide, but it was rapidly outclassed as the war progressed. Although an HE round was produced it was ineffective and issued only on a very small scale.

9. Ordnance, QF, 6-pdr 7cwt

Calibre	57 mm (2.24 in)
Length of bore in calibres	L/36 (Mark III) L/43 (Mark V)

Length of gun	
overall	100.95 in (2,565 mm)
	(Mark III)
	116.95 in (2,971 mm)
	(Mark V)
Maximum rate of	
fire	15 rds/min
Maximum range	5,500 yds (5,030 m)
Maximum range	
on sight	2,400 yds (2,195 m)
Ammunition types	
and MV	AP/T: 2,800 ft/sec (854 m/sec) (Weight: 6 lb 5 oz) in Mark III gun 2,925 ft/sec (892 m/sec) in Mark V gun APC/T: 2,775 ft/sec (853 m/sec) (Weight: 6 lb 5 oz) in Mark III gun 2,900 ft/sec (884 m/sec) in Mark V gun APCBC/T: 2,600 ft/sec (792 m/sec) (Weight: 7 lb 2 oz) in Mark III gun 2,725 ft/sec (831 m/sec) in Mark V gun AP/CR/T: 3,550 ft/sec (1,082 m/sec) (Weight: 4 lb 3 oz) APDS/T: 4,000 ft/sec (1,220 m/sec) (Weight: 3 lb 2oz) HE/T: 2,700 ft/sec (823 m/sec)
Date into tank	
service	1942

The 6-pdr was an effective anti-tank weapon when introduced, although it lacked an HE round for most of its service life. The anti-tank capability was considerably enhanced by the introduction of the APDS round in 1944, although by this time it was being supplanted by the British 75-mm, 77-mm and 17-pdr tank guns. The 6-pdr was the main armament of the Crusader III, Cavalier, Centaur I, Cromwell I to III, the Valentine VIII to X and Churchill III, IV and X.

10. Ordnance, QF, 75-mm

Calibre	75 mm (2.95 in)
Length of bore in	
calibres	L/36.5
Length of gun	
overall	118.58 in (3,011 mm)
Maximum rate of	
fire	10 rds/min
Maximum range	10,500 yds (9,603 m)
Ammunition types	
and MV	APCBC/T: 2,030 ft/sec (618 m/sec) (US APC M61: weight: 14 lb 7 oz) HE/T: US M48 round. Weight: 14 lb 11 oz Chemical: US M64 round. Weight: 15 lb 4 oz
Date into tank	
service	Spring 1944

The British 75-mm tank gun was designed to use as many 6-pdr gun components as possible and was chambered to use the readily available US ammunition. While its HE performance was satisfactory, AP ammunition was inferior to that of the 6-pdr. Luckily, by the time that calls were being made from NW Europe for the reinstatement of the 6-pdr, the 77-mm and 17-pdr were coming into service on the Comet, Challenger and Sherman Firefly. The British 75-mm tank gun served as the main armament of the Centaur III, Cromwell IV, V and VII, Valentine XI, and the Churchill VI, VII and X.

11. Ordnance, QF, 17-pdr

Calibre	76.2 mm (3 in)
Length of bore in calibres	L/55
Length of gun overall	180.35 in (4,580 mm)
Maximum rate of fire	10 rds/min
Maximum range	10,000 yds (9,146 m) (HE)
Ammunition types and MV	APCBC/T: 2,900 ft/sec (884 m/sec) Weight: 17 lb APDS/T: 3,950 ft/sec (1,204 m/sec) Weight: 8 lb 3 oz. Core weight: 3 lb 14 oz HE/T: 2,875 ft/sec (876 m/sec)
Date into tank service	Spring 1944

Originally developed as a towed anti-tank gun, the 17-pdr proved too heavy, at 2 tons, for manoeuvring and manhandling in the field and too large for mounting in British tanks of the time (1942). So an SP mounting on the Valentine infantry tank chassis was designed for it. Known as Archer, the SP 17-pdr was most successful; 665 were produced and issued to anti-tank regiments of the Royal Artillery. In the event it was also, but with some difficulty, mounted on the Challenger cruiser tank and with ease on the M4 Sherman. This version was known as the Sherman VC Firefly and about 600 were adapted from standard vehicles. It was mounted in some M10 gun motor carriages, which were known as Achilles, and as the main armament of the Centurion Mark I and the still-born Black Prince.

12. Ordnance, QF, 77-mm (3-in)

Calibre	76.2 mm (3 in)
Length of bore in calibres	L/49
Length of gun overall	136 in (3,454 mm)
Maximum rate of fire	10 rds/min
Maximum range	7,000 yds (6,402 m) (HE)
Ammunition types and MV	APCBC/T: 2,600 ft/sec (792 m/sec) Weight: 17 lb APDS/T: 3,675 ft/sec (1,120 m/sec) Weight: 8 lb 3 oz. Core weight: 3 lb 14 oz HE/T: 2,875 ft/sec (876 m/sec)
Date into tank service	Spring 1944

The 77-mm gun was a shortened 17-pdr, specifically modified by Vickers Armstrong for the A34 Comet cruiser tank. Ammunition handling in the turret was eased by virtue of the cartridge case which was shorter and larger in diameter than that for the 17-pdr. The title '77 mm' was adopted to avoid confusion with other 76.2-mm (3-in) guns coming into British and US service. It proved to be an exceptionally accurate gun, with an AP performance only slightly inferior to that of the 17-pdr. It remained in service with the British army until the last Comets were withdrawn from the Hong Kong garrison in 1959.

13. Ordnance, QF, 3-in, Close Support howitzer

Calibre	76.2 mm (3 in)
Length of howitzer overall	78 in (1,981 mm)

Maximum rate of fire	18 rds/min
Maximum range	2,400 yds (2,195 m) (HE)
Ammunition types and MV	HE/T: 600–700 ft/sec (213 m/sec) Smoke: ditto
Date into tank service	1938

In the absence of a high explosive round for the 2-pdr gun, with which the majority of British tanks in the early stages of the Second World War were equipped, it was necessary to have some tanks armed with a high explosive-firing weapon in tank units. These tanks were known as 'Close Support' (CS) tanks and they were armed with the 3-inch CS howitzer, which had itself replaced the 3.7-in (93.9-mm) CS mortar of the early CS tanks (Cruiser Tanks Marks I & II). The limited scale of issue (only two per tank squadron), short range and badly-designed ammunition gave British tank units little chance of engaging well-sited, enemy anti-tank guns in the Western Desert. It began to be replaced in 1943 by the 95-mm (3.7-in) howitzer, but remained in service until the end of the war in the CS version of the Tetrarch light tank. It was also fitted in the CS Covenanter and Crusader cruiser tanks and in the CS infantry tanks Matilda, Valentine (a New Zealand conversion) and Churchill I.

14. Ordnance, QF, 3.7-in CS mortar

Calibre	3.7 in (94 mm)
Length of mortar overall	59 in (1,498 mm)
Maximum rate of fire	18 rds/min
Maximum range	2,000 yds (1,829 m) (HE)
Ammunition types and MV	HE/T - 620 ft/sec (189 m/sec) Weight 15 lb Smoke: ditto. Weight 15 lb 5 oz
Date into tank service	1930

The 3.7-in breech-loading mortar was the first of the close-support tank weapons. Fitted to some Vickers Medium tanks, its operational use in the Second World War was limited to a few A9 and A10 tanks in France in 1939–40.

15. Ordnance, QF, 25-pdr

Calibre	3.46 in (88 mm)
Length of gun overall	106.7 in (2,710 mm)
Maximum rate of fire	6 rds/min
Maximum range (in SP role)	6,400 yds (5,854 m)
Ammunition types and MV	HE: 1,700 ft/sec (518 m/sec) Weight: 25 lb AP/T: 2,000 ft/sec (610 m/sec) Weight: 20 lb Smoke: coloured smoke, star shell, propaganda, incendiary and flare
Date into tank service	1942

The 25-pdr field gun came into service on its field mounting in 1939. Its adaptation to a self-propelled weapon began in June 1941 in response to urgent requests from the Middle East theatre. The resulting equipment, known as the Bishop, was based upon the Valentine tank chassis, the gun being mounted in a fixed, fully-enclosed mounting that left little room for ammunition, limited elevation (and hence the maximum range) to 15° and gave a total traverse of only 8°. Some 100 equipments were built and sent to North Africa; they were replaced in the Italian campaign in mid-1944 by the US-supplied M7 Priest. The 25-pdr was also mounted on the Canadian Ram tank chassis in an equipment known as Sexton; this was a much more successful SP, in which the 25-pdr was mounted in an open-topped fighting compartment which allowed greater traverse (25° left, 15° right) and 40° elevation, the latter permitting the gun to attain its normal maximum range. The Sexton replaced the Priest in British service from mid-1944, production ending in 1945 after 2,150 had been built. It remained in British service until the late 1950s.

16. Ordnance, QF, 32-pdr

Calibre	93.4 mm (3.67 in)
Length of gun overall	195 in (4,953 mm)
Maximum rate of fire	4 rds/min (est.)
Maximum range (in SP role)	Not known
Ammunition types and MV	APCBC/T: 2,880 ft/sec (878 m/sec) Weight: 32 lb APDS/T: 3,640 ft/sec (1,109 m/sec) Weight: 15.3 lb. Core weight: 6.7 lb AP/CR/T: 3,620 ft/sec (1,103 m/sec) Weight: 17.9 lb. Core weight: 6.7 lb HE: Not known
Date into tank service	1944

Based on the 3.7-in (94-mm) anti-aircraft gun, development of the 32-pdr started in 1942 as a successor to the 17-pdr. Troop trials of the prototype in 1944 proved the gun to be too heavy and cumbersome to be practical as a towed weapon, but development of the A39 had been taking place in parallel to development of the gun, and six prototypes of the complete SP, known as Tortoise, were completed in late 1944. The gun was provided with powered traverse and elevation. Troop trials were completed in BAOR in 1948. Ammunition was separate, the complete round weighing some 45 lb.

17. Ordnance, QF, 95-mm howitzer

Calibre	95 mm (3.74 in)
Length of howitzer overall	86 in (2,184 mm)
Maximum rate of fire	18 rds/min
Maximum range	6,000 yds (5,487 m) (HE) 3,400 yds (3,109 m) (Smoke)
Ammunition types and MV	HE: 1,075 ft/sec (328 m/sec) Weight: 25 lb HEAT: 1,650 ft/sec (503 m/sec) Weight: 14 lb 13 oz Smoke
Date into tank service	Late 1942

This, the last of the CS tank weapons to enter service, was an effective close-support weapon, made the more so by being provided with an anti-tank capability in the shape of a HEAT round, in addition to the normal HE and smoke shells. It was mounted in the Centaur IV and Cromwell VI and VIII cruiser and in the Churchill V, VII and XI infantry tanks, as well as in the SP equipment

Alecto. It remained in service in the Cromwell until withdrawn in the early 1950s.

18. 290-mm Petard Spigot mortar

Calibre	290 mm (11.4 in)
Length of mortar overall	86 in (2,184 mm)
Maximum rate of fire	2–3 rds/min
Maximum range	230 yds (210 m)
Effective range	80 yds (73 m)
Ammunition types and MV	HEAT: MV not known Weight: 40 lb
Date into tank service	Early 1944

This weapon was developed as a result of lessons learned in the disastrous Dieppe raid of August 1942, specifically for the demolition of bunkers, sea defences and anti-tank obstacles. Series production started in 1943; some 700 were produced, mounted in converted Churchill III and IV tanks as Armoured Vehicles Royal Engineers (AVRE). It proved to be a highly effective demolition weapon and remained in service until the late 1940s, when it was replaced by the 6.5-in (165-mm) AVRE demolition gun, mounted in converted Churchill VII AVREs. It fired a fin-stabilized bomb known as the 'Flying Dustbin'.

APPENDIX B

SP Artillery based on German Tank Chassis

TANK CHASSIS	GUN	NOMENCLATURE
PzKpfw I	4.7-cm Pak(t)	4.7-cm Pak(t) auf PzJäg I (SdKfz 101)
	15-cm s.I.G.33	15-cm s.I.G.33 auf PzKpfw I Ausf B (SdKfz 101)
PzKpfw II	7.5-cm Pak40/2 (L/46)	7.5-cm Pak40/2 auf PzJäg II Ausf A-C u.F (Marder II) (SdKfz 131)
	7.5-cm Pak40 (L/46)	7.5-cm Pak40 (L/46)auf PzJäg II Ausf D u. E (SdKfz 132)
	7.62-cm F.K.296(r)	7.62-cm F.K.296(r) auf PzJäg II Ausf D u. E (SdKfz 132)
	7.62-cm Pak36(r)	7.62-cm Pak36(r) auf PzJäg II Ausf D u. E (SdKfz 132)
	Ditto	7.62-cm Pak36(r) auf PzJäg II Ausf A-C u.F (SdKfz 131)
	10.5-cm le.F.H.18/2	10.5-cm le.F.H.182 auf Gw.II (Wespe) (SdKfz 124)
	15-cm s.I.G.33	15-cm s.I.G.33(Sf)auf PzKpfw II (SdKfz 121)
PzKpfw III	7.5-cm K (L/24)	7.5-cm K (L/24) auf Stu.G.III (SdKfz 142)
	7.5-cm Stu.K.40 (L/43)	7.5-cm Stu.K.40 (L/43) auf Stu.G.III (SdKfz 142)
	7.5-cm Stu.K.40 (L/48)	7.5-cm Stu.K.40 (L/48) auf Stu.G.III (SdKfz 142/1)
	10.5-cm Stu.H.42 (L/28)	10.5-cm Stu.H.42(L/28) auf Stu.G.III (SdKfz 142/2)
PzKpfw III/IV	8.8-cm Pak43/1 (L/71)	8.8-cm Pak43/1 (L/71) auf PzJäg III/IV (Nashorn, früher Hornisse) (SdKfz 164)
	15-cm s.F.H.18	15-cm s.F.H.18 auf Gw III/IV (Hummel) (SdKfz 165)

TANK CHASSIS	GUN	NOMENCLATURE
PzKpfw IV	2-cm Flakvierling 38	2-cm Flakvierling 38 auf PzKpfw IV (Flak Pz IV - Wirbelwind)
	3-cm MK103 Zwilling	3-cm MK103 Zwilling auf Flak Pz IV (Flak Pz IV - Kugelblitz)
	3.7-cm Flak43	3.7-cm Flak43 auf Flak Pz IV (Möbelwagen)
PzKpfw IV	7.5-cm Stu.K.40 (L/48)	7.5-cm Stu.K.40 (L/48) auf Stu.G.IV (SdKfz 167)
	7.5-cm Pak39 (L/48)	7.5-cm Pak39 (L/48) auf PzJäg IV (SdKfz 162)
	7.5-cm Stu.K.42 (L/70)	7.5-cm Stu.K.42 (L/70) auf Pz Jäg IV (SdKfz 162)
	10.5-cm le.F.H.18/1	10.5-cm le.F.H.18/1 auf Gw IVb (SdKfz 165/1)
	15-cm Stu.H.43 (L/12)	15-cm Stu.H.43 (L/12) auf Stu.G. IV (Stu.Pz.43 - Brummbär) (SdKfz 166)
PzKpfw V Panther	8.8-cm Pak43/3 (L/71)	8.8-cm Pak43/3 (L/71) auf PzJäg Panther (Jagdpanther) (SdKfz 173)
PzKpfw VI (P)	8.8-cm Pak43/2	8.8-cm Pak43/2 auf PzJäg Tiger (P) (Elefant, früher Ferdinand) (SdKfz 184)
PzKpfw VI (H) (Tiger Ausf E)	38-cm R.W.61	38-cm R.W.61 auf Stu.Mrs.Tiger
PzKpfw Tiger Ausf.B	12.8-cm Pak44 (L/55)	12.8-cm Pak44 (L/55) auf PzJäg Tiger Ausf B (Jagdtiger) (SdKfz 186)

APPENDIX C

GERMAN TANK GUNS AND AMMUNITION

AUTOMATIC WEAPONS

1. Dreyse MG13k Medium Machine-Gun

Calibre	7.92 mm (0.31 in)
Length overall	55.75 in (1,416 mm) incl. butt
Weight	23.9 lb (10.9 kg)
Rate of fire	625 rds/min (cyclic)
Cooling	Air
Feed system	Box (25 or 100 rds) or drum (50 rds)
Muzzle velocity	2,525 ft/sec (770 m/sec)
Ammunition types	Ball (Patr. SmK)
Date into tank service	1934

The tank version of this MG was used only on the PzKpfw I; all other German tanks in the Second World War were armed with its replacement, the MG34.

2. MG34 Medium Machine-Gun

Calibre	7.92 mm (0.31 in)
Length overall	40.75 in (1,035 mm)
Weight	25.5 lb (11.59 kg)
Rate of fire	800–900 rds/min (cyclic)
Cooling	Air
Feed system	150 rd belt or 50 rd belt drum
Muzzle velocity	2,525 ft/sec (770 m/sec)
Ammunition types	Ball (Patr. SmK)
Date into tank service	1937

The MG34 was the standard German MMG in the Second World War, and as such was used on all their tanks subsequent to the PzKpfw I. It was an excellent gun and very suitable for use in AFVs because of its reliability, ease of barrel change and the small opening it required in the armour. It could be dismounted for use on its bipod in the local defence role.

3. 2-cm Kampfwagenkanone 30 (2-cm KwK30)

Calibre	2 cm (0.79 in)
Length overall	76.5 in (1,943 mm)
Length of bore in calibres	L/55
Weight	139 lb (63 kg)
Rate of fire	280 rds/min
Cooling	Air
Feed system	10 rd magazine
Muzzle velocity	2,625 ft/sec (800 m/sec) (AP & HE)
	3,444 ft/sec (1,050 m/sec) (APCR)
Ammunition types	AP (Pzgr), APCR (Pzgr40) & HE (Sprgr)
Date into tank service	1937

The 2-cm KwK30 was the main armament of the PzKpfw II, and was developed from the AA gun, 2-cm FlaK30. It was also the main armament of several armoured cars, as well as of the quadruple AA mounting on the Wirbelwind (Whirlwind) SP.

4. 2-cm Kampfwagenkanone 38 (2-cm KwK38)

Calibre	2 cm (0.79 in)
Length overall	76.5 in (1,943 mm)
Length of bore in calibres	L/55
Weight	123 lb (55.9 kg)
Rate of fire	420–480 rds/min
Cooling	Air
Feed system	10 rd magazine
Muzzle velocity	2,625 ft/sec (800 m/sec) (AP & HE)
	3,444 ft/sec (1,050 m/sec) (APCR)
Ammunition types	AP (Pzgr), APCR (Pzgr40) & HE (Sprgr)
Date into tank service	1939

Originally intended as a lighter replacement for the 2-cm KwK30, the KwK38 eventually served alongside the KwK30, with which it was interchangeable. Both guns used the same ammunition and had similar performances apart from the much greater rate of fire of the KwK38.

TANK MAIN ARMAMENT
5. 3.7-cm Kampfwagenkanone (3.7-cm KwK (L/45))

Calibre	3.7 cm (1.46 in)
Length overall	67.55 in (1,716 mm)
Length of barrel in calibres	L/45
Weight	430 lb (195.5 kg)
Ammunition types	AP (Pzgr), APCR (Pzgr40), HE (Sprgr)
Cartridge case number	6331
Muzzle velocity (AP)	2,445 ft/sec (745 m/sec)
Date into tank service	1937

The 3.7-cm tank gun formed the main armament of the early models (A, B, C and D) of the PzKpfw III, but was phased out as later models of this tank armed with the 5-cm KwK (L/42) started coming into service in 1939. It compared favourably with the US 37-mm gun but was inferior to the British 2-pdr and the Soviet 47-mm in armour penetration. Like all German tank guns of the Second World War it employed electric primer firing gear and a spring-assisted falling wedge breech block with semi-automatic operation.

6. 5-cm Kampfwagenkanone (5-cm KwK (L/42))

Calibre	5 cm (1.97 in)
Length overall	82.44 in (2,093 mm)
Length of barrel in calibres	L/42
Weight	492 lb (223 kg)
Ammunition types	AP & APC (Pzgr), APCR (Pzgr40), HE (Sprgr)
Cartridge case number	6317
Muzzle velocity (AP)	2,247 ft/sec (685 m/sec)
Date into tank service	1939

The 5-cm KwK (L/42) replaced the 3.7-cm gun in Models E to early J inclusive, of the PzKpfw III. At the time of its introduction it outperformed the British 2-pdr, as well as having a high explosive anti-personnel round, which the 2-pdr lacked. After 1941 it was also provided with an APCR round (AP40 or Arrowhead) with a much higher muzzle velocity than the standard APC round and greater armour penetration over short ranges. The British 2-pdr could only achieve such velocities and penetration with a squeeze-bore attachment on the muzzle, the Littlejohn adaptor.

7. 5-cm Kampfwagenkanone 39 (5-cm KwK 39 (L/60))

Calibre	5 cm (1.97 in)
Length overall	111.35 in (2,828 mm)
Length of barrel in calibres	L/60
Weight	672 lb (305 kg)
Ammunition types	AP & APC (Pzgr), APCR (Pzgr40), HE (Sprgr)
Cartridge case number	6360
Muzzle velocity (AP)	2,700 ft/sec (823 m/sec)
Date into tank service	1942

Developed in 1939, this gun was a modification of the 5-cm KwK (L/42) with a greatly increased chamber capacity and barrel length which gave it a much-improved armour penetration performance. It formed the main armament of late Model J and Models L, M and N of the PzKpfw III. It was first in action in 1942 and was a very successful tank gun in its time.

8. 7.5-cm Kampfwagenkanone (7.5-cm KwK (L/24))

Calibre	7.5 cm (2.95 in)
Length overall	69.61 in (1,768 mm)
Length of barrel in calibres	L/24
Weight	628 lb (285.5 kg)
Ammunition types	APCBC (Pzgr39), HE (Sprgr), HEAT (Gr38Hl) Smoke (Nbgr) and case shot
Cartridge case number	6354
Muzzle velocity (APCBC)	1,263 ft/sec (385 m/sec)
Date into tank service	1938

The 7.5-cm KwK (L/24) was mounted in all models of the PzKpfw IV, up to and including the Model F1, and in the PzKpfw III Model N. It also appeared as a self-propelled gun on the Stu.G.III assault gun and an 8-wheeled armoured car, the SdKfz 263. Really a low-velocity howitzer, it was intended to give anti-personnel fire support (although provided with a relatively ineffectual APCBC round). It remained in service throughout the Second World War in one capacity or another.

9. 7.5-cm Kampfwagenkanone 40 (7.5-cm KwK40 (L/43))

Calibre	7.5 cm (2.95 in)
Length overall	138.6 in (3,520 mm) incl. muzzle brake
Length of barrel in calibres	L/43
Weight	1,041 lb (473 kg) incl. muzzle brake
Ammunition types	APCBC (Pzgr 39), APCR (Pzgr 40) HE (Sprgr), HEAT (Gr38Hl) & Smoke (Nbgr)
Cartridge case number	6339
Muzzle velocity (APCBC)	2,428 ft/sec (740 m/sec)
Date into tank service	1942

The mounting of this gun as the main armament of the PzKpfw IV Models F2 and G in 1942 marked a change in role for the PzKpfw IV from anti-personnel to anti-tank.

Provided at first with a single and then a double-baffle muzzle brake, the gun gave the PzKpfw IV a distinctive outline that led to it being called the 'Mark IV Special' by British troops in the Western Desert, as well as giving it a greatly enhanced anti-tank performance. The gun was also used in an SP equipment based on the Stu.G.III, in which capacity it was known as the Stu.K.40 (L/43).

10. 7.5-cm Kampfwagenkanone 40 (7.5-cm KwK40 (L/48))

Calibre	7.5 cm (2.95 in)
Length overall	153.6 in (3,899 mm) incl. muzzle brake
Length of barrel in calibres	L/48
Weight	1,094 lb (497 kg) incl. muzzle brake
Ammunition types	APCBC (Pzgr39), APCR (Pzgr40) HE (Sprgr), HEAT (Gr38Hl) & Smoke (Nbgr)
Cartridge case number	6339
Muzzle velocity (APCBC)	2,461 ft/sec (750 m/sec)
Date into tank service	1943

Models H and J were up-gunned with this weapon in 1943/4; it was also mounted, known as the 7.5-cm Stu.K.40 (L/48), as an SP gun in the Stu.G.III and Stu.G.IV and as the PaK 39 (L/48) in the Pz.Jäg.IV. It was an excellent all-round weapon, firing a useful HE round and having an excellent anti-armour performance, particularly at short range firing the PzGr40 APCR round. It remained in service until the end of the war.

11. 7.5-cm Kampfwagenkanone 42 (7.5-cm KwK42 (L/70))

Calibre	7.5 cm (2.95 in)
Length overall	218 in (5,537 mm) incl. muzzle brake
Length of barrel in calibres	L/70
Weight	2,390 lb (1,086 kg) incl. muzzle brake
Ammunition types	APCBC (Pzgr39), APCR (Pzgr40) & HE (Sprgr)
Cartridge case number	6387
Muzzle velocity (APCBC)	3,068 ft/sec (935 m/sec)
Date into tank service	1943

This fine weapon formed the main armament of all models of the PzKpfw Panther, as well as the 7.5 cm Stu.K.42 (L/70) on the Pz.Jäg.IV.

12. 8.8-cm Kampfwagenkanone 36 (8.8-cm KwK36 (L/56))

Calibre	8.8 cm (3.46 in)
Length overall	209.4 in (5,318 mm) incl. muzzle brake
Length of barrel in calibres	L/56
Weight	2,932 lb (1,332 kg) incl. muzzle brake
Ammunition types	APCBC (Pzgr39), APCR (Pzgr40) HE (Sprgr) & HEAT(Gr38Hl)
Cartridge case number	6347
Muzzle velocity (APCBC)	2,657 ft/sec (810 m/sec)
Date into tank service	1942

This gun was a development of the famed FlaK36 AA gun which, used in the anti-tank role in the Western Desert, proved the nemesis of any British tanks unfortunate enough to meet it in action. It was the main armament of the dreaded PzKpfw Tiger Model E, first encountered in the north African campaign in November 1942 and on the Leningrad front in August of that year. It remained in service until the end of the war, but was partially replaced by the 8.8-cm KwK43 (L/71) in the PzKpfw Tiger Model B in 1944; it was not mounted in any other AFV.

13. 8.8-cm Kampfwagenkanone 43 (8.8-cm KwK43 (L/71))

Calibre	8.8 cm (3.46 in)
Length overall	263.2 in (6,685 mm) incl. muzzle brake
Length of barrel in calibres	L/71
Weight	3,726 lb (1,694 kg) incl. muzzle brake
Ammunition types	APCBC (Pzgr39), APCR (Pzgr40) HE (Sprgr) & HEAT(Gr38Hl)
Cartridge case number	6388
Muzzle velocity (APCBC)	3,340 ft/sec (1,018 m/sec)
Date into tank service	1944

This weapon was the most powerful tank armament produced by the Germans in the Second World War, although weapons of greater calibre were fitted in self-propelled mountings. It formed the main armament of the PzKpfw Tiger Model B (Königstiger or King Tiger), the heaviest tank to appear in German army service in the war, as well as being mounted (as the 8.8-cm PaK 43 (L/71)) in the Pz.Jäg.III/IV (Rhinoceros, formerly Hornet), Pz.Jäg.Panther (Jagdpanther) and the Pz.Jäg.Tiger (P) (Elephant, formerly Ferdinand).

14. 12.8-cm Panzerabwehrkanone 44 or 80 (12.8-cm PaK44 or PaK80 (L/55))

Calibre	12.8 cm (5.04 in)
Length overall	276.4 in (7,020 mm)
Length of barrel in calibres	L/55
Weight of APCBC projectile	62.5 lb (28.4 kg)
Ammunition types	APCBC (Pzgr43) & HE (Sprgr)
Muzzle velocity (APCBC)	3,020 ft/sec (920 m/sec)
Date into tank service	mid-1944

Although not taken into German army service as a tank gun before the end of the war in Europe, the 12.8-cm gun was intended as the main armament of the Maus super-heavy tank, of which only prototypes had been built at the war's end. However, it was introduced as the armament of the Jagdtiger tank destroyer in 1944 and was first met in action in the Ardennes in December of that year. It was the only German wartime tank gun to fire separate ammunition, the round being too large and heavy to be loaded as one item; even so, two loaders were deemed necessary, to speed up the loading process.

APPENDIX D

SOVIET TANK GUNS AND AMMUNITION

AUTOMATIC WEAPONS
1. DT Light Machine-Gun

Calibre	7.62 mm (0.3 in)
Length overall	38.5 in (977 mm) shoulder piece closed 45.4 in (1,152 mm) shoulder piece fully extended
Weight	19 lb (8.6 kg)
Rate of fire	600–700 rds/min
Cooling	Air
Feed system	63-round drum magazine
Ammunition types	ball, ball/trace, incendiary, incendiary/trace, AP.
Date into tank service	1937

This machine-gun, designed by Degtyarev, is designed also to be used dismounted, on a bipod, for local defence. It was gas operated and gave automatic fire only; the barrel could not be changed when the gun was mounted in the tank. It was the standard coaxial and auxiliary armament MG for all Soviet tanks during the Second World War.

2. DShK Heavy Machine-Gun

Calibre	12.7 mm (0.5 in)
Length overall	64 in (1,626 mm)
Weight	30.4 lb (13.8 kg)
Rate of fire	550–600 rds/min (cyclic)
Cooling	Air
Feed system	50-round flexible metal belt
Muzzle velocity	2,800 ft/sec (854 m/sec)
Ammunition types	AP, AP/I, AP/I/T, HE/I
Date into tank service	1940

This heavy MG was first introduced in 1940 to tank use in the T-40 light tank, of which it formed the main armament. It was a development of a standard infantry MMG, the Degtyarev Model 1938, but was inadequate main armament for a tank in 1940 and was soon replaced by the 20-mm ShVAK cannon. It was reintroduced as a tank weapon in 1945 on the IS-3 as an AA MG, and subsequently on other medium and heavy tanks and SP guns.

3. 20-mm ShVAK automatic cannon

Calibre	20 mm (0.79 in)
Cooling	Air
Ammunition types	API, HE/T, HE/I
Date into tank service	1941

Little information is available in the UK on this weapon. It briefly replaced the 12.7-mm DShK MMG as the light tank main armament in 1941 on the T-60 light tank but, like its predecessor, was soon found to be inadequate and was replaced, on the T-70, by the 45-mm (L/46) tank gun. The ShVAK was derived from an aircraft cannon.

SINGLE-SHOT WEAPONS
4. 37-mm Tank Gun M-30

Calibre	37 mm (1.46 in)
Length overall	65.5 in (1,665 mm)
Length of bore in calibres	L/45
Weight of shot	1.5 lb (0.68 kg)
Muzzle velocity	2,378 ft/sec (725 m/sec)
Ammunition types	AP, HE
Date into tank service	1932

This weapon appeared before the Second World War as sub-turret armament on the T-26 light, the BT-2 medium and the T-35 heavy tank. It was a Rheinmetall design, built under licence in the Soviet Union. Against the German armour encountered in 1941, however, it was quite inadequate and was replaced by the 45-mm (L/46).

5. 45-mm Tank Gun M-32 (L/46)

Calibre	45 mm (1.77 in)
Length overall	81.5 in (2,070 mm)
Length of bore in calibres	L/46
Weight	275 lb (125 kg)
Weight of round (APCBC)	5.8 lb (2.6 kg)
Weight of shot (APCBC)	3.1 lb (1.4 kg)
Muzzle velocity (APCBC)	2,492 ft/sec (760 m/sec)
Ammunition types	APCBC, APCR, HE
Date into tank service	1932

The 45-mm (L/46) gun was employed as the main armament on the T-26B and T-70 light tanks and the BT-3, BT-5 and BT-7 medium tanks, and as sub-turret armament on the T-28A medium and T-35 heavy tank. This gun had, for its time, an excellent anti-tank performance but, as enemy tank armour increased in thickness and tank armament increased in calibre and weight of projectile, it became outclassed and was replaced in medium and heavy tanks by the 76.2-mm guns.

6. 76.2-mm Tank Gun PS-3 (L/16.5)

Calibre	76.2 mm (3 in)
Length of bore in calibres	L/16.5
Weight of shot (AP)	13.8 lb (6.27 kg)
Muzzle velocity (AP)	1,190 ft/sec (363 m/sec)
Ammunition types	HE, Shrapnel
Date into tank service	1932

This 3-inch calibre weapon was more of a howitzer than a gun, on account of its short barrel length and consequent low muzzle velocity. It was an adaptation of a ground weapon and was fitted as main armament in the T-28B medium, the BT-5A and BT-7A close support medium fast tanks and the T-35 heavy tank. It had little if any anti-tank capability, however, and was soon replaced in the T-34 medium and KV1 heavy tank by a gun with increased barrel length. Little information on its performance is now available.

7. 76.2-mm Tank Gun (L/30.5)

Calibre	76.2 mm (3 in)
Length of bore in calibres	L/30.5
Weight of round (AP/T)	21 lb (9.55 kg)
Weight of shot (AP/T)	13.8 lb (6.27 kg)

Muzzle velocity
(AP/T) 2,007 ft/sec
(612 m/sec)
Ammunition types AP/T, HE, Shrapnel
Date into tank
service 1940

This improved 3-inch gun was introduced in 1940 as the main armament of the BT-7M and of the first T-34 medium and KV1 heavy tanks. With a reasonable anti-tank performance it enabled the Red Army tanks to hold their own with the German PzKpfw III and IV of the time. However, as the up-gunned German tanks with their long-barrelled high velocity 5-cm and 7.5-cm guns and their thicker armour began to appear, the Soviet 76.2-mm weapon was outclassed and replaced by the longer F-34 (L/41.2) gun.

8. 76.2-mm Tank Gun F-34 (L/41.2)

Calibre 76.2 mm (3 in)
Length overall 124.6 in (3,168 mm)
Length of bore in
calibres L/41.2
Weight 1,003 lb (456 kg)
Weight of round
(AP/T) 21 lb (9.55 kg)
Weight of shot
(AP/T) 13.96 lb (6.31 kg)
(AP/CR) 6.7 lb (3.05 kg)
Weight of HE shell 13.7 lb (6.2 kg)
Muzzle velocity
(AP/CR) 3,165 ft/sec
(965 m/sec)
(APCBC & HE) 2,231 ft/sec
(680 m/sec)
Ammunition types AP/T, APCBC, AP/CR,
HE, shrapnel
Date into tank
service 1941

This gun was the standard main armament of the T-34 medium and KV heavy tanks for

much of the Second World War and proved an excellent compromise weapon until the German Tiger and Panther started to appear on the Eastern Front. It was also the armament of the SU-76 light SP gun.

9. 85-mm Tank Gun D-5T (L/51.5)

Calibre 85 mm (3.35 in)
Length overall 173.9 in (4,417 mm)
Length of bore in
calibres L/51.5.
Weight 1,282 lb (583 kg)
Weight of round
(APCBC/T) 33.2 lb (15 kg)
Weight of shot
(APCBC/T) 20.4 lb (3.27 kg)
Muzzle velocity
(APCBC/T) 2,599 ft/sec
(792 m/sec)
Ammunition types AP, APCBC, APCR &
HE
Date into tank
service 1943

The 85-mm (L/51.5) tank gun was an excellent weapon, capable of taking on the German Panthers and Tigers on an almost equal footing. Mounted in a new, larger turret, it replaced the 76.2-mm F-34 tank gun in both T-34 and KV tanks, which then became known as the T-34/85 and KV-85 respectively. A tank version of the 85-mm ground-mounting AA gun, it also formed the armament of the T-34 based tank destroyer, the SU-85, in which case it was known as the D-5S.

10. 100-mm Tank Gun D-10T (L/54)

Calibre 100 mm (3.94 in)
Length overall 220 in (5,588 mm)
Length of bore in
calibres L/54
Weight of round
(APCBC/T) 66 lb (30 kg)

Weight of shot	
(APCBC/T)	34 lb (15.5 kg)
Muzzle velocity	2,953 ft/sec
	(903 m/sec)
Ammunition types	APCBC/T & HE
Date into tank	
service	1945

With the heavier German tanks, such as the Königstiger and Maus, and tank destroyers, such as the Jagdtiger, known by the Soviets to be on the German stocks, it became necessary to replace the 85-mm guns with a more powerful weapon. One of these was the 100-mm gun D-10, which was scheduled to appear on the T-34 replacement, the T-44 medium tank, in 1945. The T-44 proved unsatisfactory and was not used in action, but the SP version of the 100-mm gun, the D-10S, did appear as the SU-100 on the T-34 chassis that year. This was an excellent all-round gun, which remained in service after the war on the T-54 series.

11. 122-mm Tank Gun D-25T (L/43)

Calibre	122 mm (4.8 in)
Length overall	233 in (5,918 mm)
Length of bore in	
calibres	L/43
Weight of round	86.5 lb (39.3 kg)
Weight of shot	
(APCBC/T)	55 lb (25 kg)
Muzzle velocity	
(APCBC/T)	2,562 ft/sec
	(781 m/sec)
Ammunition types	AP, APCBC/T & HE
	(separate ammunition)
Date into tank	
service	1944

The D-25T tank gun was introduced into the heavy tank for the same reason that the 100-mm replaced the 85-mm in the medium tank, in order to compete on an equal footing with the new heavier German tanks likely to be met with in 1944/5. As the existing KV-85 turret was not big enough, a new turret was designed to take this gun and mounted on a redesigned hull. Despite the larger turret, the gun still needed a double-baffle muzzle brake to keep the recoil within safety limits; ammunition was separate, on account of its weight and size. The new tank was named the IS, after Iosef Stalin, and appeared early in 1944. The chassis was also used as a self-propelled mount for a tank destroyer mounting the D-25S 122-mm gun, this vehicle being known as the ISU-122.

12. 122-mm Tank Howitzer M-38 (L/23)

Calibre	122 mm (4.8 in)
Length overall	110.2 in (2,800 mm)
Length of bore in	
calibres	L/23
Weight	1,593 lb (722.5 kg)
Weight of round	56.33 lb (25.6 kg)
Weight of HE shell	47.9 lb (21.76 kg)
Maximum range	(HE) 12,900 yds
	(11,800 m)
Ammunition types	HE, HEAT, AP
Date into tank	
service	1941

This howitzer was the first SP weapon to be mounted on the T-34 chassis, in which capacity it was known as the SU-122; it was contemporary with the SU-76. It had an excellent anti-personnel capacity in its large HE shell, although its anti-tank capability was negligible. It made a very useful and mobile infantry support weapon.

13. 152-mm Tank howitzer (L/20)

Calibre	152 mm (6 in)
Length of bore in	
calibres	L/20
Weight of round	104.74 lb (47.61 kg)

Weight of HE shell 88 lb (39.9 kg)
Ammunition types HE, Shrapnel
*Date into tank
service* 1940

The 152-mm L/20 tank howitzer was the main armament of the KV-2 heavy tank; this was an artillery support weapon with an excellent HE shell, mounted in a turret with 360° traverse. Ammunition was separate.

14. 152-mm Tank Gun/Howitzer M-37(L/29)

Calibre 152 mm (6 in)
Length overall 145.3 in (3,700 mm)
  less muzzle brake
*Length of bore in
calibres* L/29
Weight 2,977 lb (1,350 kg)

Weight of round 104.74 lb (47.61 kg)
Weight of HE shell 88 lb (39.9 kg)
Weight of AP shot 112.4 lb (51.1 kg)
*Muzzle velocity
(HE)* 781–1,670 ft/sec
  (238–508 m/sec)
*Maximum range
(HE)* 13,560 yds (12,400 m)
Ammunition types HE, AP
*Date into tank
service* 1943

This weapon formed the armament of the ISU-152, a self-propelled howitzer mounted on the chassis of the IS heavy tank. With a higher muzzle velocity and a longer range than the L/20 howitzer in the KV-2, it needed a multi-baffle muzzle brake to keep its recoil length within limits. It too used separate ammunition.

APPENDIX E

US Tank Guns and Ammunition

AUTOMATIC WEAPONS

1. .30 Calibre Browning Machine-Gun M1919

Calibre	0.30 in (7.62 mm)
Length overall	38 in (965 mm)
Weight	31 lb (14.1 kg)
Rate of fire	425–450 rds/min
Cooling	Air
Feed system	Belt
Muzzle velocity	2,700 ft/sec (823 m/sec)
Ammunition types	Ball, AP and AP/T
Date into tank service	1937

This machine-gun, designed in 1919, has been proved over the years to be a very reliable weapon; throughout the Second World War it was the standard US tank MG and was in service with the British army in those US tanks supplied under Cash-and-Carry and Lend-Lease. It became standard in British tanks after the war. A major advantage was the small hole (2-in diameter, compared to the 2.8 in x 3.1 in required by the British 7.92-mm BESA tank MG) which it required in the tank's armour. Disadvantages were the fabric ammunition belt, the low rate of fire, the weak feed, which was also not changeable from one side to the other, and its low endurance. Barrel change within the vehicle was just possible but not as easy as the German MG34, which also required a hole in the armour of only 1.6 inches in diameter.

2. .50 Calibre Browning Machine-Gun M2

Calibre	0.50 in (12.7 mm)
Length overall	65.13 in (1,654 mm)
Weight	84 lb (29 kg)
Rate of fire (cyclic)	400–500 rds/min
Cooling	Air
Feed system	110 rd metal belt
Muzzle velocity	2,900 ft/sec (884 m/sec)
Ammunition types	AP/T
Date into tank service	1937

The .50 cal Browning MG M2 was a scaled-up version of the .30 cal M1919, used primarily in the AA role but also as main armament on the early M2 combat car and the M1A1 light tank. It was the standard AA MG for most US tanks, including those in British service, in the Second World War.

TANK MAIN ARMAMENT

3. 37-mm Tank Gun M6

Calibre	37 mm (1.46 in)
Length overall	82.5 in (2,096 mm)
Length of bore in calibres	L/57
Weight	185 lb (84 kg)
Weight of round (APCBC)	3.4 lb (1.55 kg)
Weight of shot (APCBC)	1.9 lb (0.86 kg)
Muzzle velocity (APCBC)	2,900 ft/sec (884 m/sec)

Ammunition types	AP, APCBC, HE & canister
Date into tank service	1939

This was the standard high velocity anti-tank weapon of US light and medium tanks in the pre-Second World War period and in the early stages of that war. It should be compared with its contemporaries, the British 2-pdr, the German 3.7-cm KwK and the Soviet 45-mm tank guns. It was mounted as main armament in the M2A4, M3, M5 and M22 light tanks, as the anti-tank armament of the M2 and M3 medium tanks and as the coaxial armament of the M6 heavy tank.

4. 75-mm Tank Gun M2

Calibre	75 mm (2.95 in)
Length overall	91.75 in (2,330.5 mm)
Length of bore in calibres	L/31
Weight	783 lb (356 kg)
Weight of round (APCBC)	19.4 lb (8.8 kg)
Weight of shot (APCBC)	14.4 lb (6.5 kg)
Muzzle velocity (APCBC)	1,930 ft/sec (588 m/sec)
Ammunition types	AP, APCBC, HE & smoke
Date into tank service	1941

The 75-mm M2 (L/31) gun was the low-velocity HE-firing weapon mounted in a limited traverse barbette on the M3 (Lee & Grant) medium tank and as main armament (with a coaxial 37-mm M6 gun) on the M6 heavy tank. Its HE capability was much appreciated by those British tank units in the Western Desert lucky enough to be equipped with it; the only British tank gun then in

service, the 2-pdr, lacked an adequate HE shell.

5. 75-mm Tank Gun M3

Calibre	75 mm (2.95 in)
Length overall	118.4 in (3,007 mm)
Length of bore in calibres	L/40
Weight	893 lb (406 kg)
Weight of round (APCBC)	19.9 lb (9 kg)
Weight of shot (APCBC)	14.9 lb (6.77 kg)
Muzzle velocity (APCBC)	2,030 ft/sec (618 m/sec)
Ammunition types	AP, APCBC, HE & smoke
Date into tank service	1941

This gun, a development of the M2 gun above, was the compromise weapon selected as main armament for the medium tank M4 (Sherman), having a reasonable anti-armour capacity combined with a good HE performance. It was the standard armament of the Sherman for most of the Second World War and was also used in the British Churchill (NA75) to replace the British 6-pdr 7 cwt gun, which lacked an HE projectile until 1944. The British 75-mm tank gun was chambered to take the ammunition of the US 75-mm M3 tank gun.

6. 76-mm Tank Gun M1

Calibre	76 mm (3 in)
Length overall	163.75 in (4,159 mm)
Length of bore in calibres	L/55
Weight	1,141 lb (518.6 kg)
Weight of round (APCBC)	24.8 lb (11.3 kg)

Weight of shot	
(APCBC)	15.4 lb (7 kg)
Muzzle velocity	
(APCR)	3,400 ft/sec
	(1,037 m/sec)
Ammunition types	AP, APCBC, APCR,
	HE & smoke
Date into tank	
service	1944

The 76-mm M1 tank gun replaced the 75-mm M3 as the main armament of the Sherman, tanks armed with it being distinguished by the suffix (76) after the nomenclature. It was a high velocity gun whose prime function was to engage tanks but its anti-tank performance at the time of its introduction into service was, however, still inferior to that of the German Tiger and Panther guns. It also formed the main armament of the tank destroyers M10 and M18 (Hellcat).

7. 90-mm Tank Gun M3

Calibre	90 mm (3.54 in)
Length overall	177 in (4,496 mm)
Length of bore in	
calibres	L/53
Weight	2,300 lb (1,046 kg)
Weight of round	
(APCBC)	42.75 lb (19.43 kg)
Weight of shot	
(APCBC)	24 lb (10.9 kg)
Muzzle velocity	
(APCR)	3,350 ft/sec
	(1,021 m/sec)
Ammunition types	AP, APCBC,
	APCR & HE
Date into tank	
service	1944

This weapon formed the main armament of the M26 Pershing heavy/medium tank.

Although still not matching the anti-armour performance of the German 7.5-cm KwK42 (L/70) and the 8.8-cm KwK36 (L/56) and KwK43 (L/71), the 90-mm had a reasonable performance against armour when firing APCR, as well as an excellent HE shell; it fired separate ammunition. It performed well in its troop trials in north-west Europe between the time of the arrival of the first twenty Pershings in February 1945 and the end of the war in Europe. This gun also formed the main armament of the tank destroyer M36.

8. 105-mm Tank howitzer M4

Calibre	105 mm (3.54 in)
Length overall	295 in (7,493 mm)
Length of bore in	
calibres	L/25
Weight	973 lb (442.3 kg)
Weight of round	
(HE)	42 lb (19 kg)
Weight of shell	
(HE)	33 lb (15 kg)
Muzzle velocity	
(HE)	1,550 ft/sec
	(472 m/sec)
Ammunition types	HE, HEAT & smoke
Date into tank	
service	1943

The 105-mm howitzer M4 was a very useful infantry support weapon firing an HE shell of good capacity. As well as being mounted in some versions of the M4 Sherman, distinguished by the suffix (105), it formed the armament of two howitzer motor carriages. These were the HMC M37 on the light tank M24 (Chaffee) basis and the HMC M7 on the M3 medium tank chassis (known as 'Priest' in British service).

BIBLIOGRAPHY

PUBLISHED SOURCES: BOOKS

Chamberlain, Peter and Ellis, Chris. *British and American Tanks of World War II*, New York, Arco Publishing Co. Inc., 1969.

—*The Churchill Tank*, London, Arms & Armour Press, 1971.

—*British and German Tanks of World War I*, London, Arms & Armour Press, 1969.

Chamberlain, Peter and Doyle, Hilary L. *Encyclopedia of German Tanks of World War Two*, London, Arms & Armour Press, 1978.

Courtney-Green, P.R. *Ammunition for the Land Battle*, London, Brassey's (UK) Ltd, 1991.

Crow, Duncan and Icks, Robert J. *Encyclopedia of Tanks*, New Jersey, Chartwell Books, 1975.

Fletcher, David. *Mechanised Force – British Tanks between the Wars*, London, HMSO, 1991.

—*The Great Tank Scandal – British Armour in the Second World War, Part 1*, London, HMSO, 1989.

—*The Universal Tank – British Armour in the Second World War, Part 2*, London, HMSO, 1993.

Forty, George. *German Tanks of World War Two 'In Action'*, London, Blandford Press, 1988.

—*M4 Sherman*, Poole, Dorset, Blandford Press, 1987.

Grove, Eric. *World War II Tanks*, London, Orbis Publishing Ltd, 1976.

Gudgin, Peter. *The Tiger Tanks*, London, Arms & Armour Press, 1991.

—*Armour 2000*, London, Arms & Armour Press, 1990.

Hart, Captain B.H. Liddell. *The Tanks, Volumes One & Two*, London, Cassell, 1959.

Heigl, Fritz. *Taschenbuch der Tanks*, München, J.F. Lehmanns Verlag, 1926 and 1927.

Oswald, Werner. *Kraftfahrzeuge und Panzer der Reichswehr, Wehrmacht und Bundeswehr*, Stuttgart, Motorbuch Verlag, 1971.

Perrett, Bryan. *Soviet Armour since 1945*, London, Blandford Press, 1987.

RAC Tank Museum, Bovington

—*An Illustrated Record of the Development of Armoured Fighting Vehicles – Tanks of Other Nations:*

—*France* (1970)

—*Germany* (1969)

—*USA* (1976)

—*USSR* 1976)

RAC Tank Museum, Bovington Camp, Dorset

—*An Illustrated Record of the Development of the British Armoured Fighting Vehicle – Tanks 1915–1918*, Bovington Camp, Dorset, 1971.

—*An Illustrated Record of the British Armoured Fighting Vehicle – British Tanks 1939–1945*, Bovington Camp, Dorset, 1978.

Von Senger u. Etterlin, F.M. *Die Deutschen Panzer 1926–45*, München, J.F. Lehmanns Verlag, 1968.

Zaloga, Steven J. and Loop, James W. *Soviet Tanks & Combat Vehicles – 1946 to the Present*, London, Arms & Armour Press, 1987.

PUBLISHED SOURCES: ARTICLES

Gudgin, Peter. 'The T-34', *War Monthly*, London, December 1981.

Hofman, George R. 'The United States' Contribution to Soviet Tank Technology', *RUSI Journal*, London, March 1980.

Zaloga, Steven and Grandsen, James. 'Soviet Fast Tanks, Parts 1 & 2', *Military Modelling*, London, January and February, 1982.

UNPUBLISHED SOURCES

War Office (MI10). *Illustrated Record of German Army Equipment 1939–1945, Volume III, Armoured Fighting Vehicles*, The War Office, London, 1947.

Military College of Science (School of Tank Technology). Preliminary Report No.1/0 – 'Russian KV/1', Chertsey, Surrey, February 1944.

—Preliminary Report No.2/0 – 'Russian T/34', Chertsey, Surrey, February 1944.

INDEX